Seton Churchill

General Gordon

A Christian Hero

Elibron Classics
www.elibron.com

Elibron Classics series.

ISBN 1-4021-4798-8 (paperback)
ISBN 1-4212-7656-9 (hardcover)

This Elibron Classics Replica Edition is an unabridged facsimile of the edition published by James Nisbet & Co., Limited, London.

LITERARY OPINIONS.

Lord Wolseley says: "It gives by far the best account of the circumstances of his noble death yet published."

Sir Gerald Graham, V.C., G C.M.G., writes:— "Most interesting, and written in a spirit that will be welcomed by all Gordon's friends."

The Young Man.—"It is quite fascinating in its sustained interest. Young men should give it to their friends."

Record.—"The author is to be congratulated upon the bright and readable biography he has produced of General Gordon. The book should be in the library of every Young Men's Institute."

Christian.—"The events of this remarkable life are admirably brought together, the military, political, and social features being interpreted in the light of religious conviction and spiritual motive"

British Weekly.—"The author has told the eventful story of General Gordon's life with knowledge, skill, and sympathy. This book ought to be a very useful and acceptable present."

Church Bells—"This volume is interesting from its first page to its last."

C. G. Gordon

P.S. I am quite happy, thank God, & like Lawrence, I have "tried to do my duty"

Copied from the Original Engraving by permission of F. C. M'QUEEN & SONS, *sole Proprietors of the Copyright.*

GENERAL GORDON,

A CHRISTIAN HERO.

BY

LIEUT.-COLONEL SETON CHURCHILL,
AUTHOR OF "BETTING AND GAMBLING," "STEPPING-STONES
TO HIGHER THINGS," "FORBIDDEN FRUIT
FOR YOUNG MEN," ETC.

EIGHTH EDITION.

London:
JAMES NISBET & CO., LIMITED,
21 BERNERS STREET.

Printed by BALLANTYNE, HANSON & Co.
At the Ballantyne Press

Dedicated

TO THE

YOUNG MEN OF ENGLAND,

WITH THE EARNEST DESIRE THAT SOME OF THE NOBLE

GODLIKE CHARACTERISTICS OF THIS

CHRISTIAN SOLDIER AND HERO

MAY BE REPRODUCED IN FUTURE GENERATIONS.

LIFE OF GORDON.

CHAPTER I.

INTRODUCTION.

LORD WOLSELEY, on hearing an officer say that General Gordon was mad, remarked, in language similar to that used by George II. to the Duke of Newcastle about General Wolfe, that it was a great pity Gordon had not bitten more Generals, so that they might have been infected with some of his madness. Nor is there any reason why the motive power which could make a man do such noble deeds and lead such a splendid life should be confined to Generals. There are thousands of young men in this country who may be helped to live better lives by the study of such a Christian hero as Charles George Gordon undoubtedly was, and it is with that end in view that I have endeavoured to write a popular sketch of his life and character.

My object in adding to the number of biographies * already written of General Gordon is to meet the demand for a popular book for young men and others, which will focus the events of his life into one handy

* In certain points where I have differed from other writers, I have relied on the opinion of a near relative of the late General Gordon, as to the accuracy of the statements put forward.

A

volume, and which shall at the same time give a clear insight into the religious life of this Christian hero. This I have attempted to combine with a sketch of his military, political, and social life, setting forth not only the deeds of the man, but the motive which prompted them. The best writers on Gordon have taken up parts of his life only, so that no one can get a view of it as a whole without wading through a large number of volumes, some of them very ponderous. The best record of his career in China is a work by Mr. Andrew Wilson called "The Ever-Victorious Army." A smaller book by Mr. W. E. Lilley gives an interesting account of Gordon's life at Gravesend. The first part of his life in Africa is given in a larger volume by Dr. G. Birkbeck Hill, called "Colonel Gordon in Central Africa." The late Prebendary Barnes edited a small book, "Reflections in Palestine," and Mr. A. Egmont Hake has published a complete account of the hero's career at Khartoum in "The Journals of General Gordon," which were given to him in manuscript to be edited. In addition to this valuable work, the same writer, who is a distant cousin of Gordon's, has written two large volumes, embracing the whole of his life, under the title "The Story of Chinese Gordon."

The late Sir Henry Gordon has also written a biography; but though an able man and very fond of his brother, it is not generally considered that he did full justice to his memory. The brothers were widely separated in age, there being fourteen years between them; and owing to the younger one having spent so much of his life abroad, they had not seen much of each other. Colonel Sir William F. Butler has written the ablest and most interesting of all the biographies which embrace the whole of Gordon's life, but as he is a Roman Catholic, it could not be expected that he would enter largely into the religious views of his hero. The remarks he does make on the subject are, however, excellent and in good taste. Another capital sketch of Gordon has been produced by the celebrated war correspondent Archibald Forbes, who not unnaturally devotes most of his space to the military aspect of Gordon's career, and says but little about his religious life. From the religious standpoint the best information can be got from the "Letters of General Gordon to his Sister," edited by Miss Gordon. There seems to have been a special bond of sympathy between the brother and sister, and she seems to have been made the recipient of all his confidences, religious and otherwise.

In order to get a clear and accurate conception of Gordon's many-sided character, I have made myself acquainted with all these authorities on the subject. There is another little book to which I am indebted—"Letters from Khartoum," written by the late Frank Power, correspondent of the *Times* at Khartoum during the siege. It gives a good insight into Gordon's life in the beleaguered city. I have further had the advantage of hearing many anecdotes and incidents that throw a light upon the personality of one who undeniably ranks amongst the great men of the century. Nevertheless I feel that to represent the religious and professional life of a man like Gordon, who was so essentially original and unlike other people, is a very difficult task, so I have, as far as possible, quoted his own words in giving expression to his views.

The play of "Hamlet" without its leading character

mighty torrent must drain the waters of a continent;" and his prediction proved to be correct. When we see the deep stream of true heroism flowing from the heart of such a man as Gordon, we instinctively feel that no mere human heart could produce such a torrent of good works, but that behind the human being there must be something more. It has been my object in this memoir to show that the stream that went forth from Gordon's heart to cheer and bless all with whom he came in contact, sprang from no isolated fountain, but had its origin in the great ocean of Divine love, which has existed in all ages, but was revealed more distinctly on Calvary.

This is a material, sceptical age, when many pride themselves on their want of faith, quite forgetting that to believe too little is as clearly an indication of mental weakness as to believe too much. God suddenly raised up a man in our midst who was as strong in faith as he was indifferent to the material things of this world. It was indeed his faith in things eternal and unseen that made him so indifferent to things temporal. Gordon might have lived and died amongst us without being known beyond a limited circle, but that his Master placed him on high so that men should be compelled to hear about his life. Sir William Butler in his interesting book "The Campaign of the Cataracts" does not at all exaggerate when he says:—

"Who is this far-off figure looming so large between the rifts in the dense leaguer which the Arab has drawn around Khartoum? We cannot save him with all this host and all this piled-up treasure; but, behold! our failure shall be his triumph; for God has raised a colossal pedestal in the midst of this vast desert,

and placing upon it His noblest Christian knight, has lighted around the base the torch of Moslem revolt, so that all men through coming time may know the greatness of His soldier."

In spite, however, of the fact that many failed to appreciate him while he was alive, we may be thankful to think that there is much good left in Old England yet; for when the events of his noble career were made public, there was a widespread feeling of regret that we had as a nation failed to value adequately a man of so much true nobility.

In an interesting article in "The Young Man," Mr. William T. Stead hit off the prominent characteristic of the hero's life when he said: "General Gordon taught the world that it is possible to be good without being goody-goody. That it is possible to live like a Christ and to die like a Christ for your fellow-men, without going out of the world or refusing to do your own fair share of the day's work of the world, is one of those truths which need to be revealed anew to each successive generation by the practical demonstration of an actual life." Gordon was essentially a manly man, but with all his courage and bravery he combined the tenderness of a woman. He could be "truest friend and noblest foe." His courage and deeds of daring would have won him that much-coveted distinction the Victoria Cross, had they been performed in an English campaign; yet the sufferings of a child, or even of an animal, caused him the greatest grief. He had a keen sense of humour, and might have cultivated the mere pleasure-seeking part of his nature, and become socially very popular. It has been well said that "Humanity wants more than this; it craves to have its best and noblest powers called into play, and exercised into action that will tend in some way to promote the general good." It is for this reason that his example is such a noble one to set before young men. Most young fellows who are worthy of the name of men have within them a spirit which admires all that is manly, noble, and chivalrous; and for such it is a grand thing to have a high ideal, even if they do not attain to it. As it is true of men that they cannot habitually think mean thoughts without becoming mean, or set before themselves a low ideal without lowering themselves, so is it true that men cannot adopt a high ideal without instinctively cultivating noble and lofty aims.

Frederick Robertson of Brighton once said, "Hate hypocrisy, hate cant, hate intolerance, hate oppression, hate injustice, hate pharisaism, hate them as Christ hated them, with a deep, living, Godlike hatred." It would be difficult to point to one who was more thoroughly influenced by the teaching conveyed in this short sentence than was Gordon. But negative virtues of this kind were not enough for him. One of his most prominent characteristics was his love for that which is good, and his incessant efforts to do good. His career was one long effort to relieve the sufferings of his fellow-creatures, to inculcate Divine truths, and in every way to make the world better. Few labourers have been called to such a variety of work; but it was all one to him. He worked for God in China when fighting to quell a civil war; he served the same Master at Gravesend when he visited the sick and the dying, and rescued little street arabs from lives of sin; and the same motives prompted him when, later on, he devoted all his energies to mitigating and attempting to abolish the horrors of the slave-trade. He is dead, but his noble example still lives.

> "Press on, press on! nor doubt, nor fear,
> From age to age, this voice shall cheer;
> Whate'er may die and be forgot,
> Work done for God—it dieth not."

CHAPTER II.

EARLY LIFE AND CRIMEAN WAR.

CHARLES GEORGE GORDON was born on January 28, 1833, at Woolwich, so that he began his life among soldiers. He was the fourth son of General Henry William Gordon, who was in the Royal Artillery. His father came from a good family, which for centuries had been associated with the army. The old General appears to have been a good officer and a kind-hearted man, and doubtless the son inherited not only the instincts of a soldier, but a certain nobility of character which was conspicuous in the father. When the father held a high command at Corfu, he made a point of seeking out and paying attention to the forlorn and uninteresting, who are usually overlooked by others. Those who have been richly endowed by Nature have little difficulty in gaining the smiles of society; but in all classes there are a few unfortunate ones, who are not specially gifted and attractive, and who consequently often have the cold shoulder turned towards them. It was characteristic of Charles Gordon's father, as it was of himself in later years, that these were the ones he befriended and looked after.

If Charles Gordon inherited from his father the instincts of a soldier, there can be little doubt that on his mother's side he inherited a spirit of enterprise.

His mother was Elizabeth Enderby, the daughter of an enterprising merchant, who had ships on every sea. It is men of this class, quite as much as our soldiers and sailors, who have made England what she is. Samuel Enderby was one of the best-known among the great merchant-princes of England, and he it was chiefly who opened to commerce the previously unknown waters of the South Pacific, after the exploring expeditions of Captain Cook. It is supposed that the first batch of convicts sent to Botany Bay were conveyed in one of his ships, and, but for his whaling fleet, Australia might never have been peopled by English emigrants. His ships carried on a busy trade with America, and it was one of his fleet that carried the historic cargo of tea which was thrown into Boston harbour when the Americans severed their connection with the mother country. His daughter had a large family, numbering five sons and six daughters. Three only of the sons survived, and they all attained the rank of General in the army. One of them became General Enderby Gordon, C.B., of the Royal Artillery, who distinguished himself in the Crimean War, and also in the Indian Mutiny. Another became General Sir Henry William Gordon, already alluded to as the author of "Events in the Life of Charles George Gordon." Charlie Gordon, to use the name by which the subject of this memoir was always known among his friends, was a delicate lad, and, perhaps for this reason, was the special favourite of his mother, who appears to have been a fond parent and a sensible woman. She was always proud of her boy, and once or twice even annoyed him by speaking of him in terms of praise to others.

The Gordon family seems to have been a very happy one, which to a great extent must have been the result of the mother's influence. One only needs to read the published "Letters of General Gordon to his Sister" to see how passionately fond the two were of each other. It might well have been Gordon that Browning had in his mind when he said:—

> "I think, am sure, a brother's love exceeds
> All the world's love in its unworldliness."

A few lines from a letter of one of his brothers, written from the Crimea, shows the fond and almost parental care that the elder exhibited on behalf of the younger brother. The extract is as follows:—"Only a few lines to say Charlie is all right, and has escaped amidst a terrific shower of grape and shells of every description. You may imagine the suspense I was kept in until assured of his safety."

Like all soldiers' sons, Gordon when young had plenty of opportunities of moving about and seeing different parts of the world. In many ways this roving life is disadvantageous to a lad, as in after years he can never look back to one spot as his home, and consequently he can never localise the charming associations connected with that word. A boy also suffers considerably by being moved from one school to another. On the other hand, his wits, as a rule, get sharpened by contact with new people and new circumstances. Before Gordon was seven years old, he had accompanied his father on successive moves to Dublin, and to Leith Fort. In 1840 he went to Corfu, where his father was in command of the Royal Artillery. It was here the Duke of Cambridge first made his acquaintance, as they occupied quarters next to each other, and His Royal Highness, just forty-five years afterwards, after Gordon's death, said in a speech at the Mansion House, that he remembered the little lad then. As Gordon returned to England with his mother at the age of ten, the fact that the Commander-in-Chief remembered him at all is another proof of the wonderful faculty of memory which the Royal Family are said to possess. How differently the Duke would have thought of that little fair-haired boy with the blue penetrating eyes could he have looked into the future! It was in 1843 that Mrs. Gordon brought her son to England for the sake of his education. He went to school at Taunton for a few years, and then to Mr. Jeffery's, Shooters Hill, Woolwich, preparatory to entering the Royal Military Academy. His father had been given an appointment at the Arsenal at Woolwich, so that his holidays, as well as much of his school life, were spent at that great garrison town. There was nothing about the youth at this time that indicated what his future would be. Indeed, the very energies which in after life made him undertake so much, finding no other vent, gave him a turn for mischief and fun of all sorts. Later in life, and even amid all his troubles in the Soudan, he would in his letters recall with pleasure the boyish days spent at Woolwich.

In 1848 he entered the Royal Military Academy at Woolwich, where he remained till 1852, when, at the age of nineteen, he received his commission in the Royal Engineers. Although he was an adept at surveying and at fortification, two branches of military knowledge which served him well in after years, he was deficient in mathematics, and consequently did not make much progress. An event which took place here might have had very serious consequences, and shows that even then he had the daring nature which afterwards characterised him. For some reason it became necessary to restrain the cadets when leaving the dining-hall, the approach to which was by a narrow staircase. At the top of this staircase stood the senior corporal, with outstretched arms, facing the cadets. This was too much for one so full of fun and energy and so reckless of consequences as Gordon; so, putting down his head, he charged, and butting the corporal in the pit of the stomach, sent him flying down the staircase and through a window beyond. Fortunately the corporal was unhurt, but Gordon was perilously near dismissal, and having his military career cut short. The act of insubordination was, however, overlooked by the authorities, but that it did not subdue his spirit is evident from the fact that on another occasion, when told by Captain Eardley Wilmot that he would never make an officer, he tore the epaulets from his shoulders and threw them at the feet of his superior. This officer, afterwards General Eardley Wilmot, became one of his greatest friends. Later on, for another offence, in which many were concerned, and of which it is doubtful if Gordon really was guilty, he was deprived of half a year's seniority in the army. This punishment really did him a good turn, for it enabled him to secure a commission in the Royal Engineers, instead of the Royal Artillery, to which he would otherwise have been posted.

On the 23rd June 1852 Gordon was gazetted to the Engineers, and on the 29th November 1854 he was ordered to Corfu. As the Crimean War was going on, he was much disappointed at this order, and at first attributed it to his mother's influence, who, he thought, wanted him to be sent to a safe place. Through the influence of Sir John Burgoyne, an old family friend, his destination was changed, and on the 4th of December, during that bitterly cold winter, he writes, "I received my orders for the Crimea, and was off the same day." This was not the only time that he exhibited such promptitude in leaving his native land at the call of his country. Thirty years afterwards he left England for the Soudan the very day he received his orders.

He arrived in the Crimea on New Year's Day 1855, when all the celebrated historical battles were over. His martial ardour had doubtless been stirred by hearing how bravely our men swarmed up the heights at Alma, charged the Russian gunners at Balaklava, and drove back the sortie at Inkerman. When he arrived, the siege of Sebastopol had commenced in earnest, and for some time it was an engineer's campaign, in which the spade did more than the rifle, or, to speak more correctly, the musket; for very few of our men had rifles then. Disease and exhaustion from hardship slew far more than the bullet. Altogether, it was rather a trying time for a young officer full of fire and spirit, anxious to see service of that more dashing kind that appeals to the imagination. The slow advance of the trenches must have tried his somewhat impatient spirit, which, even in later years, when it might have been modified by time, was always more ready for a rapid march, a brilliant flank movement, or something of that kind. But though the trench-work must have been wearisome and distasteful to a degree, he threw himself heart and soul into it, meriting the following praise from Colonel Chesney, an eminent engineer officer:—"In his humble position as an engineer subaltern he had attracted the notice of his superiors, not merely by his energy and activity (for these are not, it may be asserted, uncommon characteristics of his class), but by an extraordinary aptitude for war, developing itself amid the trench-work before Sebastopol in a personal knowledge of the enemy's movements such as no other officer attained. 'We always used to send him out to find what new move the Russians were making,' was the testimony given to his genius by one of the most distinguished officers he served under." He not only exhibited the "aptitude for war" of which Colonel Chesney speaks, but it appears that he also displayed on several occasions a great deal of that personal courage for which he afterwards became so renowned. A single incident may be taken as a specimen of many. One day as he was passing along the trenches, he overheard a heated altercation between a sapper and a corporal, both belonging to his own corps. On inquiring into the cause, he discovered that the corporal had ordered a man to stand on the parapet, where he was exposed to the enemy's fire, while the corporal, under cover, was going to hand him some gabions for repairing the parapet. Gordon at once jumped on to the parapet himself and called the corporal to join him, letting the sapper hand up the gabions from a place of safety. Gordon remained until the work was completed, in spite of the fire of the Russians, and then turning to the corporal said, "Never order a man to do anything you are afraid to do yourself."

His warlike genius and his courage were by no means his only remarkable characteristics, and it may not be out of place to mention here a trifling event, which possibly had a marked influence on his whole life. It so happened that Colonel Staveley, an officer who afterwards attained to some eminence, but who at that time was of no great note beyond being the second in command of a distinguished corps, the 44th Regiment, mentioned in Gordon's hearing that he had been appointed field-officer of the day for the trenches for the following day, but owing to his having been on sick leave, was ignorant of the geography of the place. Now considering that Gordon was at this time greatly over-worked in the trenches, he might well have been excused had he allowed Colonel Staveley's remark to pass; for it must be remembered that it is no part of the duty of a young engineer officer to instruct infantry field-officers in their duties. But this was not Gordon's style. He, at all events, never limited himself to a strict routine of mere duty, and so he cheerfully volunteered assistance, saying, "Oh! come down with me to-night after dark, and I will show you over the trenches." Colonel Staveley says, "He drew me out a very clear sketch of the lines (which I have now), and down I went accordingly. He explained every nook and corner, and took me along outside our most advanced trench, the bouquets and other missiles flying about us in, to me, a very unpleasant manner; he taking the matter remarkably coolly." Napoleon somewhere remarked that "the smallest trifles produce the greatest results," an expression to which Gordon himself once referred. This Colonel Staveley afterwards became General Sir Charles Staveley, and he it was who first recommended Gordon, when quite a young captain in China, to take command of that army for which he did so much, and

return home, he was sent to Asia Minor to perform a similar duty, and was not able to return till he had been abroad three years. He was then granted leave for six months, and afterwards returned to his work in Armenia, where he remained till the spring of 1858, thus missing all chance of being employed in the Indian Mutiny, which broke out in 1857. On his return to England in 1858, he went to Chatham, where he was promoted to the rank of captain the following year.

CHAPTER III.

CHINESE WAR AND TAIPING REBELLION.

A STOUT old Scotch lady when asked about her health, replied that she was "weel i' pairts, but ower muckle to be a' weel at ane time." If the old lady was too large to be perfectly well all over at the same time, may it not be said that in this respect China resembled her in 1860? The largest empire in the world was suffering from external as well as internal troubles. A great portion of the country was given up to all the horrors of civil war conducted on an enormous scale, while the united armies of England and France were assaulting it from without.

Space does not permit a detailed account of the causes which led England to declare war on China. This war was but a phase in a dispute that had been going on since 1837 between the two countries. In 1842, to our shame it must be said, by force of arms we compelled the Chinese to receive opium from India, and thenceforward a very sore feeling existed against us. Just before the Indian Mutiny this feeling was awakened by a trifling event, and war was again declared, though, owing to the outbreak of the Mutiny, we did not press matters for a time. As soon as our hands were free in India, operations in China were actively pushed forward, the French troops joining us on account of the murder of some French missionaries. The war was practically a walk-over, for the Chinese army was quite incapable of meeting trained forces; and a treaty having been agreed upon, the representatives of the English and French returned home.

In March 1859 Mr. Frederick Bruce, brother to Lord Elgin, was sent out as Minister Plenipotentiary to China, and instructed to proceed to Pekin to exchange the ratifications of the treaty. He was to be accompanied by Admiral Hope, the English admiral commanding in China. Pekin lies inland about a hundred miles, being connected with the sea by the river Peiho, the entrance to which was commanded by the Taku Forts. For some reason, the Chinese did not want Mr. Bruce to proceed to Pekin, or at all events they objected to his proceeding by the river route, as he proposed. Obstacles to the progress of our ships were put in the way, and the Chinese refused to remove them. Mr. Bruce thereupon called upon the Admiral to take steps for their removal, and on his attempting to do so, the Chinese fired on the English ships with such telling effect that four gunboats were placed *hors de combat.* Nor was the Admiral more successful when he attempted to storm the forts. The result of that day's work was that out of 1100 men in the English force nearly 450 were killed or wounded. The feeling in England was, that though Mr. Bruce had acted very hastily in thus committing England to another war without definite instructions from home, the matter could not be allowed to rest. The French again joined us, and Sir Hope Grant, who had distinguished himself in the Indian Mutiny, was appointed to the command. This General, it may be remarked, was an earnest Christian no less than an eminent soldier. The Taku Forts were captured and the troops were marching on Pekin, when the Chinese sought to open negotiations, in order to prevent our army from entering their capital. Our representatives consented to enter into negotiations at Tungchow, a place about a dozen miles from Pekin. Some English officers, accompanied by a few of the staff of the English and French envoys, went forward to Tungchow, to make the necessary arrangements for the interview of the envoys with the Chinese commissioners. A misunderstanding arose, and twenty-six British and twelve French subjects were seized, in spite of the flag of truce, and hurried off to different prisons. Their sufferings as prisoners were frightful, the result being that half of them died, while the remainder, when released, bore evident signs of the ill-treatment they had undergone. The allied armies at once marched on Pekin, and Lord Elgin refused to treat with the Chinese till the prisoners were restored, which did not take place till the gates of the city were about to be blown in. The Chinese were compelled to pay £10,000 for each European and £500 for each native soldier captured, in addition to having their famous Summer Palace, valued by some at the almost fabulous sum of £4,000,000, destroyed.

Gordon at this time was adjutant of engineers at Chatham, a post a good deal esteemed by officers of his rank. He had lost the opportunity of seeing active service in India, but he was determined that it should be no fault of his if he were not sent out to China. He resigned his appointment at Chatham, an act which greatly annoyed his father and many of his friends.

Even a high official in the War Office considered that he was damaging his prospects for life; whereas it turned out that by going to China he got that opportunity of exercising his talents and displaying his abilities which he might otherwise never have met with. Not leaving England till the 22nd of July 1860, he was too late to take part in the principal action, the taking of the Taku Forts, which were assaulted on the 21st August. He writes to his mother from Hong-Kong, "I am rather late for the amusement, which will not vex you." He arrived at Tientsin on September 26th, and marched with Sir Hope Grant's force to Pekin. The following is his description of the only part he was allowed to take before the Chinese surrendered:—

"We were sent down in a great hurry to throw up works and batteries against the town, as the Chinese refused to give up the gate we required them to surrender before we would treat with them. The Chinese were given until noon on October 13 to give up the Anting gate. We made a lot of batteries, and everything was ready for the assault of the wall, which is battlemented and forty feet high, but of inferior masonry. At 11.30 P.M. on the 12th, however, the gate was opened, and we took possession; so our work was of no avail."

The English and French armies left Pekin on November 8th, a little over three weeks after the fall of the city, and returned to Tientsin, to take up their quarters for the ensuing cold weather. Captain Gordon was the senior engineer officer left behind, and he remained till the spring of 1862, performing the ordinary engineer duties of providing accommodation for men and horses. During his stay at Tientsin there is little of any interest to record. He wisely relieved the monotony of camp life by making a journey to the

Great Wall of China, which has been visited by very few of our countrymen. He was doubtless prompted by curiosity to undertake this expedition, but other motives were also at work. He was a born soldier, he was good at surveying, and doubtless he was anxious to ascertain by personal observation if any other route existed than the well-known one by which a Russian army could march on Pekin; but he was unsuccessful in finding one. During the journey the cold was very severe; in one place, he says, "the raw eggs were frozen hard as if they had been boiled."

It has been already mentioned that China was troubled by an extensive civil war, which had been going on for many years. It appears to have commenced in the province of Quang-Tung, and to have been headed by a schoolmaster, Hung-tsue-schuen. That there must have been good cause for the dissatisfaction which caused the outbreak is clear from the fact that not only did thousands join the rising, but that among the rebels were men of great ability. The leader seems to have been a strange mixture of good and evil, and at one time appears to have had an inclination towards Christianity. Unfortunately the evil part of his nature predominated, and his head was turned by his success. During the time the Chinese troops were engaged in war with the English, the rebels had it pretty well their own way, and large tracts of the country were devastated. Intoxicated with success, the rebels threatened to attack Shanghai, and the merchants there, seeing how incapable the Government was to protect them, subscribed to form a small army to protect their interests. The command of this force was given to an American named Ward, who appears to have been a born soldier. His career was short, but he was engaged in seventy actions and never lost one. So successful was he, that the Pekin authorities conferred on his troops the pretentious title of "Ever-Victorious Army." Unfortunately for that army, it soon lost its able commander, for in September 1862 he was killed when assaulting a city near Ningpo. He was succeeded by an American adventurer named Burgevine, who turned out a complete failure, being one of that type of unprincipled men who do so much harm in non-Christian countries. When he was dismissed, application was made to the English General to appoint an English officer to take command. Major Gordon had been ordered to Shanghai from Pekin at the beginning of May 1862, and consequently had come under the command of General Staveley, with whom, it will be remembered, he was acquainted in the Crimea. General Staveley's duty was to clear the country for thirty miles round Shanghai of the rebels, and in the performance of this task Major Gordon had been employed. The opinion that General Staveley had formed of Gordon's courage and ability in the Crimea was confirmed in the operations around Shanghai, and the following account is given by that General of Gordon's plucky conduct:—

"Captain Gordon was of the greatest use to me when the task of clearing the rebels from out of the country within a radius of thirty miles from Shanghai had to be undertaken. He reconnoitred the enemy's defences, and arranged for the ladder-parties to cross the moats, and for the escalading of the works; for we had to attack and carry by storm several towns fortified with high walls and deep wet ditches. He was, however, at the same time a source of much anxiety to me from the daring manner in which he approached the enemy's works to acquire information. Previous to our attack upon Singpo, and when with me in a boat reconnoitring the place, he begged to be allowed to land, in order better to see the nature of the defences. Presently, to my dismay, I saw him gradually going nearer and nearer, by rushes from cover to cover, until he got behind a small outlying pagoda within a hundred yards of the wall, and here he was quietly making a sketch and taking notes. I, in the meantime, was shouting myself hoarse in trying to get him back; for not only were the rebels firing at him from the walls, but I saw a party stealing round to cut him off."

There is not much more of interest to record of Gordon's doings at this period. The rebels having been cleared out of the thirty-miles radius, Gordon was deputed to commence a complete survey of the whole district, and in December we find him so engaged. This occupation gave him a thorough insight into the ways of the people and the nature of the country. In this month he writes as follows:—

"The people on the confines are suffering greatly and dying of starvation. This state of affairs is most sad, and the rebellion ought to be put down. Words cannot express the horrors these people suffer from the rebels, or the utter desert they have made of this rich province. It is all very well to talk of non-intervention, and I am not particularly sensitive, nor are our soldiers generally so, but certainly we are all impressed with the utter misery and wretchedness of these poor people."

When General Staveley was applied to for an officer to take command of the so-called Ever-Victorious Army, his thoughts not unnaturally turned to Gordon, who, by the way, had received the brevet rank of major at the end of 1862. Gordon, having seen the failings and shortcomings of our generals in the Crimea, longed for an opportunity to exercise the gifts of which he felt conscious. General Staveley, however, shrank from recommending him for such a dangerous post. He knew well the plucky, chivalrous nature of the young engineer, and not unnaturally feared that he would expose himself too much to danger. His affection for Major Gordon made him at first refuse to recommend him for the command, and it was not till Gordon repeatedly urged him to yield, and promised not to expose himself more than necessary, that he consented to submit his name to the authorities at home. A temporary commander being urgently required, he appointed the chief of his staff, Captain Holland, of the Royal Marines, to the post, pending the decision of the War Office with regard to Gordon. Before the reply arrived from England two expeditions took place, one against Fushan, under Major Brennan, and one against the city of Taitsan, in which Captain Holland commanded in person. Both were disastrous to the reputation of the Ever-Victorious Army. In the attack on Taitsan some 7500 men were engaged, about one-third belonging to the Ever-Victorious Army, while the remainder were Chinese Imperial troops. Unfortunately, Captain Holland took it for granted that the Mandarins were correct when they informed him that the moat around the city contained no water, whereas it proved to be at least thirty feet deep. This was not discovered till the assaulting party arrived without bridges, and with nothing but escalading ladders, which they attempted to use as bridges. The ladders were of course not strong enough to bear the weight of the men, and broke down. The assault was very soon turned into a rout, and the "Ever-Victorious Army" not only lost several hundred men, but allowed two guns to fall into the hands of the enemy.

Such a disaster clearly indicated that an abler man was required at the head of the Ever-Victorious Army, and forthwith Major Gordon was appointed. A letter written home at the time shows that he was conscious that his father would not be pleased at the step he had taken:—

"I am afraid that you will be much vexed at my having taken the command of the Sung-kiang force, and that I am now a Mandarin. I have taken the step on consideration. I think that any one who contributes to putting down this rebellion fulfils a humane task, and I also think tends a great deal to open China to civilisation. I will not act rashly, and I trust to be able soon to return to England; at the same time, I will remember your and my father's wishes, and endeavour to remain as short a time as possible. I can say that if I had not accepted the command, I believe the force would have broken up, and the rebellion gone on in its misery for years. I trust this will not now be the case, and that I may soon be able to comfort you on the subject. You must not fret over the matter. I think I am doing a good service . . . . I keep your likeness before me, and can assure you and my father that I will not be rash, and that as soon as I can conveniently, and with due regard to the object I have in view, I will return home."

Gordon's father has been much misrepresented by some biographers. It has been practically said that he was not able to appreciate his son's nobility of character; but there is not a word of truth in this. The old man saw that the post accepted by his son was one of great danger, made all the more dangerous by that son's daring, and the fact that he did not understand the language of the people and was not cognisant of their manner of conducting warfare. He also was of opinion that the Chinese Government ought to be able to deal with their own internal affairs, and put down any rebellions that might occur without making a cat's-paw of his son. One cannot blame the father, who only looked at the matter in a natural way, judging the circumstances from his own standpoint. It is impossible to consider the whole facts, and to read the letters concerning them, without feeling that neither father nor son had anything of which to be ashamed.

One of the most painful things in life is for a man who is fond of his parents to have to take a step which he feels will not meet with their approval, and we may be quite sure that Major Gordon gave this subject his earnest and prayerful consideration. The path of duty seemed to him to be clear, and the call was distinct. The whole country was practically deluged in blood, and not only strong men, but hapless women and children, were suffering. Could Gordon, knowing what he did, and feeling conscious of his power to put down the rebellion, have declined to enter the path so unexpectedly opened to him? Some would have done so. But opportunities such as this, not seized, are seldom repeated. His ability, his energies, and his powers might never have found full scope, and might have proved a curse to him rather than a blessing. How often one sees in life men with marked ability who are not only unhappy themselves, but make every one around them equally so. They seem to have missed the object for which they were created, and instead of doing their duty in a large sphere, as they might have done, their stunted energies prevent them from properly filling even a smaller and humbler sphere. They have missed the opportunity of being really great, and yet their abilities prevent them from being satisfied with anything short of this. The call came to Gordon to take his share in the battle of life, and to do his best to mitigate the sufferings caused by a horrible civil war, and doubtless he pondered those words, "He that loveth father or mother more than Me is not worthy of Me." He decided to take the path which appeared to him the one of duty; nor need we be surprised when we know that he was a thorough Englishman of the highest type, of whom the words are true—

> "There's a heart that leaps with burning glow
> The wronged and the weak to defend;
> It strikes as soon for a trampled foe
> As it does for a soul-bound friend."

CHAPTER IV.

GORDON'S FIRST COMMAND.

At the age of thirty, Major Gordon obtained his first independent command, thus surpassing the Duke of Wellington's achievement by four years. With Wellington, too, able as he showed himself to be, it must be borne in mind that his first appointment was due to family interest, for his eldest brother, Lord Mornington, was Viceroy of India at the time. In Gordon's case, however, personal merit was the only qualification that brought him to the notice of the General in command, and it speaks volumes for Sir Charles Staveley's insight into character that such a wise appointment was made. Sir William Butler in his biography of Gordon says, "Thus on March 24, 1863, Gordon stepped out for the first time from that inevitable environment of the mass which so often keeps entangled in its folds men on whom Nature has conferred great gifts. Fate, it is said, knocks once at every man's door, but sometimes it is when the shadows are gathering and the fire is beginning to burn slow." This was not the case with Gordon, for he was at about the age at which such famous soldiers as Alexander, Wellington, and Napoleon have shown that man is full of life and fire. Many of the brilliant successes attained by those men would never have been won had they not had opportunities of making their first attempts till mature years had sobered them down. Nothing gives a man so much confidence in his own resources as success, more especially if that success has been gained amidst trying circumstances.

There can be no doubt that the period which we are now considering is the most interesting of Gordon's life. Up to this time, he had done well all that he had been called upon to perform in the way of duty, but had had no opportunity to show of what stuff he was made. A subordinate may suggest, and a superior may reap the benefit of his brains, if he has only sufficient intelligence of his own to recognise merit in others, a quality of which many are deficient. But a subordinate cannot initiate. And his suggestions, when adopted by a superior, frequently fail, for the simple reason that only a portion of his ideas are grasped, and something is lacking. Gordon's new position gave him not only the opportunity to initiate, but the power to carry out his ideas. After the suppression of the Taiping rebellion, every one who had the power to recognise greatness at all knew that Gordon had qualities that would make him succeed in anything he liked to take up, and therefore it was no matter of surprise to see him adding laurels to his crown.

Hitherto I have refrained from making any allusion to Gordon's personal appearance, having reserved the point till this period of his history, when, for the first time, he takes a prominent part on the stage of life. There have been numerous pictures sold representing him, and perhaps still more numerous descriptions written. The best that I have seen are accounts written by two intimate friends. Sir Gerald Graham, who knew him as a cadet at Woolwich, and was one of the last Englishmen ever to see him, says:—

"Not over five feet nine inches in height, but of compact build, his figure and gait characteristically expressed resolution and strength. His face, though in itself unpretending, was one that, in common phrase, 'Grew upon you.' Time had now streaked with grey the crisp, curly, brown hair of his youth, and traced lines of care on his ample forehead and strong clear face, bronzed with exposure to the tropical sun. His usual aspect was serene and quiet, and though at times a ruffling wave of constitutional impatience or indignation might pass over him, it did not disturb him long. The depth and largeness of Gordon's nature, which inspired so much confidence in others, seemed to afford him a sense of inner repose, so that outer disturbance was to him like the wind that ruffles the surface of the sea, but does not affect its depth. The grace and beauty of Gordon's whole expression came from within, and, as it were, irradiated the man, the steadfast truthful gaze of the blue-grey eyes seeming a direct appeal from the upright spirit within. His usual manner charmed by its simple unaffected courtesy; but though utterly devoid of self-importance, he had plenty of quiet dignity, or even imperious authority, at command when required."

Colonel H. G. Prout, an American officer, who served under Gordon in the Soudan, writing in *Scribner's Magazine* says:—

"He was rather under than over medium height, of well-proportioned figure, by no means heavy, but muscular and vigorous in all his movements. His hair was brown, and curled rather closely. His complexion was ruddy. He wore a short moustache and small whiskers, and shaved as carefully when he was in the heart of Africa as when he was in London. His mouth was resolute, but full of humour. His smile was quick, and his whole expression was kind, bright, and ready, but absolutely self-reliant. Only a dull person could fail to see that here was a man who had nothing to ask or to fear. His most striking feature was his eyes. These were bright blue, and the blue and white were of that pure unclouded quality that one sees only in the eyes of a baby. Only a baby's eyes could be so direct and sincere. You felt that they looked right into your soul and laid bare your motives."

Both these descriptions speak of him as seen in the Soudan, but they are so graphic, that it requires little imagination to see the man before us a few years younger. At the age of thirty, he was of course much younger looking; but his general appearance was not one that changed much. Considering the hardships through which he passed, it was wonderful how little he exhibited their effects. It will be remarked that in both of the foregoing descriptions reference is made to his blue eyes, which certainly were a very prominent feature in his personality. If we may anticipate events a little, as we are considering this subject, it is interesting to record that a little native boy named Capsune, whom General Gordon rescued from the slave-dealers in 1870, asked the lady who had charge of him after Gordon's death whether she was quite sure that Gordon Pasha still kept his blue eyes, and did she think he could "see all through me now?" Another day he said he was "quite sure Gordon Pasha could see quite well in the dark, because he had the light inside him."

This, then, is the man whom the fortunes of war called to fill about as difficult a position as it is possible to imagine. The enemy he was to disperse were flushed with victory, having for years been able to defy all who had attempted to suppress them. Their numbers were overwhelming as compared with the handful of men the merchants of Shanghai were able out of their private resources to put into the field; and, as if these were not sufficient advantages, they had possession of all the large cities and places of importance for many miles outside the thirty-miles radius around Shanghai. The army Gordon was called upon to command possessed a high-sounding name, justly earned by a former commander, but with his death had passed away all that made the title justifiable. It was a relic of greatness that had departed, and to one like Gordon, who had a keen sense of humour, it must have sounded ridiculous in the extreme. The army consisted of about 3000 Chinese, with 150 officers, the latter being principally foreigners. The officers were by no means wanting in pluck, nor deficient in military skill, but there appears to have been a great want of discipline among them, to say nothing of the existence of keen jealousies of one another. The fact that in one month eleven officers died of *delirium tremens* speaks volumes as to their character. Colonel Chesney says, "Among them were avowed sympathisers with the rebels, and avowed defiers of Chinese law; but all classes soon learnt to respect a General in whose kindness, valour, skill, and justice they found cause unhesitatingly to confide; who never spared himself personal exposure when danger was near; and beneath whose firm touch sank into insignificance the furious quarrels and personal jealousies which had hitherto marred the usefulness of the force."

The head-quarters of this little army was a place called Sung-kiang, to the west of Shanghai, and close to the border of the thirty-miles radius around that city.

Gordon proceeded on the 24th March 1863 to assume his command, and it was thought by many that he would endeavour to take the city of Taitsan, and thus wipe out the reproach of his predecessor. But his military instinct showed him a far more important step to take. About twenty miles inland and fifty miles from Gordon's head-quarters was a city called Chanzu, which was the only one in that neighbourhood loyal to the Imperial cause. It had been held by the Taipings, but the chief had persuaded his men to abandon the cause of the rebels and throw in their lot with the Emperor. No sooner had their decision been taken, than the Taiping General marched a strong army on the city to punish them. The defenders were holding out bravely, but they were reduced to starvation, and were suffering terribly. It would have been both impolitic and cruel to have left this city to its fate; so Gordon determined to relieve it. Chanzu was, however, cut off from the sea by an intervening city called Fushan, which commanded the river; so Gordon decided that, with the object of relieving the Chanzu garrison, Fushan must be captured. As has already been mentioned, one expedition against this place had signally failed. Gordon took two steamers, packed 1000 men into them, 200 of whom were artillerymen, and with this small force proceeded to attack Fushan. In spite of the overwhelming numbers against him, the enemy being able to draw reinforcements from the army investing Chanzu, he captured the place. No sooner had it fallen than Gordon set to work to relieve Chanzu. This he had very little difficulty in doing, for as soon as the rebels found that they were between two armies and exposed to attack in opposite directions, they moved off.

This brilliant achievement accomplished, Gordon retired to his head-quarters at Sung-kiang. By Imperial decree he was made a Tsung-Ping or Brigadier-General. He had passed through his first ordeal, and had come out of it with credit. He had not only struck a blow, but had done it with such promptitude, that every one began to get confidence in this young "General," as he was hereafter termed by the Chinese. To take a handful of men, not stronger than a full-sized English regiment at that time, to transport them in one day fifty miles, and to capture a city with overwhelming odds against him, exhibited capacity combined with promptness of action equal to anything recorded in the annals of the greatest soldiers. His predecessor, with an army numbering 7500—for he had a large force of Imperial troops in addition to his own—had been terribly beaten in his attempt to take Taitsan. But Gordon with a force of only 1000 men had captured one city and relieved another, at a much greater distance from head-quarters, and that with the loss of only two killed and six wounded. In the account of the attack, no light is thrown on the question why Gordon succeeded so brilliantly when others failed. He simply pounded away with his artillery, which was not strong, for three hours, and having effected a breach, he ordered an assault of infantry, which swept everything before it. This in itself is such a simple operation, and so much like what had been done before, that it does not account for his success. As the question will doubtless often occur to the reader, why Gordon so often succeeded where others failed, it may be well to quote a few words written by Colonel Prout, dealing with this very subject:—

"Gordon took and kept his unquestioned place as a chief, not by force of gold lace, banners, and salutes of trumpets and guns, but *by doing things.* He filled Carlyle's definition, *King*, *Könning*, which means *Can*-ing, Able-man. All who are at all familiar with his character and deeds must recognise the fact that he was a man of great qualities, both of mind and character. He did not do things accidentally or by mysterious means. Whatever business he had in hand, he knew it thoroughly in all its details. He knew his men and their motives, and he grasped all the minutiæ of his material. He was a highly educated modern soldier, and from the principles of grand strategy down to mending a gun-lock or loading a cartridge he knew his profession. He was not a great student of books, but his quick and strong mind seized and held facts with wonderful power. His most remarkable intellectual quality was directness."

This paragraph from a magazine article throws light on the cause of much of Gordon's success. Lord Beaconsfield used to say that genius was the art of taking pains. It will be remembered that the principal reason why Gordon's predecessor failed at Taitsan was, that he took it for granted that he was rightly informed when he was told that the ditch around the city was dry, and consequently he came unprovided with bridges. Gordon, on the other hand, took nothing for granted. Every detail was personally looked into, every difficulty anticipated by his eager restless brain. Consequently everything he took in hand succeeded; and yet to the superficial observer it all seemed so simple. The power of anticipating and providing against difficulties is one of those gifts which go a long way towards ensuring success in any calling in life, and that gift Gordon possessed to a remarkable degree. Whether it was innate, or whether it was cultivated, is difficult to say. Possibly it was implanted by nature to a certain extent, and in addition he cultivated and developed the natural gift.

A brief allusion has already been made to Burgevine, the American who for a short time commanded the Ever-Victorious Army after the death of Ward. This man plays a somewhat important part in connection with Gordon's operations, so it may be well here to give an account of his history, for just at this time an order arrived from Pekin that he was to be reinstated in his command, if the Governor of the province approved. The career of Burgevine is, it is to be feared, an illustration of the lives of many adventurers who, having failed in some civilised country, go out to seek their fortunes among a non-Christian people, and bring disgrace upon Christianity. Without principle, destitute of all honourable feelings, they imbibe all that is low and bad in the countries to which they go, yet all the time they are called Christians, and looked upon as such by the natives. In almost every large city belonging to a non-Christian people will be found one or more of this type, to whom the lines might with truth be applied—

> "Hast thou with Asiatic vices filled thy mind,
> And left their virtues and thine own behind?"

Burgevine was by no means deficient in military skill or courage, but he was utterly unprincipled, and, as the sequel will show, he was as ready to sell himself to the enemy as he was to fight for the Imperialists. The immediate cause of his dismissal from the command of the Ever-Victorious Army was that he went to the Chinese treasury officer with a hundred men of his body-guard and demanded money for arrears of pay. That official being unable to comply, Burgevine struck him and ordered his followers to seize 40,000 dollars. No sooner was he dismissed, than he went to Pekin to plead his cause there, and got the American ambassador to back him up, the latter of course being ignorant of his real character. The authorities at Pekin yielded, and sent him back to Shanghai to assume command, provided the local Governor had no objection. A shrewd suspicion exists that this was but a diplomatic way of getting out of a difficulty, as the authorities at Pekin must have known that the Governor could not possibly consent to receive Burgevine back after what he had done. This Governor was Li Hung Chang, a man of considerable power, who could see that he had in Gordon a man of ability; and though he did not at that time appreciate him as he afterwards did, still the fascination of Gordon's character, that so endeared him to many others, had already begun to work. Consequently the Governor strongly opposed the return of Burgevine, and at the same time took the opportunity of informing the Pekin authorities that Gordon was gaining the confidence of his men, as well as of the merchants and others at Shanghai. This for a time closed Burgevine's career, though we shall hear of him again.

The city of Chanzu was relieved on April 5th, but it was not till the end of that month that Gordon again took the field. His brief but brilliant campaign had shown the weak points in his force; so he spent some three weeks at head-quarters in getting his little army better in hand. Among other things, he put his men into a uniform of dark serge with green turbans, so as to make the enemy suppose that they were Europeans. At first this little reform was very unpopular, as most reforms are, and the men were called by their countrymen "Imitation Foreign Devils." When the Ever-Victorious Army regained its right to its title, the men became proud of their uniform, and would not have exchanged it for their old costume. Dr. Wilson in his interesting account of this period tells us that Woo, the Tautai of Shanghai, even went so far as to purchase thousands of boots of European make, such as were worn by Gordon's men, that their footprints might be seen about, as the rebels were so impressed with fear of the disciplined Chinese troops! Not only uniform, but every other detail necessary to the improvement of the army, was during that short space of time gone into, and on April 29th Gordon once more commenced active operations.

This time the object of attack was the city of Quinsan, about thirty miles to the north-west of his camp; but, when *en route*, he heard that his Imperialist allies, who were besieging the city of Taitsan, had been most treacherously treated. The rebels had proposed to surrender, and had permitted upwards of 1500 men of the Imperial army to enter their city. Suddenly they closed the gates and captured these men, beheading some 300 of them, including the brother of Li Hung Chang. This disaster to his allies decided Gordon to turn aside and lend his aid in reducing Taitsan, the city where his predecessor had suffered such a terrible defeat. It must have been an anxious time when he led his small army against a place which would remind them so forcibly of the greatest disaster they had experienced.

The city of Taitsan had a garrison of some 10,000 men, with a considerable sprinkling of white men, some of whom were deserters from the English and French armies, together with American sailors and others. Gordon's army consisted of only 3000 men; so that not only had his opponents the benefit of walls, from behind which they might deliver their fire, but they outnumbered his little force by more than three to one. Taitsan was, however, a great prize to be aimed at, for its fall would blot out the remembrance of the disaster which had occurred when it was last attacked. Captain Holland on that occasion had assaulted it from the south. Gordon's quick military eye showed him that he ought to seize the canal leading into the town on the western side. He had little difficulty in possessing himself of this water-way, and he made use of it to bring his guns and ammunition to within 600 yards of the walls. At that distance he opened fire, under cover of which he pushed forward some of his guns to within 100 yards, concentrating all his fire on one spot, with the object of effecting a breach in the walls. At each discharge of his guns at this short range masses of masonry fell, forming a gradual slope, up which the assaulting party could rush. Steamers and boats came up the canal and turned into the moat, forming a perfect bridge across the water. The defenders, seeing their danger, wisely concentrated their fire on the temporary bridge, and rushed to defend the breach. Captain Bannen, who led the attack, was killed, and the assaulting party were for a time driven back. Another column was formed for the assault, and this time Gordon kept up an incessant artillery fire over the heads of his own men as they advanced. Again they met with a determined resistance, but after a severe hand-to-hand struggle, the attack was victorious, and the defenders, seized with panic, actually trampled down many of their own side in their haste to escape.

Thus on May 1, 1863, fell this important stronghold; but the victory cost Gordon dearly, as his killed and wounded were very numerous for such a small force. The vacancies, however, were filled up by volunteers from among the prisoners he took, and these men made admirable fighting soldiers, though they had of course somewhat lax notions on the subject of discipline. Although Gordon received little or no help from the Imperial troops, they caused him a good deal of pain and annoyance by an act committed on the fall of Taitsan. Capturing seven retreating rebels, the Imperial troops tied them up, and, according to their own horribly cruel custom, forced arrows into their flesh, flayed bits of skin off their arms, and thus exposed them for several hours previous to execution. This was supposed to be in revenge for the treachery of the Taipings, already alluded to, and they contended that these seven men were specially to blame. Be that as it may, a very natural sense of indignation was awakened throughout the civilised world, and questions were asked in Parliament about the incident, it being assumed that Gordon and other British officers were concerned in these atrocities. As Gordon, in spite of his bravery and his being habitually brought into the presence of bloodshed, was one of the most tender-hearted of men, it need hardly be said that he was deeply grieved and pained by the whole circumstance, and it was through his influence that General Brown, then in command of the British troops at Shanghai, informed the Chinese Governor that, on a repetition of such barbarity, all the British officers would be withdrawn.

CHAPTER V.

PROGRESS OF THE REBELLION.

BEFORE Gordon captured Taitsan, it will be remembered, he was on his way to attack the city of Quinsan. Having accomplished his purpose of assisting his allies, the Imperial troops, he reverted to his original object. He wanted to leave Taitsan to be held by the Imperialists, and at once to march on Quinsan; but owing to the want of discipline in his army, he was unable to do this. His men had taken a large amount of loot from Taitsan, and were anxious to dispose of it, and their young General, much against his will, had to accept the inevitable. With an army such as that which Gordon had under his control, it does not do to draw tight the reins of discipline too suddenly. It had for a long time been in a lax condition, and Gordon saw that he must gain the men's confidence before sharply asserting his authority. With an army well in hand, the right thing would have been to follow up his victories immediately, so that the enemy should not have time to recover themselves. But instead of being able to go on at once from Taitsan to Quinsan, he had to return to head-quarters, and there wait till the end of May, reorganising and making preparations. So bad was the discipline among his officers, that just before he started for Quinsan, all the majors commanding regiments resigned, simply because he promoted his commissary-general, an English officer named Cooksby, to the rank of colonel. This step was taken because Gordon found that disputes were always occurring about rations and quarters between the commissary-general and the regimental commanders. As the latter had, and the former had not, military rank, the commissary was in an awkward position. Gordon therefore decided that, the commissary being one of his most important staff officers, he ought not only to have military rank, but that his rank should be of a superior kind. It is worthy of note that in this respect Gordon was just twenty years ahead of the War Office authorities, for it was not till the year 1884 that commissariat officers in the English army were accorded military rank. The amusing part of the outbreak of insubordination amongst Gordon's majors was, that though they resigned their commissions, they asked that they might be allowed for the sake of loot to accompany the expedition to Quinsan. Gordon accepted the resignations, but declined to let the majors take part in his expedition. But he had to yield this point; for on the following day, when the "fall in" sounded, the men supported their commanding officers, and refused to obey. The majors, however, seeing that there was only one General, and that he might be killed, in which event the command would probably devolve on one of themselves, thought better of the matter, and fell in with their men as usual. The only wonder is that, with such an army and such disorganised material, the young commander should have been able to accomplish so much against overwhelming numbers.

When Gordon reached Quinsan, he found the Imperial troops under Governor Li and General Ching in a most unfortunate position. They were supposed to be besieging the city, but the enemy were practically besieging them. Gordon quickly drove off the enemy that were seeking to encompass the Imperialists, and then he found that General Ching was anxious to attack the eastern gate of the city, a proceeding that did not at all commend itself to him. He saw at a glance that the western gate would probably be the better one to attack, as the enemy would be less prepared there. Quinsan was an important place, and was strongly defended; it was held by at least 15,000 men, and the moat round the fortification was forty feet wide. Before coming to a definite decision, Gordon made a reconnaissance in a steamer, taking the Governor and General Ching with him. Being convinced by personal observation that he was right in the step he intended to take, he informed the Chinese General to that effect, and in a letter written some little time after the event he says, "General Ching was as sulky as a bear when he was informed that I thought it advisable to take these stockades the next day, and to attack on this side of the city."

At dawn on the 30th May, having surrounded the city with his own and the Imperialist troops, he took a small force by water to a point on the main line of communication between Quinsan and Soo-chow, only defended by a weak stockade, which was easily taken. Gordon then took the celebrated little steamer the *Hyson*, and went towards Soo-chow. Meeting a large force of the enemy on the way to reinforce Quinsan, he opened fire upon them. Little anticipating an attack in this direction, they got into confusion and fled, the steamer following them. Having inflicted heavy loss on the retreating army and steamed right up to Soo-chow, he turned round and went at full speed till he got back to Chunye, where he had that morning left a small detachment of riflemen. It was 10.30 P.M. and a rather dark night. His intention was to wait till the next morning and renew the conflict by attacking the city. But the rebels within the walls had been seized with panic, and knowing that the city was invested on three sides, they made a rush for Soo-chow. In doing so they met Gordon's steamer returning. Again she opened fire and blew her whistle, the sound of the latter doing much damage by adding to the noise and increasing the panic among the rebels. The men were in dense masses, and each shell mowed them down in large numbers. Gordon says, "The mass wavered, yelled, and turned back." The city had fallen, and by 4 A.M. on May 31st everything was quiet, and it was reckoned that from three to four thousand of the enemy must have been killed, drowned, or taken prisoners. The little steamer had won the day, having fired some eighty or ninety rounds; the troops had done little or nothing. Only two men on Gordon's side were killed and five were drowned.

Thus in a single day had fallen this important city, which was the key to the position of Soo-chow. Indeed, the impetuous young commander was anxious to dash on and seize Soo-chow itself, but he could not inspire the Imperialist General with his spirit. He says, "I have no doubt of my having been able to take Soo-chow the other day, if the Mandarins had been able to take advantage of our success." The capture of Quinsan was one of the most brilliant strokes of success Gordon had during the whole of the campaign, and he attributed it to the fact that the lines of communication between that city and Soo-chow were neglected, and that he was permitted to get his steamer into the canal, which ran parallel with the only road. Both the armies which he defeated were compelled to march along the road, as on each side of the road there was water. Through the men marching thus in dense masses, the shot and shell from the steamer carried death and destruction, creating much confusion. The Tai-ping rebels were evidently not prepared to fight such an amphibious general as Gordon proved himself to be.

It may be well to remark here on the fertility of resource and the initiative power which this young commander possessed. It mattered not what difficulties arose, his fertile brain sooner or later devised a method by which he could overcome them. It is said that the best doctor is not necessarily the cleverest man, but the one who is most fertile in resource. If disorders of the human frame refuse to yield to one kind of treatment, another must be tried, and so on, until at last the right method is discovered. There can be no question that this is also true of the military and other callings in life. The man of a fertile brain, ever ready to suggest new methods when old ones have failed, is the most likely to succeed. It was to this cause, more than to any other, that Napoleon at first owed his success. When he was a young man, it was the custom in Europe to imitate blindly the tactics of Frederick the Great of Prussia, and to rely on ponderous heavy squares and a slow stiff method of moving. Napoleon was the first to see that, however suitable such tactics had been during the time of the great Prussian general, before the development of artillery, they were not adapted to the changed circumstances under which battles were fought in his own time; and so in 1806 at Jena he smashed to pieces the Prussian force, which came against him in all the pride of inherited traditions, handed down from one of the greatest generals of his age. While it is almost a truism to say that what is appropriate to one age is not suited to another, it is only men of the type of Napoleon and Gordon who are quick enough to see the necessity for a change of method, and sufficiently resourceful to adopt new plans. Ninety-nine generals out of a hundred would never have thought of utilising a little steamer to destroy a land force, but would have proceeded in the old-fashioned methods of a siege, and perhaps have lost an enormous number of men in the process. The enemy are always more or less prepared for conventional methods of fighting, but it stands to reason that they are unprepared for new ideas. Hence much of Gordon's success.

In addition to this fertility of resource, Gordon displayed wonderful courage in carrying out his ideas. No sooner had Quinsan fallen than he saw that it would be a good thing to make a change in his head-quarters, and to transfer them thence from Sung-kiang. With the old centre were associated all sorts of traditions connected with the army before his time, in the days when discipline was lax, and the one idea of the soldiers was that the war was being carried on for the sake of providing them with loot. There were loot agents and other means by which the officers and soldiers could easily dispose of their booty. All this was demoralising, so Gordon decided on an immediate change. But the army looked at the matter from a different standpoint, and a mutinous spirit arose. Mr. Wilson informs us that the artillery threatened to blow the officers to pieces, and a written notification to that effect was sent to the General. Gordon at once summoned the non-commissioned officers, who he knew were at the bottom of the plot, and threatened to shoot every fifth man if the name of the writer of the notice were not revealed. Immediately they all commenced to groan, one corporal making himself specially conspicuous by groaning very loudly. Whether Gordon had any suspicions with regard to this particular man, we are not informed, but he directed him to be seized, and ordered a couple of infantry soldiers standing by to shoot him. He then had the others confined, and again repeated his threat to the effect that one in every five would be shot if the name of the writer were not given up. Events proved that the corporal already shot was the culprit. No doubt many in this country will judge Gordon harshly with regard to this summary method of dealing out justice; but it must be remembered that a civil war was going on in which thousands of lives were annually sacrificed. Gordon knew perfectly well that he could suppress it if he had a disciplined force under him. He also knew what a frightful scourge an undisciplined army might become. According to the tradition of all nations, each man in Gordon's army had forfeited his life by disobedience in the presence of the enemy. What was the life of one man compared with the thousands of women and children who were suffering through the horrors of that war? We in England have been for so long mercifully spared the misery of war in our own country, that possibly public opinion has become a little too sentimental. During the Trafalgar Square riots in 1887, it was suggested by some that the Fire Brigade should pump cold water on to the rioters in order to disperse them; and one writer seriously deprecated such a step, on the ground that possibly the poor fellows who got the ducking might catch cold! It is possible to go from one extreme to another, and, while wishing to avoid harshness and cruelty in any form, to become too sentimental, and thus do harm in an opposite direction. Sentimental people too often forget the sufferings of the many innocent victims when contemplating those of a few culprits. War is too stern a thing for us to trifle with, and those whose duty it is to be engaged in it must be prepared to suppress with a strong hand anything in the form of incipient mutiny.

With regard to the threat which Gordon held out of shooting one man in five, such a form of punishment is by no means uncommon in countries more civilised than China. It has been frequently resorted to in Russia, and as recently as 1876, during the Russo-Turkish war, on symptoms of a mutiny exhibiting themselves among the Russian troops, the commander-in-chief threatened to shoot one in every ten of the men, and thus quelled the manifestation. There can be no question that Gordon's acting as he did was far more plucky than all the personal exposure to danger through which he went. Many men who would be willing to sacrifice their own lives in the path of duty would have shrunk from taking such a step.

But though Gordon was quite prepared to fight as long as he could benefit his fellow-creatures by so doing, he was essentially a man of peace, and he loathed the horrors of war. On the 29th June he says: "The rebels remain very quiet, and we are engaged in organising another attack upon them. I have, however, sent a letter to the rebel chiefs, offering my good services towards any arrangements they may be inclined to enter into with the Imperialists, by which more fighting may be avoided. I am most anxious to have as little fighting as possible, and shall do my best to bring about a pacific solution of the question." This was the more magnanimous when we consider that he was perfectly confident in the ultimate result of the conflict, and that in the way of glory acquired by brilliant victories he had everything to gain in terminating the war by force of arms instead of by diplomacy.

The rebels at this time had received a great addition of strength by Burgevine going over to them, together with upwards of 300 English, American, and other adventurers. On this subject Gordon says:—

"The fact that Burgevine has joined the rebels will no doubt very much prolong the rebellion, which, humanly speaking, would almost have been put down this year, or at the latest next spring; but the force at my command is too small to do everything, and one has to act with great caution. I feel that I have so many lives intrusted to me, that these are, as it were, at my disposal, and I will not risk them in an enterprise I consider rash. Burgevine is a very foolish fellow, and little thinks of the immense misery he will cause this unhappy country, for of the ultimate suppression of the rebellion I have little doubt."

In another letter he says, "I think the rebels will

soon get very tired of their auxiliaries, and the latter of the rebels."

The worst thing, however, that Gordon had to fear was treachery on the part of his own officers and men. Burgevine knew most of them well, and had managed very skilfully to associate his own dismissal from the command of the Ever-Victorious Army with the fact that he was striving for the interests of the men and officers. Consequently he was to a certain extent a martyr in their eyes, and he made the most of this fact in endeavouring to corrupt some of Gordon's officers. But Burgevine was not more successful in alluring Gordon's army from its allegiance than in defeating it in open conflict. Having made one or two unsuccessful attempts, and discovered that the brilliant young commander was more than a match for him, he asked Gordon to meet him at an appointed place, where he told him that he had determined to desert the rebel cause. This did not surprise Gordon. What did astonish him was that Burgevine went on to propose that Gordon and he should together capture Soo-chow, throw off all allegiance to either Imperialists or rebels, organise an army 20,000 strong, and set up an independent kingdom of their own. Being a mere adventurer himself, he little understood the man of honour with whom he had to deal. Gordon at once cut short further communications. Burgevine and his men, however, being so disgusted with their masters, decided to leave them at all costs, and sent to inform Gordon that at a signal-rocket being fired by him they would rush out under pretence of a sortie and join him. The signal was given, the sortie was made, and a good many got away, but Burgevine and a few others had been suspected and detained. When Gordon discovered this, he generously wrote to the rebel chiefs, explained to them that it was against their interests to compel men to fight against their will, and asked for their release. The messenger who bore the letter was interrogated as to whether he thought it possible for Gordon to be bought over, and his reply was of course in the negative. Strange to say, Gordon's request was granted, and Burgevine was released and handed over to the British Consul. Dr. Wilson informs us that:—

> "At the very time Burgevine was negotiating with Gordon in regard to his relief, he had proposed to Jones, his lieutenant, a plan for entrapping the man whose efforts were being directed toward the succour of him and his followers. Jones revolted against treachery so base, and he and Burgevine had a 'difficulty.' Jones told the story thus: Burgevine drew out his revolver, which he cocked and discharged at my head from a distance of about nine inches. The bullet entered my cheek and passed upward; it has not yet been extracted. I exclaimed, 'You have shot your best friend!' His answer was, 'I know I have, and I wish to God I had killed you.'"

We hear no more of Burgevine in connection with Gordon, so we here part company with him. According to Mr. Wilson, he had subsequently a very chequered career, and finally was reported to have been drowned by accident when a prisoner in the hands of the Imperialists. This writer says, "I have no reason to suppose that the account of his death given by the Chinese authorities was untrue; and if they did drown him purposely, they saved themselves and the American authorities a good deal of trouble." The only wonder is that a scoundrel who so thoroughly deserved to be hanged should ever have found a watery grave.

After the Taipings had got rid of Burgevine and his followers, they began to lose heart, for they felt that the principal reason why these men had deserted their cause was that it was a losing one. They thought that their chances of holding Soo-chow against the ubiquitous Gordon were slight, and, as is often the case under such circumstances, they underrated their own resources, and overrated those of their opponents. They made sure that Gordon would soon assault the city, but this he had no intention of doing. "With the small force at one's command," said he, "I am not at all anxious to pit myself against a town garrisoned by seven, or even ten times our number, if it can be avoided." Instead of attempting an open assault, which must have resulted in a desperate loss of life, Gordon gradually surrounded the city with his own and the Imperial troops, capturing all the smaller places around it, so that it might be completely invested. Here again he exhibited his quick perception of the weak points in his opponents' character. Even the greatest coward amongst our own countrymen would fight desperately if he felt that all his means of retreat were cut off; but, strange as it may seem, this is not a characteristic of all nations. Once let a Chinaman feel that his means of retreat are destroyed, and he is filled with panic. Gordon says, "The great thing in taking stockades from the rebels is to cut off their retreat, and the chances are they will go without trouble; but attack them in front, and leave their rear open, and they will fight most desperately."

Interesting as it would be to many, space does not permit us to follow the details of the siege, and the severe struggles Gordon had in different places, when capturing strongholds of the enemy in order to cut off their supplies. There are, however, a few personal incidents that occurred at this time which deserve mention, in order to show what marvellous escapes he had, and what great personal danger he was often in. Once when sitting on the Patachow Bridge, a somewhat celebrated structure of fifty-three arches and 300 yards long, which he had captured from the enemy, a couple of shots from his own camp struck the bridge close to him. He was alone, and he could not account for the firing. Leaving his seat to ascertain the cause, he got into his boat and started to row across the river, when suddenly an enormous mass of masonry fell from the very spot where he had been sitting, and nearly struck the boat. These two accidental—or shall we more correctly call them providential?—shots saved his life. Again, on the assault of Leeku, he discovered that one of his officers, Lieutenant Perry, had been in communication with the enemy. When challenged, this officer made an excuse which Gordon accepted, saying, "I shall pass over your fault this time, on condition that, in order to show your loyalty, you undertake to lead the next forlorn hope." But Gordon forgot his decision, and was leading the forlorn hope himself, when suddenly an officer next to him was struck down. That officer was Lieutenant Perry, who fell into the arms of his commander. Many of Gordon's officers were brave men, but not a few of them exhibited the white feather, and he had, in order to set an example of personal courage, often to take the lead. Sometimes he would take one of these timid ones by the arm, and, in his quiet way, conduct him into the thick of the fight. His men used to think he had a charmed life, and they termed the little cane which he always carried in place of a sword "the magic wand of victory."

There is one incident which should be mentioned here, although the public did not hear of it for many years after it occurred. When the Ashantee expedition was contemplated, and speculation was rife as to whom the command should be offered to, somebody wrote to the *Times*, signing himself "Mandarin," and, among other things which he mentioned about Gordon, said that during the month of September, before the capture of Soo-chow, Gordon had decided to attack certain detached forts around that place. For some reason his men again mutinied, and refused to march off the parade-ground.

"At this juncture General Gordon arrived on the spot, with his interpreter. He was on foot, in undress, apparently unarmed, and, as usual, exceedingly cool, quiet, and undemonstrative. Directly he approached the leading company, he ordered his interpreter to direct every man who refused to embark to step to the front. One man only advanced. General Gordon drew his revolver from an inside breast-pocket, presented it at the soldier's head, and desired the interpreter to direct the man to march straight to the barge and embark. The order was immediately complied with, and then, General Gordon giving the necessary word of command, the company followed without hesitation. It was generally allowed by the officers, when the event became known, that the success in this instance was solely due to the awe and respect in which General Gordon was held by the men; and that such was the spirit of the troops at the time, that had any other but he attempted what he did, the company would have broken into open mutiny, shot their officers, and committed the wildest excesses. In less than a week the spirit of the troops was as excellent as before, and gradually the whole garrison joined in a series of movements which culminated in the fall of Soo-chow."

CHAPTER VI.

END OF THE REBELLION.

The city of Soo-chow was in the possession of seven rebel generals, each exercising an independent command, but all recognising one of their number, Moh-Wang, as their head. Though the rebels had upwards of 40,000 men in the city, they were badly provided with food, and dissensions broke out among them. Most of the generals were for yielding, but the brave old chieftain, Moh-Wang, opposed such a step. Some of the generals made overtures to Gordon and General Ching, making no other condition than that their lives should be spared. But overtures were of no use so long as Moh-Wang refused to acquiesce. A council of war was summoned, and hot words passed. One general seized the brave old warrior, whose spirit was so invincible, stabbed him, and severed his head from his body. That night, November 29, 1863, Soo-chow, which had been held by the rebels since 1860, was surrendered. In order to prevent his men from looting it, Gordon sent them back to Quinsan, but he asked Governor Li to grant them two months' extra pay, which was denied, though later on one month's pay was granted. This meanness on the part of the civil Governor to a body of men who had done so much for the country very nearly led to a mutiny.

The culminating point of the young commander's grievances against his employers was yet to come. On December 6th, when Gordon visited the captured city, he discovered that the rebel generals who had surrendered had all been killed, in spite of the stipulation that their lives were to be spared. It is said that Gordon was so enraged with this cowardly treachery that he burst into tears, and then went forth, revolver in hand, to seek the Governor, in order to shoot him. It is to be regretted that Sir Henry Gordon, in his biography of his brother, denies this circumstance. Nothing is gained by attempting to screen the faults of a great man. The commander of the Ever-Victorious Army was undeniably a great man, but it is also true that he had his share of human failings, among them a tendency to act on the impulse of the moment. His honour had been touched, he felt that he had been disgraced and would appear in the light of one who could trample on a fallen foe, and there can be no question as to the accuracy of the fact, that in his impulsiveness he did seek the life of Li Hung Chung; though the Governor afterwards became a bosom friend of his. Mr. Wilson, another biographer, who has already been quoted, read his MS. over to Gordon, so that his account is likely to be accurate. In it he says:—

"His first impulse, when his two steamers came in sight, was to obtain hold of the Futai (Governor Li) and inflict summary justice on that high official. General Ching, however, gave timely warning of Gordon's incensed state, and Li very wisely hurried into the city, thus avoiding a meeting. For some days after this Gordon's anxiety to meet with the Futai was only equalled by that of the Futai to keep out of his way, and this was the only period of his campaign during which the commander of the Ever-Victorious Army *burdened himself with carrying arms.*"

The last words of this quotation, which I have italicised, clearly indicate what the nature of the summary punishment would have been had the two men met. Gordon had an opportunity of striking out those words, but he was too honest to do so, for he knew they were true. Even though we may blame him for his actions, we cannot but admire the honesty that would not allow the fact to be concealed.

Both as a matter of policy and a matter of honour, Gordon saw what a fearful mistake had been made. He was of opinion that had an honourable understanding been come to with the rebels at this time, every other city in their hands would have yielded, and thus the rebellion would have been terminated. He at once demanded an investigation into the conduct of Governor Li and General Ching, and refused to co-operate with them further. While Gordon was taking action in this matter, Governor Li was sending despatches to Pekin claiming far more credit than was fairly due for the Imperial troops, though he did not forget to praise Gordon as well. The Emperor sent the young commander 10,000 taels (about £3500) in token of his approbation, together with money for the troops and the wounded. The latter was accepted, but the former was indignantly declined, and that in a very few stiff sentences written on the back of the paper containing the order:—

"Major Gordon receives the approbation of his Majesty the Emperor with every gratification, but regrets most sincerely that, owing to circumstances which occurred since the capture of Soo-chow, he is unable to receive any mark of his Majesty the Emperor's recognition, and therefore respectfully begs his Majesty to receive his thanks for his intended kindness, and to allow him to decline the same."

Writing home he said, "To tell you the truth, I do not want anything, either money or honours, from either the Chinese Government or our own. As for the honours, I do not value them at all, and never did. I should have refused the 10,000 taels even if everything had gone well, and there had been no trouble at Soo-chow."

Gordon's army remained at Quinsan till the end of February 1864. They had received £7000 from the Chinese Government, but this, of course, did not compensate them for being prevented from taking their share of loot, and not only were they dissatisfied, but their inaction was doubtless doing them much harm. Moreover, the rebel forces were recruiting rapidly, and all the good work that Gordon had accomplished appeared likely to be undone. Gordon heard all the excuses that Governor Li had to offer, and came to the conclusion that Asiatics must not be judged according to the standard by which Englishmen, with a higher sense of honour, measure themselves. He therefore made up his mind to emerge from his retreat, and, stipulating that in the event of future capitulations nothing should be done without his consent, he once more took the field with the object of terminating the rebellion.

On the 17th February 1864 he had been promoted to the rank of lieutenant-colonel by the War Office authorities. This, of course, made no difference to his position as general in the Chinese army. His resumption of hostilities was marked by similar tactics to those which he had previously found so successful. Blows rapidly struck at distant points appear to have been his aim. Having captured Soo-chow, the next place of importance was Nankin, the second largest city in China, about 100 miles to the north-west. The rebels were in strong force there, and the place was too distant to make it practicable to capture it, at once, as there were several cities *en route* still in the hands of the rebels. Gordon decided to take these latter in detail, and he commenced with Yesing, which fell easily on March 1st. He then proceeded to Liyang, which yielded even more easily. The horrors witnessed on this march were awful. Gordon said of the inhabitants:—

> "Those who still remained alive had been driven to eat human flesh, and the unburied bodies of the dead were in a condition which showed that much of this revolting food had been consumed." "The scenes I have witnessed of misery are something dreadful; and I must say that your wish for me to return with the work incomplete would not be expressed if you saw the state of these poor people. The horrible furtive looks of the wretched inhabitants hovering about one's boats haunts me. . . . I hope to get the Shanghai people to assist, but they do not see these things: and to read that there are human beings eating human flesh produces less effect than if they saw the corpses from which the flesh is cut."

Gordon's fate was to be hampered by the blunders of his friends. On March 20th he marched on Kintang; but just as he was about to commence operations, an alarming despatch reached him from the Imperial commander. The Imperialists had actually not been able, with their immense force, to hold cities that Gordon with his small one had captured and handed over to their charge. Fushan had fallen, and Chanzu was in danger. However, Gordon thought that as he was so close to Kintang, he might as well take it, and so he made an assault. It did not, however, yield so easily, and Major Kirkham, one of his best officers, was badly wounded. Gordon himself was also wounded below the knee. A soldier who saw him struck was about to proclaim the event, when Gordon stopped him for fear he should discourage the men. He went on fighting till he fainted from loss of blood, and Dr. Moffitt * had to carry him out of action.

Sir Frederick Bruce, the British representative, wrote to Colonel Gordon after he was wounded at Kintang:—

"Be cautious of yourself. I beg you not to look upon your position merely from a military point of view. You have done quite enough for your reputation as a gallant and skilful leader. We all look to you as the only person fit to act with these perverse Chinese, and to be trusted with the great interests at stake at Shanghai. Your life and ability to keep the field are more important than the capture of any city in China."

Gordon had to abandon further attempts to take Kintang, and retire on Liyang. Here he took to his steamer, as he could no longer march owing to his wound, the first and last that he ever had. With 1000 men he started on March 24th for Woosieh, to find that the rebels who had been threatening that place had fallen back. On the following day, lying on his back in a steamer, and accompanied by a flotilla, Gordon made a dash with the 1000 men he had right into the midst of the country held by the rebels, in order to ascertain their disposition of troops. Well might Colonel Chesney say, "One scarcely knows here whether most to admire the pluck, or to wonder at the confidence of the wounded com-

* Surgeon Moffitt of the 67th Regiment was a man of ability and courage. He became a great personal friend of Gordon's, and afterwards married one of Gordon's sisters. He died in the year 1882. He was the only officer who remained with Gordon from the beginning to the end of the campaign.

mander!" He quickly took in the whole situation, and made up his mind that a place called Waisso, which was held by the enemy in some force, was the point at which to aim. Unfortunately, he was unable to get about himself, yet he could not take the entire force, which had been increased by one more battalion, on board. Consequently he had to divide it, leaving a detachment to go by land. The officers put in charge seem to have fallen into every mistake it was possible for soldiers to make. The attacking regiments did not co-operate, their flanks were left unprotected, and a long gap was permitted to occur between two regiments. To make a long story short, the assault failed, the assailants narrowly escaping annihilation. Unquestionably this signal failure was due to the fact that the commander, being wounded, could not see to details himself, and was obliged to leave his principal arm, the infantry, to the direction of others.

Fortunately the Imperialists with 6000 men came to Gordon's assistance. The Imperial force had been doing remarkably well in their recent conflict with the enemy, but unfortunately had lost their commander, General Ching. This man, who at first had been so jealous of Gordon, had afterwards learnt to know and respect him, and Gordon had acquired quite an affection for him in spite of his faults. Gordon was deeply grieved to hear of his death, indeed it is said that he burst into tears. It is touching to read an account of the death of this heathen general, who, it will be remembered, had been a leading man among the rebels before they degenerated. Mr. Hake's account is founded on the statement of Governor Li, who says that even when he knew his wound was fatal, he concentrated his mind on the affairs of the country. He pointed out that though the rebels had been beaten, their strength was not to be despised, and begged his colleague to order his officers to be careful in battle. He remarked that brave men were not easily to be found, and he bitterly regretted his own fate, by which he was prevented from doing his duty to his country. When gradually sinking, he ordered his servant to bring the yellow jacket presented to him by the Emperor, and to assist him on with it. He then bowed his head towards the Imperial Palace, and thus he yielded up his brave patriotic spirit.

After the junction of the Imperialists with Gordon's force there was little difficulty in the capture of Waisso, and with the fall of that place on April 6th it became evident that the campaign was fast drawing to a close, the only places of any importance remaining in the hands of the rebels being Nankin and Chanchufu. The former Gordon left to the Imperialists, who felt confident of victory, and were very jealous of the successful young soldier. Indeed, it is evident that they could easily have taken Chanchufu also, but they apparently were in no hurry to close the campaign. Many of them were mere mercenaries, who did not want to remove the *raison-d'être* for their existence as an army. Strong suspicion exists that an incident which occurred soon after Gordon reached Chanchufu, and when he was making preparations for the attack, was really an attempt on his life. He and Major Tapp, a clever artillery officer, were engaged in the construction of a battery, when suddenly one of the picquets fired a volley at the battery, and the rebels, not knowing the cause, fired also. Gordon and his party were thus between two fires, and Major Tapp and several others were killed.

The first assault on Chanchufu was made by the Imperialists, and defeated. Gordon was then asked to co-operate in another assault, which he did; but not being supported by the Imperialists, he also failed. After this a combined assault was made, and again it failed. Seeing that the place was too strongly defended for an ordinary assault, Gordon taught the Imperialists how to approach it by means of trenches. Another assault was made by the Imperialists, who were on the point of being driven back again, when Gordon came to their rescue, and the stronghold was taken. When the rebel commander was captured he said that, except for the aid of Gordon and his men, he could have defied all the Futai hosts to take the city from him. The garrison was 20,000 strong; the place was skilfully fortified; and the rebels, thinking that they would receive no quarter, fought with great desperation and recklessness of life.

With the capture of Chanchufu ends the list of Gordon's fights in China. His next care was to break up the Ever-Victorious Army. He knew this to be very important, for he felt that they would be a standing danger to the country. With men like Burgevine about, who were not wanting in skill, and were as unprincipled as they were daring, it was impossible to say what might happen if the command of such an army fell into bad hands. The Chinese Government behaved very generously, giving each wounded officer £900, and others on a similar scale. In a letter written home, Gordon says:—

"The losses I have sustained in this campaign have been no joke: out of one hundred officers I have had forty-eight killed and wounded; and out of 3500 men, nearly 1000 killed and wounded; but I have the satisfaction of knowing that, as far as mortal can see, six months will see the end of this rebellion, while if I had continued inactive it might have lingered on for six years. Do not think that I am ill-tempered, but I do not care one jot about my promotion or what people may say. I know I shall leave China as poor as I entered it,* but with the knowledge that through my weak instrumentality upwards of eighty to one hundred thousand lives have been spared. I want no further satisfaction than this."

A large sum of money was offered to Gordon and at first declined; but when pressed to accept it, he decided to do so, and divide it among his men. His pay had been good, being over £3000 per annum, but, in his usual generous manner, he had spent it almost entirely on his men, especially in providing comforts for the sick and wounded.

The last fight had taken place on May 11th, and by June 1st Gordon had disbanded his army, his promptness exhibiting itself to the very last. "So parted the Ever-Victorious Army," says Colonel Chesney in his "Essays on Modern Military Biography," "from its general, and its brief but useful existence came to an end. During sixteen months' campaigning under his guidance it had taken four cities and a dozen minor strong places, fought innumerable combats, put *hors de combat* numbers of the enemy, moderately estimated at fifteen times its own, and finding the rebellion vigor-

* It may be well to note here that his predecessor, Ward, who was killed in action, accumulated the sum of £60,000, although he was not very long in command, and was not considered at all an unscrupulous man.

ous, aggressive, and almost threatening the unity of the Chinese Empire, had left it at its last gasp, confined to the ruined capital of the usurper."

Gordon paid a visit to the Imperialists who were investing Nankin, where he interested himself in their mode of conducting the siege, and gave a good deal of useful advice as to the future existence of the Imperial army. Beyond this he took no active part. Nankin fell; the "Heavenly King," who was the author of the rebellion, committed suicide; and Chung Wang, his celebrated general, was beheaded, permission being given to him at his own request that he might first write his autobiography. One cannot but feel that it would have been an act of policy as well as of clemency had the Emperor spared the life of this noble fellow Chung Wang, more especially as the so-called Heavenly King had committed suicide. As long as he was alive Chung Wang showed a loyalty to him that was worthy of a better cause. He might easily have escaped with his life but that he was anxious to save the life of the son of the Heavenly King, a worthless individual, with all the faults of his father and none of his ability. Chung Wang gave up his fleet-footed horse to the young man, who did not even know how to make use of the chance thus given him. The loyalty Chung Wang displayed to the rebel chief might easily have been transferred to the Emperor. Governor Li we shall hear of again, for when Gordon revisited China in 1880 he found his old friend still alive and active. There can be no doubt that Gordon's personal influence over this man was considerable, and when we next hear of him it is as standing almost alone among his countrymen, pleading for a peaceable policy. The latter part of the following letter, which he wrote to Gordon when in the Soudan, shows that he had imbibed a good deal of that public spiritedness which made Gordon so willing to sacrifice himself for the good of others. The letter was dated March 22, 1879. Li Hung said:—

"I am right glad to hear from you. It is now fourteen years since we parted from each other. Although I have not written to you, I often speak of you, and remember you with very great interest. The benefit you have conferred on China does not disappear with your person, but is felt throughout the regions in which you played so important and active a part. All these people bless you for the blessings of peace and prosperity which they now enjoy. Your achievements in Egypt are well known throughout the civilised world. I see often in the papers of your noble works on the upper Nile. You are a man of ample resources, with which you suit yourself to any kind of emergency. My hope is that you may long be spared to improve the condition of the people among whom your lot is cast. I am striving hard to advance my people to a higher state of development, and to unite both this and all other nations within the four seas under one common brotherhood."

An amusing circumstance was the utter bewilderment of the Regent of China, Prince Kung, as to how he could reward Gordon. The money offered he had refused for himselt, and as for honours and distinctions they had no charms for him. He accepted the yellow jacket, the highest distinction the Chinese Emperor could confer (corresponding to our Knight of the Garter), but this he did only to please his parents, not because he valued it himself. Prince Kung called on the English Minister at Shanghai and said, "You will be surprised to see me again, but I felt I could not allow you to leave without coming to see you about

Gordon. We do not know what to do. He will not receive money from us, and we have already given him every honour which it is in the power of the Emperor to bestow; but as these can be of little value in his eyes, I have brought you this letter, and ask you to give it to the Queen of England, that she may bestow on him some reward which would be more valuable in his eyes."

Gordon had already been awarded a brevet lieutenant-colonelcy in the Royal Engineers, so he was now made a Commander of the Bath; but he was as indifferent to English honours as to those of the Chinese. As for Prince Kung's letter to Queen Victoria, we are informed by Mr. Hake that he has good reason to believe it never reached the Queen, but was allowed to remain in a pigeon-hole in the Foreign Office! Well may we quote the words of Axel Oxenstiern to his son, to which the late Prince Consort once referred in a letter to the late Emperor of Germany, at that time Crown Prince of Prussia, "Oh my son, mark how little wisdom goes to the government of states." Mr. Hake also informs us that when General Gordon presented himself at the War Office, the Secratary of State seemed hardly to have heard his name, and knew nothing of his work in China. Yet this was the man that at the age of thirty had saved from ruin the largest empire of the world! We are indeed a marvellous people. We are always manufacturing sham heroes, and parading them before the world. Yet when we have a real one in our midst we utterly ignore him. When one thinks of the many campaigns in which England has been engaged since the Chinese war was over, the public may well be astonished at a military system which allowed one of its ablest soldiers to live in obscurity, and not even be consulted in the affairs of the nation. Sir William Butler with withering scorn says :—

> "Nay, he was almost a stranger in his own land, and, when nearly a generation had passed away, and the fruit of many blunders had accumulated in Egypt a load of disaster that seemed too heavy to be borne, Gordon was at last called from the obscurity in which he had been so long consigned,—he was, his own brother has told us, as a person who was now heard of for the first time."

A report has been circulated that he was offered the command of the Ashantee Expedition and declined it. This report has absolutely no foundation. The truth of the matter is that he never was offered a command on active service of any kind by the British authorities. Those who manage the affairs of other nations were able to recognise the merits of this remarkable man, and to find opportunities for him to exercise his powers, but our own authorities seem to have been absolutely blind to his qualities. Yet this was he of whom Colonel Chesney, a great writer on military matters, said, "If there is a man in the world who can conduct a war with honour, thoroughness, and humanity, and bring it to a satisfactory close without needless delay or expense, England has that man in 'Chinese Gordon.'" It is, of course, quite possible that every army has some men of military genius, whose services are never utilised in positions of importance, for the simple reason that they are unknown to the authorities. There is no profession in which it is more difficult to pick out the born leaders than is the case in the army. Plenty of men who promise well when in a subordinate position prove miserable failures when in command. Men who can pass examinations with flying colours are not always able to make use of their knowledge in the field. A foreign power had, however, provided a field in which one of our officers was able to show what wonderful military instincts he possessed. It is therefore all the more difficult to find excuses for those who were responsible for the fact that, as far as England was concerned, Gordon was allowed to live in obscurity, and was never even offered a command of any sort in any of the campaigns in which his countrymen were engaged.

CHAPTER VII.

AT GRAVESEND.

When Lord John Russell visited Elba, he was asked by Napoleon, then a prisoner there, whether he thought that his rival, the Duke of Wellington, would be able to live without the excitement of war, which Napoleon used to call "a splendid game." It seemed incredulous to Napoleon that a man who had shown himself so good a soldier as Wellington should retire into the position of a simple citizen, and Napoleon, little knowing the great man, thought that he would probably use his influence as a statesman to involve his country in war again. To some it may possibly seem strange that Gordon, who had distinguished himself as a soldier, and had saved an empire, should again take up the humble avocation of an engineer officer, but so he did. He was in reality only a captain of engineers, though a brevet lieutenant-colonel in the army, when in February 1865 he returned home. He took a few months' leave, which he spent quietly at Southampton with his father and mother, shunning all publicity.

On the expiration of his leave he was sent to Gravesend, to superintend the building of some forts for the protection of the Thames. During one of our periodical panics as to the safety of the country, large sums of money were voted for defensive purposes. Gordon's duties were very subordinate as far as these defences were concerned. The plans were made out by others, and his duty was merely to see them executed. Though he worked very hard in the performance of his duty, he made no secret of the fact that he thoroughly disapproved of the way in which the national money was being wasted. It is said that one day, when the Commander-in-chief came to inspect the progress of the work, Gordon denounced the whole thing most vehemently, and exposed its worthlessness. It is characteristic of the man that he had the courage of his opinions at all times. He must have been carried away a good deal by his feelings, for when he got home that day he said that he might have been put under arrest for the way in which he had denounced the work of his superiors. As it was, his Royal Highness smiled good-naturedly at his vehemence, and took no further notice. But though Gordon thoroughly disapproved of the nature of the defences on which he was engaged, he worked very hard at them, and it certainly is through no fault of his if the Thames fortifications are not all they should be. He was an early riser and a hard worker, and as he hardly ever went into society, and did not go in for games, he found time to engage in all kinds of religious and philanthropic work, in addition to his other duties. He spent six years at Gravesend, and, although this is not a popular station with many officers, he found so much to be done, that in after years he used to look back upon the time spent there as the happiest of his life. After the stirring scenes through which he had passed in the Crimea and in China, it may have appeared to some a very commonplace, uninteresting sort of life to eke out for so many years, but no one more than Gordon felt the force of the truth conveyed in the lines:—

"'A commonplace life,' we say and we sigh;
But why should we sigh as we say?
The commonplace sun in the commonplace sky
Makes up the commonplace day.
The moon and the stars are commonplace things,
And the flower that blooms, and the bird that sings;
But dark were the world, and sad our lot,
If the flowers failed, and the sun shone not;
And God, who studied each separate soul,
Out of commonplace lives made His beautiful whole."

One remarkable characteristic of Gordon was the persistent way in which he avoided publicity of any sort, evading every effort to bring him forward. When he first came to Gravesend no one knew him, and he used quietly to take a seat in the gallery of the parish church. As soon as it was discovered that the stranger who occupied such a humble place, was no other than the renowned "Chinese Gordon," great efforts were made to induce him to take a more prominent position. But it was in vain. What was good enough for the poor was good enough for him, and he did not approve of the rich and the eminent occupying all the good seats, to the exclusion of the poor, whose souls were just as valuable in the sight of God. Again, he steadily refused to take the chair at all public meetings. It was not that he could not speak at such gatherings, for, although he was not a good speaker, he was by no means a bad one, and he was always willing to conduct services for the poor. He had a horror of taking a prominent position, and the only occasion on which he ever broke through his rule as to taking the chair, was at a meeting of some three hundred children over which he presided. He was, however, very much at home when sitting in front of a class of children, and this he infinitely preferred to giving formal addresses even to children. Only once was he persuaded to address the whole school collectively. Speaking to a large number of children requires a special gift, and this he did not possess. His strength with children lay in the fact that he obtained a personal influence over each one individually. With a small class he could get to know each by name, and win the affections of all one by one. The words, "He loved little children," which were the only epitaph on the tomb of a certain Sunday-school teacher, might well be applied to Gordon. It is difficult to say what kind of teacher he was, or whether he availed himself of the latest developments in the art of instructing children; but this is quite clear, that he had one of the best qualifications a teacher can possess, love for his pupils. There is a tale of a lady visitor who once asked a little boy why he went so far to his Sunday-school, when there were as good ones nearer at hand. The reply was, "They may be as good, but they are not so good for me;" and when the lady asked him "Why not?" he said, "Because they love a fellow over there." Love is a qualification that is too often lacking in teachers, but it was one that Gordon displayed very prominently. Need we wonder that the "dear little fellows," as he used to call them, responded by loving him in return?

Nor was it only in the Sunday-school that Gordon's love for the young was exhibited; he also had a class in the ragged school, and used to invite his boys to his house for instruction in the evening on week days, as well as on Sunday evenings. When three or four of them had scarlet fever, he nursed them in his own house, and would sit up at night talking to them, till he could get them to drop off to sleep. He used to call these boys "kings," a name suggested to him when reading Rev. i. 6, "And hath made us kings and priests unto God." He exclaimed to his sister, "Why then, these are little 'kings,'" and he stuck to the name. He took great pains to secure good posts for his boys in ships going to sea, and on a map on his wall he kept a number of little flags representing the boys he had sent abroad. These flags he used to move about as he heard from time to time where the lads were. We need not be surprised that among these boys were some who ardently loved him, and that they used to give expression to their feelings by scribbling on the wall with a piece of chalk, as boys will do, "God bless the Kernel," "C. G. is a jolly good fellow," or "Long life to our dear teacher, Gordon." The ragged school at Gravesend still retains the Chinese flags which he presented to the boys, flags which he had himself captured from the Taiping rebels. They are now kept as precious relics, to be displayed only on special occasions. Sir Henry Gordon says, that when the news reached England of the death of the heroic defender of Khartoum, a young man, about twenty-five years of age, called on him to inform him that he and others who had been Gordon's boys at Gravesend, wished to put up some kind of memorial to his memory, and that he was willing to give £25. He was much overcome when speaking of all that Gordon had done for him.

Another writer relates that on one occasion when Gordon was watching some workmen, he saw among them a lad looking very unhappy. On his inquiring, the lad said, "Mother has left us, and gone away from home; and everything there is so miserable that it is not like home at all." At once the boy was invited to spend his evenings at the Fort House, where he was instructed in the night school class, and taught to read his Bible. Some little time after this he fell ill, and the doctor decided that he ought to be taken to the local infirmary. "Shall I see you there, Colonel?" he asked with wistful eyes; "I know I am going to die." "But you are not afraid," replied Gordon, "for now you know who says, 'I am the Resurrection and the Life.' He will be as near to you in the infirmary as here, and as near to you in death as in life." "Oh, yes, I know Him now;" and so he did, for as the narrator said, "The Colonel had led him to Christ by his life and teaching." When in the hospital the young lad said to a nurse, "Read the Bible to me, there is nothing like it." "But you are very tired," said the nurse. "Yes, I am very tired. I do long to go to Jesus." This is a briefly narrated incident, and is but a specimen of many that might be recorded if space permitted.

Gordon also took special pleasure in visiting the workhouse and talking to the paupers, remembering that—

> "Down in the human heart, crushed by the tempter,
> Feelings lie buried that grace can restore;
> Touched by a loving heart, wakened by kindness,
> Chords that were broken will vibrate once more."

Workhouse inmates are, as a rule, a very disheartening class to visit. A large percentage of them have been brought there by faults of their own, and most of them are beyond the age when one may reasonably hope for reform. Gordon's kind heart was proof against disappointment, and he persistently used to visit the old people, supplying tobacco to the men, and tea to the women, and chatting away to them, in an effort to help them to forget their troubles. He was mindful, too, of the sick, caring not who the sufferer was nor what his complaint; so long as he was in need, so long was Gordon a regular visitor at his sick-bed. Frequently when he heard that the doctors had ordered delicacies beyond the reach of a patient, he would purchase what was required, and administer it with his own hands. Mr. Lilley says:—

> "On one occasion he visited a poor, wretched woman, in an apparently dying condition. He at once lighted a fire, made some gruel for her, and fed her with his own hand. He afterwards appointed a nurse to look after her, and sent a doctor to her, and it is believed that she is still residing at Gravesend, a living testimony to his generous care."

The people so loved him, that often instead of sending for the clergyman when in sickness or trouble, the poor would send for the Colonel living at Fort House, the official residence of the officer commanding the Royal Engineers.

Even his house and garden seem to have been placed at the disposal of the poor in the neighbourhood. A visitor once remarked to his housekeeper on the beautiful vegetables his garden produced. She replied that the Colonel never touched them, but used to let the poor people come in and cultivate plots of ground in the garden, and grow their own vegetables; and even when presents of fruit were sent him by friends, he used to take them to the bedside of some sick person, who he thought needed them more than he did.

As for his own food, nothing could have been more simple and plain. The Rev. S. H. Swaine says, "Coming home with us one afternoon late, we found his tea waiting for him—a most unappetising stale loaf and a teapot of tea. I remarked upon the dryness of the bread, when he took the whole loaf (a small one) and crammed it into the slop-basin, and poured all the tea upon it, saying it would soon be ready for him to eat, and in half-an-hour it would not matter what he had eaten." It is said that some of the boys whom he invited to live in his house were a good deal disappointed when they saw the kind of fare that was put before them. They had fondly imagined that the occupant of such a grand house would have sumptuous meals, which they would share, and they were not prepared for the plain salt-beef, and other good but very plain food, to which the Colonel was in the habit of sitting down. But though he denied himself luxuries of any sort, he often used to take grapes and other dainties to the sick and the dying.

All forms of distress aroused his interest; and when the late Canon Miller of Greenwich was collecting money for the suffering people at Coventry, during the cotton famine, Gordon took a large and valuable gold medal, that had been presented to him by the Empress of China, and having with a gouge scooped out his name, which was engraved upon it, put it into an envelope and despatched it to the Canon, merely notifying briefly the object for which it was sent. Efforts have been since made to discover the fate of the medal, which was of the best gold, and twice the size of a crown piece, but owing to the death of Canon Miller, they have hitherto been unsuccessful.

Gordon was, indeed, generous to a fault, and sometimes he was taken in by impostors; but as he had a good knowledge of human nature, he was not deceived so often as many with his generous heart would be. His generosity was only limited by his purse, and there were times in his life when he drew the line too fine, for, as he himself once said, "I assure you that many a time I have not known where my food was to come from, nor if I should find a place in which to lie down at night." So long as there was money in his pocket, so long had he money to give away; but on many occasions he forgot that he had a long railway journey before him, and that the generosity he displayed to the needy would not be extended to him at the railway ticket office. But on the whole, his money was well laid out; many is the lad he started in life, many the waif he picked up from the gutter, who, now a well-to-do respectable member of society, might, but for him, have been a criminal, getting into trouble himself, and leading others astray.

It would be interesting to follow more in detail the career of this remarkable man at Gravesend, but space forbids. Gordon only spent six years at this kind of work, and much of the time was engaged in his official duties, yet the results were so good, that one cannot but regret that a longer part of his career was not passed in the same way. From his letters written in the Soudan, it is evident that he often thought of devoting his old age to work among the poor, had he been spared. It was, however, willed otherwise, and we are only permitted to see how much can be done by a man in six years, when his heart is thoroughly in the work.

It has been remarked more than once, that Gordon's military career reminds one of the great soldier Cromwell, who did so much to rescue England from the degenerate condition into which it had fallen under the miserable rule of the Stuarts. In the same way the six years spent by Gordon at Gravesend, very forcibly remind us of the great religious philanthropist, Lord Shaftesbury, who did perhaps more than any other man of this nineteenth century, or any other century, to relieve human suffering, and to solve some of those difficult problems that are associated with the condition of the poor. Lord Shaftesbury had little in common with Cromwell, except that both loved God and hated tyranny and injustice. Their ways of going to work were very different, but one cannot help seeing that Gordon combined much of both characters; and had his lot fallen in different times or different circumstances, he might have undertaken the work of either. He had all the martial instinct of a Cromwell, and, with it, the love of relieving suffering which so characterised Lord Shaftesbury. His one object seems to have been to—

> "Rescue the perishing, care for the dying,
> Snatch them in pity from sin and the grave;
> Weep o'er the erring ones, lift up the fallen,
> Tell them of Jesus, the Mighty to save."

Gordon was never allowed to carry on any work for any great length of time, and the six years at Gravesend passed very quickly. In 1871 he was appointed British representative on the European Commission to superintend the improvement of the mouth of the Danube, so that it might be made more navigable for ships. He was engaged in this work for two years, with his head-quarters at Galatz; and the eminent war correspondent, Archibald Forbes, says that he "found his memory still green there in the early years of the Russo-Turkish war, fourteen years after he had exchanged the mosquitoes of the Lower Danube for the not less venomous insects of the Upper Nile."

Apart from the testimony of Archibald Forbes, we may be quite sure that he did some good work at Galatz, for it would be difficult to imagine him doing nothing but the ordinary routine of official duties. He always discovered an opening of some sort by which he could help his fellow-creatures, and his active mind and sympathetic nature were, in the words of Jean Ingelow, always asking the question of those with whom he came in contact—

> "Are there no briers across thy pathway thrust?
> Are there no thorns that compass it about?
> Nor any stones that thou wilt deign to trust
> My hand to gather out?"

The time had now come when he was to be called to a new form of work, one to which he was to give the best years of his life, and for which ultimately he was to sacrifice life itself. In the Crimea and in China, he had shown what he could do as a soldier; at Gravesend he had set a noble example to the world of what a Christian philanthropist might do in his spare hours; and now he was to be called to wage war with the horrors of slavery. We had him in our midst for six years, and we found no work for him worthy of his abilities; but while we overlooked his merits, other nations were not so blind. Just as later on the King of the Belgians was anxious to secure his services which we were allowing to remain idle, so now Nubar Pasha, the far-sighted minister of Ismail Khan, Khedive of Egypt, persuaded him to enter the Egyptian service, and go to Africa as Governor of the Equatorial Provinces.

But before we follow him into the Soudan, it may be well to dwell for a little on the distinctly religious aspect of his life.

CHAPTER VIII.

*SIMPLE FAITH.**

THERE are few young men who cannot remember having, in their boyhood, taken a caterpillar and shut it up in a box. Before long the creature assumed a chrysalis form, and finally developed into a butterfly, with a completely new power not possessed by the caterpillar. Instead of only being able to grovel on the ground, the creature in its new existence is able to soar high into the air. This is one of Nature's conversions, and is a faint illustration of the spiritual change which takes place in the human heart, when the natural man becomes a new creature with new powers. It is customary for some to sneer at the doctrine of conversion, scorning the idea of a distinctly spiritual change taking place in the human heart. It would, however, be difficult to find any other term by which accurately to describe the change that took place in Gordon's life.

Up to a certain period, while he had done well all that he was called upon to do, and had completely outstripped his peers, showing himself, in his profes-

* In this and the following chapter, I have, in order to give Gordon's views, selected quotations from his letters at different periods of his life, but not always in chronological order. For want of space a large number of extracts have had to be omitted; those that are given must be taken as specimens.

sional capacity, to be a head and shoulders above his fellows, there were nevertheless latent powers within him, which had not yet been called into play. Who can study his life without being convinced that he had a power with God, in later life, that he did not possess earlier? Christ said, "I, if I be lifted up, will draw all men unto Me." He was lifted up before Gordon's eyes, and there was a distinctive response to the magnetic influence of the Cross; and, as in the laws of magnetism, the instrument that has been charged can in its turn charge metal brought into contact with it, so in the life of Gordon we see, that not only had the Redeemer a distinct influence on his whole nature, but that he was himself so charged with Divine love, that he was able to exert a magnetic influence over others. Ecclesiastics may fight and wrangle about names and terms; we have to deal with facts. It matters little by what name we call it, the fact remains that a distinct spiritual change came over Gordon, leaving him a man who had power with God. But though the effect of this change in Gordon's life was most marked, it is not so obvious when it took place. As a boy and a cadet he was full of animal spirits, and somewhat given to practical joking; but, though not a religious boy, he never was bad in the ordinary acceptation of the term. After he had obtained his commission, before he went out to the Crimea, there were distinct indications of a feeling after God, and some have affirmed that this was brought about through the influence of his mother. That good mothers are blessed by God as the means of conveying spiritual light to their boys, is a fact so frequently evident, that writers and others are often led to assume it must always be the case.

Now, though Gordon possessed an excellent mother, of whom he was very fond, and who in later years became a true Christian, as a matter of fact in early life she was somewhat worldly. She was always a remarkably clever and sensible woman, but in the matter of religion she never attempted to influence her son. Whatever of spiritual good there was in him, was therefore not due to her. That he had great affection for her is clear, even if there were no other evidence, from a letter written during her illness in October 1873, when he was abroad, to his sister, in which occurs this passage:—

"Kiss my dear mother, and do not fret for me. I have, thank God, all comfort, peace, and happy reminiscence with the knowledge that the Comforter is with you all; that He is able, willing, unselfish, and kind, and that He will keep you all till you reach the land where the 'sun never sets,' and where you will see Him, and know why 'Jesus wept' at Lazarus' grave. Feed by the living pastures; they will fatten you."

A few days later he says:—

"By keeping my watch at your time, I feel enabled to know what you are doing. It will be a sore trial for you to see my dear mother leave her worn-out shell, but you will feel that God takes her to Himself. My dear mother has spent a useful, hard-working life, and a happy one; it seems as if it is for you she is kept."

Still the truth expressed in the following lines applied to Gordon's case:—

"They talk about a woman's sphere,
As though it had no limit.
There's not a place in earth or heaven,
There's not a task to mankind given.
There's not a blessing or a woe,

There's not a whispered yes or no,
There's not a life, or death, or birth,
That has a feather's weight of worth,
Without a woman in it."

Writers have too often ignored the influence of an elder sister in the formation of a man's character. There can be little doubt that even before Gordon went out to the Crimea, he was indebted to his sister for much spiritual help, as the following letter, written from Pembroke in 1854, shows:—

"MY DEAR AUGUSTA,—Write another note like the last, when you have time, as I hope I have turned over a new leaf, and I should like you to give me some hope of being received.

. . . . . I got your very kind letter to-day, and am very much obliged to you for it. I have not had time to look out the texts, but will do so to-morrow. I am lucky in having a very religious captain of the 11th, of the name of Drew; he has on the mantelpiece of his room the 'Priceless Diamond,' which I read before yours arrived. I intend sending to you, as soon as possible, a book called 'The Remains of the Rev. R. McCheyne,' which I am sure you will be delighted with. I told Drew to go to Mr. Molyneux; and he did so, and of course was highly pleased. I cannot write much in favour of our pastor; he is a worldly man, and does not live up to his preaching; but I have got Scott's 'Commentaries.' I remember well when you used to get them in numbers, and I used to laugh at them; but, thank God, it is different with me now. I feel much happier and more contented than I used to do. I did not like Pembroke, but now I would not wish for any prettier place. I have got a horse and gig, and Drew and myself drive all about the country. I hope my dear father and mother think of eternal things. Can I do or say anything to either to do good? When you get my book, read the 'Castaway.'

"You know I never was confirmed. When I was a cadet, I thought it was a useless sin, as I did not intend to alter (not that it was in my power to be converted when *I* chose). I, however, took my first sacrament on Easter day, [16th April 1854], and have communed ever since.

"I am sure I do not wonder at the time you spent in your room, and the eagerness with which you catch at useful books—no novels or worldly books come up to the Sermons of M[c]Cheyne or the Commentaries of Scott. I am a great deal in the air, as my fort is nine miles off, and I have to go down pretty often. It is a great blessing for me that in my profession I can be intimate with whom I like, and have not the same trials among my brother officers as those in a line regiment have. I ought not to say this, for 'where sin aboundeth, grace aboundeth more fully;' but I am such a miserable wretch, that I should be sure to be led away. Dearest Augusta, pray for me, I beg of you."

For several years after the date of the above letter, he alludes very little to religion, and if we may accept his own statement on the subject, in a letter from China, dated Taku Forts, 15th March 1862, it is probable that he went back for a time.

"The climate, work, and everything here suits me, and I am thankful to say I am happy both in mind and body. I have had a slight attack of small-pox—it is not necessary to tell my mother this, as it will trouble her. I am glad to say that this disease has brought me back to my Saviour, and I trust in future to be a better Christian than I have been hitherto."

Then followed the stirring adventures he went through in command of the Ever-Victorious Army in China; but that he could not, during that period, have had the full assurance which characterised him later on, and which arises from the witness of the Holy Spirit, is evident from the fact that he once remarked to his aunt, Miss Enderby, that he could not make out how it was that he had feared death so little, when all the time he did not know that he was prepared to die.

On the 19th September 1865, his father passed away

a few months after he had taken up his appointment at Gravesend. This event seems to have marked an important crisis in his spiritual life. He shut himself up in complete retirement for a few days, and emerged a very different man from what he had been before. From that time to the day of his death, he was known as an out-and-out Christian. During the previous ten years it is clear, from his letters, that he was in the highest and truest sense a child of God, but there seems to have been something wanting in his character. From the time of his father's death, he seems to have had such a firm assurance in Christ, that religion was the prevailing element of his life.

It is interesting to note that Gordon dedicated himself to the service of God not only in the full vigour of health and strength, but at a time when he might have been, had he chosen, one of the world's favourites. In the case of some, broken health, advancing age, or disappointed hopes and ambitions, are the causes that lead to a search for something more lasting than this world can offer. Thankful as we may be when any man yields to the higher claims of his Heavenly Father, whatever the prompting cause may be, it is satisfactory to be able to record an instance in which apparently none but the highest motives were at work. Gordon at the time of his father's death was only thirty-two years of age, and though young, he had done deeds of heroism which might make many a Victoria Cross hero envy his opportunity and courage. He had seen what the world had to offer, and he decided that there was a nobler life to be led. To that new life he dedicated his remaining years, and, it need hardly be added, he never regretted the choice. As late as the 26th March

1881, after he had just recovered from a severe illness, he remarks: "B—— said, when dying, how glad he was he had sought God in his time of strength, for when he was sinking he could not do so, and so I feel."

If we may form any opinion from expressions in his letters, dating from this time to the day of his death, Gordon's religion brought him that "peace of mind which passeth all understanding," and which the world can neither give nor take away. The following are but specimens of many remarks which he let fall from time to time on this subject:—

"I may say that I have died suddenly over a hundred times; but in these deaths I have never felt the least doubt of my salvation."

"I would that all had the full assurance of life. It is precisely because we are despicable and worthless that we are accepted. Till we throw over that idea that we are better than others, we can never have that assurance."

Nor must it be thought that the joy and happiness he experienced in religion arose from any inward sense of self-satisfaction. Never had a man a humbler estimate of himself than Gordon, but his faith in this respect took a very healthy form. Instead of morbidly looking into his own heart for evidences of his union with Christ, he ever kept his eye on the precious work of his Saviour for him. Space will not permit many quotations from his writings, so the two following must suffice. The one was written soon after his conversion, the other near the end of his life.

"*May* 3, 1867.—We are *born* corrupt, and, if the devil had his way, we should be kept in ignorance of it; our permitted transgressions show us our state; it is the root that is evil, and evil must be its emanations, yet we feel much more oppressed by the outward sin than by the inward corruption."

"*May* 7, 1883.—Give me a ream of foolscap and I will sign it: it may be filled with my demerits and unworthiness, which I agree to; but my so doing is a proof of how much I accept the free gift of God. Unless our Lord's sufferings were in vain, it is just that sheet of demerits that I have signed which gives me my right to Him; had I a clean sheet I should have no right to Him."

Gordon's, however, was not a faith which contents its possessor merely with a sense of the forgiveness of sins. That he possessed this happy assurance, is evident. But no sooner had he entered into possession of some of his privileges as a child of God, than he pressed on to obtain more spiritual advantages. The indwelling of God in his heart was a truth to which he attached much importance, and the following extracts are but specimens of much that might be quoted showing that he held the same truth from a period very soon after his father's death to the year which preceded his own death.

"*July* 31, 1867.—I have had very nice thoughts on 1 John iv. 13—'Whosoever shall confess that Jesus is the Son of God, God dwelleth in him, and he in God.' I think it is the key to much of the Scripture. I am more than ever convinced that the secret of happiness and holiness is in the indwelling of God. The same truth is shown in many other verses, but the above, to my mind, shows it more clearly. Let a man seek the teaching of the Holy Spirit on such verses, and he will grow much in grace. As we believe *that* text, so we shall realise the presence of God in our hearts, and, having Him there, we have as a sequence holiness and love. He alone can make us believe the truth and keep it in mind."

"*March* 15, 1882.—It had struck me before, in 1865, that the ordinary Christian life of *non-assurance* was not a sufficient gain to have come from Christ's incarnation and death; then I learnt *assurance*, then followed the knowledge of His indwelling, then the solution in my mind of the problem of the safety of others; and then I halted, having given up the thought that in this life it was possible to regenerate the body, putting down its failings as venial and connected with our human infirmities. In time it came to me that surely some growth, some improvement, ought to be made, some increased sanctification ought to be expected, one ought not to be so very barren; glimpses of selfishness, self-seeking pride, and a certain weariness of one's *châteaux d'Espagne* came to me, and led to this—Christ dwelleth in us, and His light enlightens all dark places."

He held very strongly the teaching of the Apostle in Rom. vii., that we have two natures contending for the mastery, the one good and the other evil. Writing to his sister he says:—

"We are torn in twain by our two natures, namely, our own judgment and our faith, and the result must be inconsistent work. How can it be otherwise? In appearance the Bible is inconsistent, and so must we be who fulfil it. The only consolation is to fall back on the text, 'Trust in the Lord with all thine heart, and lean not unto thine own understanding.'"

And again on the 6th October 1878:—

"You cannot evade it: we are each composed of two beings—one of which we see, which is temporal, which will fulfil certain works in the world; and one unseen, eternal, and which is always in conformity with God. One is sometimes uppermost, sometimes subdued, but rules in the long run, for it is eternal, while the other is temporal."

Gordon was a remarkable instance of the truth of the text, "The people that do know their God shall be strong, and do exploits," a truth which is as applicable to individuals as it is to nations. Gifted by nature with a strong character, its strength was greatly developed by the way in which he came into personal contact with God in the study of His Word. He yielded no slavish subservience to any Church or priest, however good, but tested all doctrines by the unerring standard of God's truth. "Take the Holy Spirit," he used to say, "for your teacher, and you will never want another word from man on questions of doctrine." He never shrank from facing difficulties, or new theories, as some do who are not quite sure of the ground on which they stand, but would ask all who propounded novel doctrines for chapter and verse for their authority. When difficulties arose, he used to treat them as that great scholar, the late Dean Alford did, as shown in the following words: "I find difficulties in the Bible as well as others, but I am so convinced of the general truth of that sacred volume as a whole, that I can easily afford to suspend my judgment on those matters which for some purpose perhaps God has not permitted me to understand."

The Bible was to Gordon a living oracle, to which he used to apply at all times. Here are extracts from two of his letters showing how he regarded it:—

"Out of commiseration for our dual condition, God *has* given us an oracle which will answer any question, advise, instruct, and guide us; now this oracle must be His voice, for, if not, it would not be His word. He has in His infinite wisdom incarnated His voice in the Scriptures; His voice is to be understood by the highest or lowest intellect; it gives answers, &c., through all time. To the carnal man it is an ordinary book, to the spiritual man it is alive and makes alive."

"Whether we may apprehend it or not, the Scripture contains the mind of Christ, and is, when illuminated with the Spirit, as if Christ was ever talking to us. Now, we should think that if Christ was ever near to talk with us, *that* should suffice us, and consequently, *as I believe that in theory*, I try to realise it in practice."

Knowing the high value that Gordon placed on the

Word of God, we shall not be surprised to hear that he took intense pains to study the sacred volume. He incidentally mentions that one page of his Bible had been so worn by use that he could hardly read the words. The energy and thoroughness ever evinced in his professional duties, he also practised in the earnest search for God's truths. He used to apply the text, "In the sweat of thy face shalt thou eat bread," to the soul as well as to the body, to the living Bread of Life as well as to the bread that sustains physical life. At one time he devoted a great deal of time to studying the book of Revelation, although he admitted that it was the most difficult book in the Bible to understand. He did not profess to understand it all, but he used to quote that saying of Dr. Mackie's, "The blessing to be looked for does not come by comprehension, but by the reading of the revelation God has given us in His Word, Rev. i. 3." But though he read and studied his Bible as earnestly as he would any other book, he never forgot the fact that only the Holy Spirit can teach us the truths contained in it.

"We can see the *history* of the Bible, and may understand it, but we forget that we are blind to its secret mysteries, unless God shows them to us; our Saviour says, 'Unto you it is *given.*' Only the Spirit *in* man finds God."

He contended, moreover, that there could be but little benefit from a mere theoretical study of the Bible, and that consequently the best school in which to learn the sacred truths it contained was that of the discipline of life.

"I feel sure that no study without trial is of avail; life must be lived to learn these truths. I believe, if a man knows his Bible fairly, and then goes forth into the world, God will show him His works. The Jews learnt the Scripture by heart, and so I expect our Saviour did; He therefore had no need to study it. He applied its teachings to life and its trials."

Nor did Gordon study his Bible only when he was alone, for he was very fond of reading it in company with those who, like himself, valued it. Thus Mr. Pearson, of the Church Missionary Society, who was at Nyanza, gives a brief account of his visit to Khartoum in 1878, and says, "After the work of the day was finished, Gordon would say, 'Let us have reading and prayer;' and in that very palace which was, perhaps, the scene of his death, we used to meet and pray, not separating sometimes until one in the morning."

Before leaving Gordon and his Bible, it is interesting to note that the actual copy of the Scriptures which he had for a long period, including the time of his first visit to Khartoum, is now at Windsor Castle in the possession of the Queen. The following is the Queen's letter on the subject:—

"WINDSOR CASTLE, *March* 16, 1885.

"DEAR MISS GORDON,—It is most kind and good of you to give me this precious Bible, and I only hope that you are not depriving yourself and family of such a treasure, if you have no other. May I ask you, during how many years your dear heroic Brother had it with him? I shall have a case made for it with an inscription, and place it in the Library here, with your letter and the touching extract from his last to you. I have ordered, as you know, a Marble Bust of your dear Brother to be placed in the Corridor here, where so many Busts and Pictures of our greatest Generals and Statesmen are, and hope that you will see it before it is finished, to give your opinion as to the likeness.—Believe me always, yours very sincerely, VICTORIA R. I."

It is not a little remarkable that in the history of all

eminent Christians, those who attach great importance to the study of the Word of God invariably make a point of spending much time at the throne of grace, waiting on God in prayer. These two means of grace seem to be almost inseparable, and we seldom find one much in use without the other. Some people talk about being too busy to spare time for prayer or study of the Scriptures, but Luther used to say that the more work he had to do, the more necessary did he find it to hedge-in time during which he could be alone with God. The more work there is to be done, the more strength is needed, and therefore the more important is it to make use of those means which alone can bring strength for work. Few men get through more work in the course of the year than Gordon did, but he made a great point of so arranging his work as to enable him to find time for private communing with God.

When in the Soudan as Governor-General he used to hoist a flag outside his tent to indicate to outsiders that he was not to be disturbed except under very urgent circumstances, and that flag became the signal that the occupant of the tent wanted to be alone with his God, to seek for guidance * and strength, which he felt he needed so much in conducting the affairs of the province over which he was called to rule. Like

* It is sometimes said that Gordon used to "toss up" when he was in any doubt, and that such a step indicates want of faith in prayer. As a matter of fact, he did appeal two or three times to lot in this way, and he used to quote Acts i. 26 as a precedent; but it is not true that he often decided questions thus, nor is it true that he resorted to an appeal to lot instead of seeking guidance in prayer. He would pray first, and ask God to indicate His mind in this modern form of appeal to lot.

all men who begin by praying much for themselves, his heart was soon drawn out in prayer for others; and it is evident that he interceded much for his enemies, as well as for those with whom he was officially brought into contact. Thus in one letter he says: "I believe very much in praying for others; it takes away all bitterness towards them;" and on another occasion:—

"The only remedy with me is to pray for every one who worries me; it is wonderful what such prayer does. In heaven our Lord intercedes for us, and He governs heaven and earth. Prayer for others relieves our own burdens. God turned the captivity of Job *when he prayed for his friends*, who had been as thorns in his side. I feel strongly that the grace God gave me to pray for my enemies in the Soudan led to my success, though I certainly used the sword of Cæsar on them."

Those who are opposed to the doctrine that salvation is not to be obtained by human merit, but by simple faith in the Lord Jesus Christ, sometimes assert that the Gospel teaches people to be selfish, by thinking first of their own salvation. As a matter of fact, the most active Christians are those who hold this doctrine; and never has the Church of our country been so fruitful of good works, as when her children have been careful to make it clear that salvation is not to be obtained by them. It is not selfishness for a man to think of his own soul first, when he knows that he cannot do much good to others till its salvation is assured. The happy combination between a natural unselfishness, and a newly developed love for the temporal and spiritual welfare of his fellow-creatures, had very blessed results in Gordon's case. No sooner was he thoroughly convinced of the importance of religion, than his unselfish nature exhibited itself in a marvellous development of the missionary spirit at home and abroad. When Gordon secured anything good, his unselfish nature at once prompted him to let others share it. It is sometimes supposed that only men of strong faith are in earnest about the propagation of their faith, but this is not altogether a correct way of stating a fact. The young man who makes good use of the muscular power given to him by Nature acquires greater strength, whereas he who fails to do so finds that he has to pay the penalty of his neglect in having his muscles grow flabby and feeble. And so it is with faith. The unselfish man who starts with a weak faith, but is determined to let others derive as much benefit as possible, finds his faith growing stronger and stronger, as he continues to witness evidences of the influence of that faith on others. Had Gordon, like one in the parable, wrapt his faith up in a napkin, instead of making good use of it by putting it out to usury, he might never have acquired the strong faith which so characterised him. As it was, he not only to the last day of his life had cause to thank God for the full assurance he enjoyed, but the number of orphans, of widows, and of others, who derived benefit directly or indirectly from his faith, will never be known.

There are some to whom one might apply, though in a slightly different sense, the words of Naaman's servants, "If the prophet had bid thee do some great thing, wouldest thou not have done it?" While willing to exercise this faith in the performance of great deeds, they overlook numerous smaller opportunities of working for their Master, and fail to do anything because they are always looking out for great opportunities. The great change in Gordon's life took place at Gravesend, and it was there he commenced to show that intense longing to do good to others which characterised him to the end. Nothing was beneath his notice, nobody too insignificant for him. The gutter children, and the inmates of the workhouse, might have been passed over by many in his position who had higher aims. It was not so with Gordon, and consequently he quickly cultivated the missionary spirit, and soon reaped a rich harvest, proving the truth of Browning's lines about the humble-minded man, who finds nothing too insignificant for his energies:—

"That low man sees a little thing to do,
Sees it and does it:
This high man with a great thing to pursue,
Dies ere he knows it.
That low man goes on adding one to one,
His hundreds soon hit:
This high man aiming at a million
Misses an unit."

Here was a man, who had already made a great name for himself in the world, and might, had he wished, have been far better known, planning out for himself a future career, the main object of which was to spread abroad a knowledge of those spiritual truths which had so greatly benefited him, and that not by the formation of some great society, some splendid organisation, but by simply putting himself into touch with some of the humble city missionaries, and, through their instrumentality, getting at the poor. Witness these two passages from his letters:—

"*January* 8, 1881.—I hope, D.V., to put myself in communication with some of our Scripture-reader people, and shall try and visit Christ, who is in the East end in the flesh (Matthew xxv. 34). I feel this is what I shall like; these truths were not given to make a man idle."

"*September* 24, 1881.—I have been down for two Sundays to meet a lot of Chinese, and have spoken to them as well as I could. I have not yet touched on Jesus and His sacrifice, but spoke of God's indwelling. It was satisfactory, and they were pleased."

It is also interesting to note how, from time to time, he kept on reproaching himself for not being more alive to his responsibilities, and making better use of his opportunities to do good. He even seemed to begrudge himself the few months' holiday he spent in Palestine recruiting his health and energies. Writing on August 14, 1882, he says:—

"Fancy, since I left Mauritius, with the exception of twenty-nine days on board ship, I have been living at hotels, and, I may say, have not talked of the pearls to more than a dozen people."

And again from Palestine he wrote:—

"You know I do not like idleness; I want to get to a place where I can find sick people to visit, feeling sure that is the necessary work for me; I think He will direct me, so I seek no advice elsewhere. I leave it to God, to decide in His time. I do not like the ways of the polished world, and my dislike has increased during the time I have been here."

However much Gordon might reproach himself, it must not for one moment be supposed that, in the ordinary acceptation of the word, there was any cause for it. He was in truth a most indefatigable worker, and no matter how hard his official work was, he always seemed to find time to do something for his Master. A case in point is the time he spent in South Africa, when it is difficult to understand how he got through all the official work he managed to compress into his brief sojourn. Yet we find that the herculean task of reorganising the colonial army was not the only thing that occupied his attention, for on the 12th August 1882 he writes to his sister:—

"How odd, those leaflets* being in Dutch, and my wanting them, and your sending them just as I am about to go up to the Free State, when, as in the 'Auld time long ago,' I shall be dropping them along the road near the Boer towns. What hundreds I did give away; how I used to run miles, if I saw a scuttler (boy) watching crows in a field! If I, or any one else, went now to Gravesend and dropped them, how quickly men, now grown up, would remember that time. Send me the whole lot out unless you want them, I mean of all languages; it is the loveliest leaflet I ever saw, and it still looks fresh."

Francis de Sales, an eminent saint of the Roman Catholic Church, when a famine was prevailing, and he wanted to preach in a certain village, purchased twelve waggons and packed them with bread. He sent the waggons forward one at a time, going on the last one himself. "For," said he, "we must get at the poor through their physical natures. They will be the more willing to receive our message for their souls when they see that we care about their bodies." Gordon used to act on the same principle, and made a great point of caring for the physical wants of any he found in trouble. It would be difficult to enumerate all the instances of this to which publicity has been given, but a few cases may suffice. One lad who exhibited con-

* This leaflet consists principally of a few choice and carefully selected passages of Scripture, and shows how intensely he valued the *ipsissima verba* of God's own word, as a means of reaching the human heart.

sumptive tendencies he sent at his own expense to Margate. The boy recovered, grew up to be a man, and christened his eldest son "Gordon," in memory of one who, he used to say, had "saved both his body and soul." Another story is told of a case in which Gordon handed over a dirty little urchin to one of his lady friends, with the remark, "I want to make you a present of a boy." Under good influences the lad grew up until he became a respectable member of society. Years after, when he was earning good wages at sea, and was about to be married, he fell from the topmast of his vessel, and was conveyed to the Gravesend Infirmary with a fractured skull. In his last moments, however, he did not forget his benefactor, and, in trembling tones, asked his adopted mother to tell the Colonel how he valued the truth contained in that beautiful hymn he had taught him, "Jesus, Lover of my soul." The same writer mentions also the history of a boy called Albert who, through Gordon's kindness, was apprenticed to a tradesman at Gravesend. Subsequently the lad went into a business house at Southampton, where he was placed in a department which he did not understand. Fearing that his services would be dispensed with, he communicated with his friends, and they, in turn, wrote to General Gordon, who happened to be staying in Southampton at his sister's house. Without loss of time the General called on "Little Albert," whom he scarcely recognised in the youth of six feet two inches who presented himself, and had a consultation with his employer. The result was that the young man was retained in his situation, and placed in a department with which he was well acquainted.

It is by no means uncommon to find that those who

are eager about the spread of spiritual truths among professing Christians, are also keenly alive to the importance of mission work among non-Christian people. Gordon was a remarkable instance of this happy combination. The chapter that deals with his life in Palestine gives an insight into this part of his character, but a few words will not be out of place here to show his opinion on this subject in other countries. He had a very high ideal of what a missionary should be, and a supreme contempt for bad missionaries. He was on the whole fortunate in the class of men he came across in Palestine, the Soudan, and South Africa. In the first of these two places the missionaries belonged to the Church Missionary Society, an organisation with which he was much in sympathy. But he also met men of other societies, and his large-hearted sympathies went out to them too. He was a great admirer of Livingstone, and spoke of him with much respect and affection. The spirit of heroism which has characterised so many of our missionaries attracted him greatly. "Do not send lukewarms," he once wrote to Mr. Wright, the Honorary Secretary of the Church Missionary Society; and one of the first things he did at Gravesend was to support the Moravian Missions by becoming their local treasurer. Later on in Africa he writes, "How refreshing it is to hear of the missionary efforts made in these countries."

We may not quite agree with all that Gordon said on the subject of foreign missions, and some may think that the standard he set up was too high for frail human nature to aim at. Moreover, recent events in Uganda, and elsewhere, may have shown us that good work can be done by men who fall far short of Gordon's standard. Nevertheless, we cannot but feel that he was himself, in the truest sense of the word, a missionary, and that the Earl of Harrowby did not at all exaggerate the truth when he said about Gordon, after his death :—

"I believe that one effect of that man's example was to lift up a noble standard for the cross in a way that no professional missionary could have lifted it up, and to oblige devotees of pleasure and people who had thought but little of such things to acknowledge the power of the Gospel. Many who saw him and spoke to him could not understand him. It was to them a marvellous sight to witness, and I feel that we can hardly be grateful enough to that great man for the infinite benefits which he has bestowed upon us as friends of missions."

Apart from any direct work that he did to advance the cause of missions, an illustration has recently been given us in *The Jewish Intelligencer*, showing what an influence his life had on Mohammedans and others with whom he came in contact. The writer describes a conversation he had with a shereef from Mecca, a man who was held in the greatest veneration by all loyal Mohammedans. He was a well-informed man, and had travelled much. In speaking of Gordon, he said: "Oh! the English lost a great man, it is true, but the unhappy Mussulmans have lost in him a benefactor, a father, and a servant of the true God. Before I knew him I hated the Christians, but Gordon has taught me to love them; and I see more clearly every day that a religion which makes such heroic, faithful, and disinterested men, can only be a religion coming from the true God." And, believe me, the whole Mohammedan world has felt, and still feels every day, the loss of the noble defender of Khartoum.

CHAPTER IX.

HIS CATHOLICITY.

So many Churches and parties have laid claim to Gordon's patronage, and such extraordinary views have been attributed to him on religious subjects, that it may not be out of place to say something on the point. His mind was very comprehensive, and his whole nature sympathetic, consequently many, differing widely from each other, have regarded him as an ally of their own cause. When he became Private Secretary to Lord Ripon, on the appointment of the latter, who is a Roman Catholic, as Governor-General of India, it was stated in some of the Indian papers that the new Viceroy had been urged by Mr. Gladstone to accept a Baptist as his Private Secretary, in order to conciliate the Nonconformist and Protestant element in England. There was not a word of truth in the statement. The Baptist Church has possessed some very eminent men, such as Sir Henry Havelock, Dr. Carey, Dr. Judson, Dr. Angus, and Mr. Spurgeon, but General Gordon was not one of their number. He was baptized as a member of the Church of England, and though he was never confirmed, yet he lived and died a communicant of that body. In many ways he was a thorough type of that catholic generous class of Churchmen, so characteristic of our National Church, which, taking a large-hearted view of Church membership, recognises all that is good, noble, and pure in other systems, and is not afraid of losing caste by associating with Nonconformists. Nor would it be fair to say that his catholicity developed only in the direction of the Nonconformists, for no man ever tried more than he to see good in other systems of religion, such as the Roman Catholic and Greek Churches, and even Mohammedanism. He had a remarkably open mind, and was always anxious to distinguish between persons and principles. He fully recognised the errors of certain religious systems, but this did not in the least interfere with his recognition of good in the individuals who adhered to them. The catholicity of his own views may be gathered from the following extracts made from his letters at different times:—

"I do not think much of getting help from only one particular set of men; I will take Divine aid from any of those who may be dispensing it, whether High Church, Low Church, Greek Church, or Roman Catholic Church; each meal shall be, by God's grace, my sacrament."

"I would wish to avoid laying down the law: you may look at a plate and see it is round; I look at it, and see it is square; if you are happy in your view, keep it, and I keep mine; one day we shall both see the truth. I say this, because we often are inclined to find fault with those who do not think as we do, 'who do not follow *us*.' Why trouble others and disturb their minds on matters which we see only dimly ourselves? At the same time I own to repugnance to the general conversation of the world and of some religious people; there is a sort of 'I am holier than thou' in their words which I do not like, therefore I prefer those subjects where such discussions do not enter."

"Join no sect, though there may be truth in all. Be of the true army of Christ, wear His uniform, *Love*: 'By this, and by no other sign, shall men know that ye are My disciples.'"

If we may judge of a man by his friends and his books, few can surpass General Gordon in catholicity. He used to say that he learnt certain truths from certain individuals. Thus, from the writings of an eminent Plymouth Brother, C. H. Mackintosh, he learnt the doctrine of the two natures within himself, and from a Mr. Jukes he learnt the lesson of the crucifixion of the flesh. "Mr. Mylne," he used to say, "taught me the importance of intercessory prayer, and Colonel Travers taught me the importance of bringing forth the fruit of the Spirit." He valued also Bishop Pearson's work on the Creed, and the standard work on the Thirty-nine Articles by the lately-retired Bishop of Winchester. "The Imitation of Christ," by Thomas à Kempis, was a favourite book, and one which he gave away largely. "Christ's Mystical," by Hall, and "The Deep Things of God," by Hill, were also much valued, and given away to his friends, as well as Clark's "Scripture Promises," and Wilson on "Contentment." He was an admirer of the eminent preacher Charles H. Spurgeon, about whom he says:—

> "I found six or seven sermons of Spurgeon in the hotel, and read them. I like him; he is very earnest; he says: 'I believe that not a worm is picked up by a bird without direct intervention of God, yet I believe entirely in man's free will; but I cannot and do not pretend to reconcile the two.' He says he reads the paper to see what God is doing and what are His designs. I confess I have now much the same feeling; nothing shocks me but myself."

He was personally very fond of the late Bishop of Lincoln, Dr. Christopher Wordsworth, describing him as "imbued with the indwelling of God; only one fault—he is hard on the Roman Catholics." The last phrase gives a good insight into the working of Gordon's mind. Romish Catholicism, as a religious system, was about as opposed as anything could be to his own views, which were all in favour of comprehensiveness, and a large display of individuality. But though he had no sympathy with the narrow exclusiveness of that ecclesiastical survival of the dark middle ages—the Roman system—he had the greatest sympathy with earnest individuals, who in spite of their system possessed the Spirit of Christ. He had many sincere friends who were members of the Church of Rome, and he used to remark that some of them set a noble example of devotion to many Protestants, who did not act up to their own principles. Writing on the 5th January 1878, he says:—

"Why does the Romish Church thrive with so many errors in it? It is because of those godly men in her who live Christ's life, and who, like as Zoar was spared for Lot's sake, bring a blessing on the whole community. For self-devotion, for self-denial, the Roman Catholic Church is in advance of our present-day Protestantism. What is it if you know the sound truths and do not act up to them? Actions speak loudly and are read of all; words are as the breath of man."

But in spite of his large-hearted toleration he had no hesitation in speaking out against the tendency of Romanism which unduly exaggerates the position of the priests, and puts the laity into a subservient position with regard to them. Writing from Khartoum with regard to the Abyssinians he says:—

"The excommunication of the priests is the great weapon—it is terrible; far worse than, or quite as bad as, that of the Inquisition. It amuses me to hear the Catholic priests here [Khartoum] complain of it, and say that the priests want to keep the people ignorant, so as to rule them. Is it not what *they* would do elsewhere, if they could?"

It may be supposed by some that General Gordon was a member of what is known as the Evangelical party in the Church of England, but though he held perhaps more in common with that party than with any other, it would be inaccurate to say that he belonged to it. Religious party views are always rather difficult to describe, and it will be found that in every party there are some whose minds do not run on partisan lines. An eminent bishop was once asked to define the three parties of the National Church, and he replied, that the High Churchman always asked what the Church taught, the Broad Churchman could be distinguished by his asking what reason taught, and the Evangelical was known by his asking what the Bible taught. If such a rough-and-ready system of classification be applied to General Gordon, there can be no question that his loyalty to the Bible would stamp him at once. In addition, however, to this characteristic, which was the most prominent one in his life, he held in common with the Evangelicals, and far more strongly than the majority of them, the doctrine of Election, and the wise policy of cultivating friendly relations with Nonconformists, to whose places of worship he frequently went, as also the doctrine of personal assurance, and that of the utter depravity of human nature. But Gordon was not of a type of mind that can ever go completely with a party. He had such a strong individuality, that it would have been impossible for him to do as many do—sink his own views on questions not of vital importance, so as to be enabled to work with the party with which he was most in accord. He was nothing, if not original and genuine; he sought the truth for himself, and would not receive stereotyped views of religion where he did not see that they were in harmony with the Bible.

> "He that cannot think is a fool,
> He that will not is a bigot,
> He that dares not is a slave."

His fearlessness in the search for truth made him frequently touch on subjects on which his own mind was not fully made up. The fate of those who had not accepted Christ as their Saviour was one of these points. Though he frequently spoke of his own salvation, through the merits of Christ, he believed that God had provided some means of saving those who had never had opportunities of hearing of Christ, but he never dogmatised on what those means were. Referring to his Mohammedan secretary, Berzati Bey, he writes on the 12th April 1881:—

> "He will ever be one of those who have taught me the great lesson, that in all nations and in all climes there are those who are perfect gentlemen, and who, though they may not be called Christians, are so in spirit and in truth. They may not see how Christ is their Saviour, but they die with a sense that all their efforts are useless, and with the conviction that unless God provides some way of satisfying His justice, they have no hope."

The fate of the heathen who are suffering, not from any personal rejection of true religion, but on account of the sins of some distant ancestors who forsook the worship of the true God, is a mysterious subject, and one on which true Christians have differed. The most that any of us can do is to take comfort in the conviction that—

> "The love of God is broader
> Than the measure of man's mind."

It must not, however, be thought, because Gordon held that the ignorance of the heathen was no bar to their salvation, that he in any way undervalued the benefits of the Christian faith. Again and again, in view of his being asked to become a Mohammedan in order to save his life, he says in substance what he wrote on September 10, 1884, when Khartoum was surrounded with bigoted Mahdists: "If the Christian faith is a myth, then let men throw it off; but it is mean and dishonourable to do so merely to save one's life, if one believes it is the true faith."

He also believed that heathen magicians had influence with God. Writing to his sister shortly after a repulse that his men received from some natives near Moogie, in the Equatorial Province, he says: "Did I not mention the incantations made against us by the magicians on the other side, and how somehow, from the earnestness that they made them with, I had some thought of misgiving on account of them? These prayers were earnest prayers for celestial aid, in which the Pray-er knew he would need help from some unknown power to avert a danger. That the native knows not the true God is true; but God knows him, and moved him to pray, and answered his prayer."

But while General Gordon held much in common with the liberal Evangelicals, there was one point on which he differed from them very strongly, and on which he was more in sympathy with the Broad Church party in the National Church, or those amongst the Nonconformists known as the Down Grade party; this was the doctrine known as Universalism. Whether we agree with him or not, we must in honesty recognise the fact that Gordon held a modified form of the doctrine that there is no such thing as future punishment. Writing on the 13th October 1878 he gives his views thus:—

"I look on universal salvation for every human being, past, present, or future, as certain, and, as I hope for my own, no doubt comes into my mind on this subject. Is it credible that so *many* would wish it to be otherwise, and fight you about it? And among those *many* are numbers, whose lives, weighed truly as to their merits by the scale of the sanctuary, would kick the beam *against* those *they* condemn.

"Once I did believe that some perished altogether at the end of the world—were annihilated, as having no souls. After this, I believed that the world was made up of incarnated children of God and incarnated children of the evil spirit; and then I came to the belief that *the two are in one.*

"With reference to the doctrine of annihilation, I do not think it gives the same idea of God as is obtained from this other view. It may show force to annihilate, but we should think more highly of a monarch who would, by his wisdom, kindness, and long-suffering, turn a rebel people into faithful subjects, than of him who had the land wasted and utterly destroyed his rebellious subjects. I do not think that after the declaration, 'It is *finished*,' there can be any more probation; punishment brings no one to God."

Once more, writing on the 16th May 1883, he says:—

"I have become much more timid about speaking of these matters of universal salvation, yet perforce one comes to this question. If every one lives, then he must live by the fact of his possession of an emanation of the Life of Life, which must be good, and never can be evil. This emanation is the cause of his existence, his life in fact, and that I regard as the '*he*.'"

Perhaps the best answer will be found in Sir William Butler's "Life of Gordon." Dealing with Gordon's difficulty about future punishment, he says with truth :—

"Yet never lived there man who in his own life had seen more of the vast sum of human wrong-doing which has to be righted somewhere, and on which no sword of justice ever lights in this world. He does not seem to have asked himself the question, If I am shooting and hanging these maker of orphans ; if I am punishing with stripes and chains these sellers and buyers of human flesh, and doing it in the name of truth and right, is the Great Judge of all to be denied His right to use the sword of justice upon those who are beyond my reach? Are nine-tenths of the evil-doers on earth not only to escape the penalty of their crimes, but often and often to be favoured reapers in the harvest of the world's success? You catch the common robber, or the man who steals, perhaps through starvation, penury, or through knowing no better, and you imprison him for years or for life ; and is the rich usurer who has wrung the widow's farthing from her, is the fraudulent bankrupt, is the unjust judge, is the cruel spoiler of war to pass from a world that in millions and millions of cases gave them wealth and honours, and stars and garters, instead of ropes and bars and gallows, to go forthwith to free pardon, to everlasting light and endless rest beyond the grave? It would indeed be strange justice that meted to Jude and Judas the same measure of mercy in the final judgment."

It must be borne in mind that Gordon was not a trained theologian but an earnest Christian soldier. As his brother, Sir Henry Gordon, reminds us, he led a very lonely life, and consequently often lost opportunities of hearing both sides of a question. He might come across a book on one side, and thus adopt a certain set of views without hearing the opposite side. No man was more capable of forming a sound opinion, when arguments *pro* and *con* were fairly laid before him, but his peculiar style of life often prevented him from doing justice to his own judgment.

If Gordon was likely to err in one direction more than another, it was in that of an exaggerated form of kindness. He had a tender loving heart, which unduly influenced his judgment. It would be well for all students of God's Word if it could be said that their only failings arose from exaggerated virtues. All have some weak points, and it would be ridiculous to claim for Gordon immunity from error.

> "Find earth where grows no weeds, and you may find
> A heart wherein no error grows."

No writer would be doing justice to Gordon if he failed to deal with his views on the subject of God's Sovereignty, for from the beginning to the end of his religious life he attached the greatest importance to this doctrine. He was avowedly what is generally called a Calvinist, though as a matter of fact he very seldom made use of the term. That sainted prelate, the late Bishop Waldegrave, when once he heard a young clergyman sneering at the doctrine which so frequently goes by the name of Calvinism, remarked: "Young man, before you denounce Calvinism, take care that you properly understand what the term means, or possibly you may find yourself contending against some of God's truths." Now that it is so fashionable to denounce Calvinism, it is perhaps well to act on the good bishop's advice, and see whether we thoroughly comprehend it, or whether all the time we are not contending with a creation of our own imagination which is but a caricature of the thing itself. Even Froude, the great historian, who, whatever else he is.

is not a Calvinist, inquires how it is that Calvinistic doctrines have "possessed such singular attractions for some of the greatest men who have ever lived? If it be a creed of intellectual servitude, how was it able to inspire and sustain the hardest efforts ever made by man to break the yoke of unjust authority."

Of course in Calvinism, as in the opposite doctrine, some have gone to great extremes and brought ridicule on the subject, but as Gordon's views were strictly moderate and eminently practical, it is not necessary to consider to what extreme lengths some may go who differ from him on either side, nor is it necessary to consider all the revolting doctrines which have been attributed to Calvin by his enemies, nor some of the things he may even have said in the heat of argument. Gordon was distinctly of the moderate school of Calvinists; he believed that the heart of man was so corrupted by the Fall, that he could not of his own accord turn to God, and that consequently in the case of those who did turn, it must have been God's work, drawing the heart to Himself. He contended that to look at Christianity from the opposite standpoint, that of Human Responsibility, pandered to the pride which is innate in the human heart. Thus the individual would be always tempted to think that it was *his* wisdom, *his* foresight, *his* strength, *his* decision, or *his* something, that made him close with the offer of mercy, and so looking around him, and seeing many going astray, he would be tempted to congratulate himself on *his* success, when so many failed, and to fondly imagine that it was a case of the survival of the fittest. Once let the Christian grasp the actual truth, and he is deprived of this element of self-glorification. His title to honour is removed by the thought that an exterior power, unknown to himself, drew him with the cords of love, or drove him with the lash of fear. There are numerous passages in which Gordon expressed himself on this subject, but perhaps the following states his views as well as any:—

"To accept the doctrine of man having no free will, he must acknowledge his utter insignificance, for then no one is cleverer or better than his neighbour; this must be always abhorrent to the flesh. 'Have not I done this or that?' 'Had I naught to do with it?' For my part, I can give myself no credit for anything I ever did; and further, I credit no man with talents, &c. &c., in anything he may have done. Napoleon, Luther, indeed all men, I consider were directly worked on, and directed to work out God's great scheme. Tell me any doctrine which so humbles man as this, or which is so contrary to his nature and to his natural pride."

Although writers have often attempted to show that Gordon was an extreme Calvinist, there is no evidence that he ever stated his views on the subject in any stronger language than that used in Article XVII. of the Prayer-Book of the Church of England, which says:—"Predestination to life is the everlasting purpose of God, whereby (before the foundations of the world were laid) He hath constantly decreed by His counsel secret to us, to deliver from curse and damnation those whom He hath chosen in Christ out of mankind, and to bring them by Christ to everlasting salvation, as vessels made to honour." However it may be with others, Churchmen at all events have no right to sneer at Gordon's views on the doctrine of God's Sovereignty, or Fatalism, as he more frequently used to call it.

Nor did Gordon confine his views on Election

merely to the initial stage of the Christian life; he believed that the same loving Father, who in the first instance had drawn him into the fold, watched over him, and ordained for him what was to happen. Some fatalists, seeing that a certain thing is *likely* to happen, say that God has ordained that it shall be, and they fold their hands, and make no effort to avert a catastrophe. Not so with Gordon; until the thing had actually happened, he would exert all his powers to prevent it; but when he failed to avert any impending trouble, he would find comfort in the thought that it was ordained by God, and would fret no more about it. In a letter to his sister he said:—

"It is a delightful thing to be a fatalist, not as that word is generally employed, but to accept that, *when things happen* and *not* before, God has for some wise reason so ordained them. We have nothing further to do, when the scroll of events is unrolled, than to accept them as being for the best; but *before it is unrolled*, it is another matter, for you would not say, 'I sat still and let things happen.' With this belief all I can say is, that amidst troubles and worries no one can have peace till he thus stays upon his God—*that* gives a superhuman strength."

It has been asserted that Gordon was very hard on the clergy, and that he did not believe in a divinely appointed order of ministry. This has probably arisen from certain statements of his that have appeared in a disconnected form. Take the following passages from letters written at different periods of his life:—

From the Crimea.—"We have a great deal to regret in the want of good working clergymen, there being none here that I know of who interest themselves about the men."

From Gravesend.—"The world's preachers and the world's religion of forms and ceremonies are hard and cold, with no life in them, nothing to cheer or comfort the broken-hearted. Explain, O preachers, how it is that we ask and do not get comfort, that your cold services cheer not. Is it not because ye speak to the flesh which is at enmity to all that is spiritual and must die (joy is only from the spirit)? . . . You preach death as an enemy instead of a friend and liberator. You speak of Heaven, but belie your words by making your home here. Be as uncharitable as you like, but attend my church or chapel regularly. . . . Does your vast system of ceremonies, meetings, and services tend to lessen sin in the world? It may make men conceal it. Where would you find more hardness to a fallen one than you would in a congregation of worshippers of the Church of this day? Surely this hardness is of the devil, and they who show it know not God."

From the Soudan, April 20, 1876.—"The sacerdotal class have always abounded; they are allied with the temporal civil power, who need their aid to keep the people quiet. 'By whose authority teachest thou these things?' is their cry; from them alone must come the authority."

From Jaffa, July 11, 1883.—"I believe the deadness in some of the clergy is owing, firstly, to not reading the Scriptures; secondly, to not meditating over them; thirdly, to not praying sufficiently; fourthly, to being taken up with religious secular work (Acts vi. 2–4). I wonder how it is that, when a subject of the greatest import is brought up, one sees so very little interest taken in it; and how willingly it is allowed to drop with a sort of 'Oh, yes, I know all about that.'"

Yet it is quite incorrect to say that Gordon undervalued the work of hard-working clergymen. He was of a critical turn of mind and used to criticise their methods of working, but no one recognised more fully than he did the good that was being done by many devoted workers, and these he would of course exclude when administering blame for the shortcomings of the others. He had a way of speaking and writing in general terms that might be a little misleading to those who do not understand him, but he always took it for granted, in his private letters to his sister, or to his intimate friends, that they would understand to whom he meant his words to apply. There are plenty of his statements which show that he valued highly the ministry of some of the more spiritually minded among the clergy. Those who preached the truth of the indwelling of God had in his opinion a great influence over those to whom they ministered. Writing from South Africa on 5th June 1882, he says:—"Both clergymen here preach the great secret, the indwelling, but not as strongly as I could wish. Their churches are full, while, where it is not preached, they are comparatively empty."

It would indeed quite misrepresent Gordon's views to say that he ignored the work of the ministry as a body. He was one of those who believed that it was the duty of every one to be a labourer in the vineyard, whether he was ordained or not, and he himself set a noble example in working for his Master. At the same time he never called in question the principle which the Bible, and also the Prayer-Book of the National Church, recognise, that it is for the good of Christianity that there should be a division of labour, and that, while all should be workers, some should give themselves wholly to the work of the ministry. Apparently, in Apostolic days, every one who was converted became a labourer, and there certainly was no hard-and-fast line of demarcation between laymen and ministers. Perhaps we have gone too far in the other direction, and made too much distinction between lay and clerical workers, but it is only due to the National Church of this country to say, that this is the result of custom and of secular law, rather than of ecclesiastical law. Considering that the Prayer-Book was written or compiled by the clergy, it is wonderful how carefully they avoided setting up undue claims, so as to magnify their own office. There is indeed only one expression in the Prayer-Book to indicate that the authors believed that the ministry was of Divine appointment, and that is a sentence, occurring three times over in the Ordination Service, which runs: "Almighty God, who by Thy Divine Providence hast appointed divers orders of ministers in Thy Church, &c." This merely asserts that the Bible teaches that there were deacons and elders, or ministers, in Apostolic days, and it is difficult to read the New Testament without recognising this fact. Certainly Gordon did not deny it. Indeed no body even of the Nonconformists does so except the Plymouth Brethren. Gordon's shrewd common sense showed him that, apart from any Divine sanction to the principle, there must be a division of labour, there must be specialists in every department of life, and religion was no exception to the general rule. Though he would resent the pretentious claims of an exclusive ministry, he never opposed the principle of a scriptural ministry. He had friends who were in the ministry, and he derived great benefits from their teaching.

The truth is that Gordon thought more of the man than he did of the profession or calling. Shovel hats, wideawakes, long-tailed black coats, and white ties were nothing to him. What he valued was the man who was to be found beneath the clerical costume. Was he a true man, or was he merely a professional hireling? Had he a heart to sympathise with the sufferings of his fellow-creatures, and to help them to wage war with sin and temptation? If so he would find a true friend in Gordon; but it mattered little in his eyes what the external profession was, if there was an absence of the internal reality. Gordon hated everything that was not genuine, and of all the shams in life the religious one was to him the worst.

It is not a little interesting to note that while some considered him almost a Plymouth Brother on the one hand, others have attributed to him extreme party views in an opposite direction on the subject of the Lord's Supper. It may not, therefore, be out of place to show exactly what his views were, for though apparently peculiar, they were certainly not extreme. For many years he appears not to have given much thought to the subject of Holy Communion, but in 1880 the Rev. Horace Waller directed his attention to it, and after that time he took up the subject very warmly, as the following passages will show:—

"*December* 4, 1880.—'This do in remembrance of *Me*.' I mean, with God's blessing, to try and realise the truth that is in this dying request. I hope I may be given to see the truth and comfort to be derived from the Communion. I have in some degree seen it must be a means of very great grace; but of this in the future. It is a beautiful subject. Do not peck at words. Communion is better than sacrament, but communion may exist without the eating of the bread, &c. Sacrament means the performance of a certain act, which is an outward and visible sign of spiritual grace. You need not fear my leaving off this subject, it is far too engrossing to me, and is extremely interesting."

"*March* 26, 1881.—I had looked forward to a Communion, but could not go. I must confess to putting great (but *not salvation*) strength on that Sacrament."

"*February* 18, 1882.—What a wonderful history! these thoughts of eatings and sacraments Eat in *distrust of God*, and *trust in self*, and eat in *distrust of self*, and *trust in God*. It is very wonderful, as is also that the analogy should be so hidden. Eve knew no more what would happen to her by her eating, than we do by our eating."

"*January* 10, 1883.—I hear that at my village the Greek-Russian Church give the Lord's Supper to all who present themselves, without query; they give it in both kinds—bread and wine, so I shall go there. It is odd that no queries were asked when we poisoned ourselves in Eden; but that, when we wish to take the antidote, queries are asked. It is sufficient for me that the Greek Church is Christian, and that they 'show forth the Lord's death till He come.'"

But though Gordon never adopted extreme views, or in any way exaggerated the benefits of that sacred meal to which all Christians attach importance, still, from the somewhat peculiar way in which he sometimes stated his views, they might be thought very fanciful. For instance, he used to contend that as sin came into the world by eating, it was only natural that by "eating, spiritually and actually, Christ who is the Life," sin should be destroyed. "I cannot repeat it too often, that as the body was poisoned by the eating of a fruit, so it must be cured from its malady by absorbing an antidote. To the world this is foolishness. I own it, but the wisdom of God is foolishness to man" (*Observations on Holy Communion*, p. 12). In other words, the evil came in by eating, so the antidote to sin should come by the same means. Plainly stated, this does unquestionably sound somewhat fanciful; but then it must be remembered that Gordon was neither a theologian nor a lawyer, and consequently he never studied accuracy of definition. The fact is, that many have completely misunderstood his views for the simple reason that they have interpreted his words too literally, and made no allowance for poetic imagination and figurative language. There is a sense in which he was correct. No orthodox Christian doubts the fact that sin came into the world through our ancestors eating the forbidden fruit. The antidote to sin is Christ, and for us to partake of the benefits of His death we must appropriate Him by faith, or, in other words, we must by faith feed on Him, which is the same as a spiritual participation. By "eating," Gordon meant, not the mere swallowing of the symbols, but the whole process of participation in the death of Christ. Every sound Christian theologian must admit that this is necessary to salvation, and more than this Gordon did not mean.

It is interesting to note that this independent searcher after truth was by no means singular in his views, and that traces of them are to be found in the works of Augustine and other patristic writings, which possibly he had never seen. One writer has remarked that in the garden of Eden the command was "Eat not," and we know too well how that injunction was disobeyed. When Christ, the antidote to sin, came, He bade His followers "Take, eat," but with the perversity of human nature that characterises fallen man, too often that command is also neglected.

There is another point to which reference should be made. When at Khartoum, Gordon wrote to a friend, "There is no eating up here, which I miss." Some have contended that in this sentence he showed that he recognised the necessity for the presence of a priest, to make the Lord's Supper a valid ordinance. As a matter of fact, he never believed that the presence of a clergyman was necessary for Holy Communion. There were besides himself only two Englishmen at Khartoum during the siege, and one of them was Power, a Roman Catholic, who, although a great admirer of Gordon, probably would, from early training, have had conscientious scruples about taking the Lord's Supper without the presence of a priest. The other Englishman was Colonel Stewart, who, despite his friendship for Gordon, was not in sympathy with him in regard to religious matters. Had the three Englishmen been like-minded, there can be no question that that sentence in Gordon's letter would never have been written.

This is a subject that touches Christian men in the army and navy, as well as in the merchant service, very closely. Frequently such men for months together never see a clergyman, and it would be absurd to say that under such circumstances they must neglect the dying command of their Saviour.

It is told of three officers, who were great friends, that on the night before the battle of Waterloo, they agreed to partake together of the Holy Communion. The senior of them took an ordinary glassful of wine and some bread, and they knelt together, and asked God to bless the sacred rite. They rose, and the senior administered to each, using the beautiful words of the Church of England Communion Service. They never met together again on earth, but who can question the validity of that sacred meal, and who would dare to say that the ceremony would have been more acceptable to God if a clergyman had been present? The Bible nowhere asserts that the presence of a minister is necessary, and our National Church has very wisely followed the example of the Bible. The Church of

Rome does teach that the presence of a priest is necessary to make Holy Communion a valid ordinance. Our National Church, in common with the various bodies of Nonconformists, recognises, as a matter of ecclesiastical order, that under ordinary circumstances, an officiating clergyman should be present. But his presence in no way affects the validity of the sacrament, being merely a wise precaution against the admission of unworthy communicants. The laity surrender into the hands of the clergyman, or the minister aided by elders or deacons, their power of admitting or rejecting worthy or unworthy persons. But under abnormal circumstances, such as those in which Gordon was placed at Khartoum, ecclesiastical order would be suspended, and any two or three Christian laymen would have a perfect right to partake of the Holy Communion in accordance with the Word of God. This is the view that Christian officers in the army and navy have always taken, and those who were pained to think that Gordon gave his support to their opponents, may rest assured that no man contended more than he did for that liberty which is the very essence of Christian teaching.

CHAPTER X.

AS GOVERNOR OF THE EQUATORIAL PROVINCE.

It has already been mentioned that when Colonel Gordon was at Galatz he met Nubar Pasha. In September 1873 Nubar asked him to enter the service of the Khedive of Egypt. While waiting to know whether the British Government would sanction this step he wrote home as follows:—

"For some wise design God turns events one way or another, whether man likes it or not, as a man driving a horse turns it to right or left without consideration as to whether the horse likes that way or not. To be happy, a man must be like a well-broken, willing horse, ready for anything. Events will go as God likes. It is hard to accept the position; the only solace is, it is not for long. If I go to Egypt or not is uncertain; I hope He has given me the strength not to care one way or the other; twenty years are soon gone, and when over it will matter little whether I went or not."

The proposed step was sanctioned by the authorities, and so, at the age of forty-one, Gordon became the governor of the immense Equatorial Province. *En route* to Egypt he writes from Paris: "I remember that God has at all times worked by weak and small means. All history shows this to be His mode, and so I believe if He will He may work by me."

Of course some little time had to be spent in Cairo; the Khedive Ismail was anxious to make the acquaintance of his new governor, and certain preliminaries had to be settled. Gordon had a suspicion that his appointment was a sham, and that he would not have the power he needed to suppress the slave trade. He was determined that *coûte qui coûte* he would not be made a tool of to blind the European public, so at the very outset he showed his colours, and let the Khedive clearly understand that he was not a mere hireling anxious to secure a well-paid billet. As for his pay, though his predecessor had received £10,000 per annum, he decided to cut it down to £2000; for, as he said, the whole would be wrung out of the unfortunate natives, who could ill afford the high taxation to which they were subjected. Writing home at this juncture, he said:—

"My object is to show the Khedive and his people that gold and silver idols are not worshipped by all the world. They are very powerful gods, but not so powerful as our God; so if I refuse a large sum, you—and I am responsible to you alone—will not be angry at my doing so. From whom does all the money come? From poor miserable creatures who are ground down to produce it. Of course, these ideas are outrageous. 'Pillage the Egyptians!' is still the cry.

"I am quite prepared not to go, and should not think it unkind of God if He prevents it, for He must know what is best. The twisting of men carries out some particular object of God, and we should cheerfully agree now to what we will agree hereafter when we know all things."

His characteristic outspokenness—a style of thing to which Egyptian officials were not accustomed—somewhat alarmed a few of his friends, and on one occasion he was urged not to make an enemy of Nubar

Pasha, who was a very powerful minister, and could, it was said, do him a great deal of harm. At this Gordon fired up, and before those present said that he would like to see the man who was capable of injuring him. Shakespeare has well said :—

> "What stronger breastplate than a heart untainted!
> Thrice is he armed that hath his quarrel just,
> And he but naked, though locked up in steel,
> Whose conscience with injustice is corrupted."

Though Nubar showed his powers of appreciation in recognising merit in Colonel Gordon, when he met him at Galatz, there can be no question that he little understood the honest, straightforward character of the man with whom he had to deal. He must have often wished that he had never met Gordon, for, whilst the new governor was not a man to seek office for the sake of the "loaves and fishes," once in power he was not one of those pliant characters who will act as mere dummies in the hands of others. Men with great strength of character, good abilities, and honest intentions are invaluable, when their official superiors are capable of appreciating their merits; but when those under whom they serve have ulterior purposes to attain, weak, pliant natures make better servants for their purposes. In Colonel Gordon's own mind his mission at this time was to combat slavery, and in every possible way to ameliorate the sufferings of the unfortunate people over whom he was called to rule. Nubar Pasha held very different views from the newly-appointed governor on many points that were likely to arise in connection with these duties. The Soudan and the Equatorial Province were so frightfully mismanaged and cruelly governed that, Gordon says, "when Said Pasha, the Viceroy before Ismail, went up to the Soudan with Count F. Lesseps, he was so discouraged and horrified at the misery of the people that at Berber the Count saw him throw his guns into the river, declaring that he would be no party to such oppression. It was only after the urgent solicitations of European consuls and others that he reconsidered his decision."

It is quite amusing to see the efforts that were made at Cairo to break in the new governor, and to fit him for his post, in accordance with the traditions of the country. As soon as everything was settled, Gordon, with his usual promptness, and absence of all love of display, was anxious to be off to his post of duty, and for that purpose to utilise the ordinary passenger steamer from Suez. But about states such as Egypt was before the British occupation, there is a strange mixture of reckless expenditure combined with paltry meanness. Although the Egyptian authorities once refused to pay the travelling expenses of an official travelling on duty from Alexandria to Cairo in connection with Colonel Gordon, yet they insisted on this occasion that it would be unbecoming to the dignity of a governor to travel by an ordinary steamer, so a special one was set apart for this purpose. Gordon afterwards calculated that had he been allowed his own way, he would at the outset have saved at least £400! For the sake of peace he yielded the point, and went from Cairo in a special train, and from Suez in a special steamer, accompanied by a large number of useless servants. He had his revenge, however, for owing to an engine getting off the line, there was a long halt, and finally he had to proceed by the ordinary train. Gordon was a remarkable instance of the general rule, that the greater the ability of a man the less affection has he for display, and for all the official trappings of office. The only display that Gordon ever cared for was that of intrinsic merit and hard work, and these qualities he always looked for in his subordinates.

Colonel Gordon reached Suakim on February 25th, 1874, and writing home, he records his impressions of Cairo and its officials. "I think the Khedive likes me, but no one else does; and I don't like them, I mean the swells, whose corns I tread on in all manner of ways. Duke of This wants steamer, say £600. Duke of That wants house, &c. All the time the poor people are ground down to get money for all this. 'Who art thou to be afraid of man?' If He wills, I will shake all this in some way not clear to me now. Do not think I am an Egoist; I am like Moses who despised the riches of Egypt. I will not bow to Haman." Little did he then foresee that before eight years had passed British guns would be shaking the stronghold of Alexandria, and that 10,000 Egyptian soldiers would yield the citadel of Cairo to a small force of some 300 troops carrying the British flag. From Suakim he went on a camel to Berber, and thence by steamer to Khartoum, the first time he ever visited a place which now can never be mentioned without awakening in the mind associations of this noble servant of God, who feared neither man nor devil.

At first Gordon was to a certain extent subordinate to the Governor-General of the Soudan, through whom he had to get supplies. But by September 8th he was enabled to write: "I have now entirely separated my province from that of the Soudan. When I came up I had instructions to ask for all I wanted from the Governor-General of Khartoum, who was ordered to supply me. Now this was from the first a fruitful source of quarrel, and must have been so, for I could not be continually writing to the Khedive about the non-supply of things and money; it would have worn me and every one out. Now I am quite independent, raise my own revenue, and administer it, and send the residue to Cairo, which residue is all they care for there."

The Equatorial Province lies considerably to the south of Khartoum, and is bisected by the Nile. As a matter of fact the equator does not run through any part of the province, though the southern part comes very close to it, just touching the Victoria Nyanza, through the north of which the equator runs. The hold that Egypt had at any time on this province was indeed very slight, and considering how little capable she was of managing even her own affairs, it does seem ridiculous in the extreme that she should ever have attempted to annex an enormous country outside her borders. When Egypt was really strong and powerful, as in olden times, it does not appear that she ever held territory beyond Wady Halfa, and it is in reality only within this century, during the whole of which Egypt has been weak, that she has extended her territory down to the equator. Far from gaining either money or prestige, she has lost greatly by her annexations. Had the Nile, which is the only highway, been easily navigable for ships of any size, possibly the tide of civilisation might have gone south as well as north, and the history of these provinces might have been very different. But the Nile is full of rapids, or cataracts, as they are called, and at certain seasons of the year is absolutely impassable for large boats, while the paucity of wells makes regular travel by land impossible. From Khartoum to Gondokoro, which was the capital of Colonel Gordon's new province, a distance of about 1000 miles, another obstacle presents itself, in the form of an almost impassable barrier, known as a "sudd," which forms on the river, and puts a stop to traffic. Gordon said that the sudd is formed by an "aquatic plant with roots extending five feet in the water. The natives burn the top parts, when dry; the ashes form mould, and fresh grasses grow till it becomes like *terra firma*. The Nile rises, and floats out the masses; they come down to a curve and then stop. More of these islands float down, and at last the river is blocked. Though under them the water flows, no communication can take place, for they bridge the river for several miles."

Gordon left Khartoum on March 23, 1874, for Gondokoro, and on the 26th he writes: "Last night we were going along slowly in the moonlight, and I was thinking of you all, and the expedition, and Nubar, &c., when all of a sudden from a large bush came peals of laughter. I felt put out; but it turned out to be birds, who laughed at us from the bushes for some time in a rude way. They are a species of stork, and seemed in capital spirits, and highly amused at anybody thinking of going up to Gondokoro with the hope of doing anything." Gordon was full of hope, and very sanguine of success; but from the day when he reached Cairo, croakers all along the route had been whispering into his ear the hopelessness of his mission, and how utterly impossible it was to reform anything connected with such a corrupt administration as that of Egypt. Fortunately, though he used at times to have terrible fits of depression, he possessed a great deal of dogged perseverance. It was this that in China had enabled him to overcome all obstacles in fighting the enemy, and the same indomitable spirit now made him persevere and hope on, when every one else despaired. Not only were there real foes in every direction, determined if possible to frustrate his mission, but in addition there was physical suffering to endure from climatic and other causes. "No one can conceive," says he in a letter written on April 10th, "the utter misery of these lands, heat and mosquitoes day and night all the year round. But I like the work, for I believe that I can do a great deal to ameliorate the lot of the people." Two days after this he passed through a place called St. Croix, which had been a Roman Catholic mission station, but so unhealthy was it that it had at last been abandoned. After thirteen years of work not a single convert had been made, although during that period the missionaries had plodded on in the face of discouragement, and in spite of the appalling havoc that death and sickness had made in their ranks. Out of twenty missionaries thirteen had died of fever, two of dysentery, and two had been invalided. A few banana trees were all that remained of the settlement at which these heroes had been sacrificed.

Gordon reached Gondokoro on April 16th, just twenty-four days after leaving Khartoum. Everybody was much surprised to see him, for it was not even known that he had been appointed. He remained only six days, and then started back to Khartoum, in order to get his baggage. Not finding it there, he went on to Berber to hurry up the escort, but not till he had given the corrupt Governor of Khartoum a bit of his mind. "I have had some sharp skirmishing with the Governor-General of Khartoum," said he in a letter home, "and I think I have crushed him. Your brother wrote to him and told him he told *stories*. It was undiplomatic of me, but it did the Governor-General good." Having secured his baggage, he returned to Gondokoro. *En route* he writes from the entrance of the Sanbat River:—

"We arrived here from Khartoum a week ago, and I have made a nice station here, and made great friends with the Shillock natives, who come over in great numbers from the other side of the river. They are poorly off, and I have given them some grain; very little contents them. I have employed a few of them to plant maize, and they do it very fairly. The reason they do not do it for themselves is, that if they plant any quantity they would run the chance of losing it, by its being taken by force from them; so they plant only enough to keep body and soul together, and even that is sown in small out-of-the-way patches."

He reached Gondokoro the second time on September 4th, receiving the salaams and salutes of the officers, men, and functionaries, together with the submission of all the neighbouring chiefs. In the whole of his province Egypt had only two forts, one at Gondokoro, the capital, with 300 men, and one at Fatiko, further south, with 200 men. "As for paying taxes," said he, "or any government existing outside the forts, it is all nonsense. You cannot go out in any safety half-a-mile, all because they have been fighting the poor natives and taking their cattle. I apprehend not the least difficulty in the work; the greatest will be to gain the people's confidence again. They have been hardly treated."

The chief culprit, to whom much of this misgovernment was due, was Raouf Bey, whom Gordon found at Gondokoro. This man had been in office for six years, and proved a miserable failure. "Raouf had never conciliated the tribes, never had planted dhoora; and, in fact, only possessed the land he camped upon." Yet he made it a grievance that Gordon refused to employ him, and the present Khedive of Egypt many years afterwards made him Governor-General of the Soudan when Gordon resigned.

What most astonished Gordon was the apparent want of affection on the part of the natives for their offspring, and it pained him none the less when he reflected that this was entirely due to the slave trade, and the sufferings the poor people had endured. One man brought Gordon two of his children of 12 and 9 years old, because they were starving, and sold them for a basketful of grain, and though the father often came to the station after this, he never asked to see them. Gordon mentioned another case, of a family in which there were two children. Passing their hut one day, and seeing only one child, he asked the mother where the other was. "Oh," said she, "it has been given to the man from whom the cow was stolen"—her husband having been the culprit. This was said with a cheerful smile. "But," said Gordon, "are you not sorry?" "Oh, no! we would rather have the cow." "But you have eaten the cow, and the pleasure is over." "Oh, but all the same, we would sooner have had the cow!" Gordon adds, "The other child of twelve years old, like her parents did not care a bit. A lamb taken from the flock will bleat, while here you see not the very slightest vestige of feeling." Such an incident shows how the human heart can, under certain circumstances, degenerate to being "without natural affection." It is not the people who are to blame, but their cruel conquerors. Not many miles away from this place, in a district which the tyranny of slavery has not yet reached, Dr. Schweinfurth says of the natives: "Notwithstanding that certain instances may be alleged which seem to demonstrate that the character of the Dinka is unfeeling, these cases never refer to such as are bound by the ties of kindred. Parents do not desert their children, nor are brothers faithless to brothers, but are ever prompt to render whatever aid is possible." The famous negro prelate, Bishop Crowther, and the celebrated traveller, Mr. Stanley, bear similar testimony. There can be no question that the African, in his normal condition, is as capable of affection as the native of any other country.

Slavery has been, is, and as long as it exists will be, the curse of Africa. "Not a soul," said Gordon, "to be seen for miles; all driven off by the slavers in years past. You could scarcely conceive such a waste or desert." Such was his comment when at the entrance of the river Sanbat, and such would have frequently been a correct description of the country blighted by this cursed traffic.

Speaking generally, slavery exists now only in Mohammedan countries (though there are a few exceptions), yet it cannot be called a Mohammedan institution. The Prophet sanctioned only the taking of slaves in war. The custom of his time was to kill and often to torture prisoners taken in war, so that really it was a step in advance to suggest that these captives should be utilised as servants. To a great extent, if not entirely, slavery as an institution is due to the low moral standard set up by the Koran. Were it not for love of sensual indulgence, slavery would long ago have died a natural death. Over and over again has it been proved that voluntary service is far cheaper than enforced labour. An Indian coolie will work all day, and ask for little more than enough to keep body and soul together. This much the slave-owners are compelled to give to keep their slaves in health. Slaves are valuable property, and it is cheaper to feed them well than badly. But over and above the food, the slave-owner has to bear the cost of transit from their bright happy homes in Central Africa, through hundreds of miles of scorching desert, which demands a frightful death-toll. Only the strongest ever reach the slave-markets, and it has been calculated that at least 500,000 lives are annually sacrificed during transit. Indirectly the slave-owner has to pay for these. When slaves were taken in war, they cost nothing to transport; but when Mohammedan conquests ceased, the supply ceased with it, for Mohammedans are not allowed by the Koran to make slaves of men of their own creed, though they do sometimes infringe this rule.

It is generally supposed that the slave trade originated in the fact that in certain parts of Central Africa there are no horses or beasts of burden, as owing to the existence of the tetse-fly no animal can live. Consequently ivory and everything else has to be carried on the heads of porters. These porters were engaged by the Arab ivory dealers in the interior, and marched in large gangs to the seaports. Having reached their destination, and given up their loads, the question of transport back to their villages would arise. The Arab traders found that it would suit their purpose best to sell the porters as slaves. Who was to know whether or not they were taken in battle? In Mohammedan countries, so long as plenty of backsheesh is forthcoming, those in authority ask few questions. Soon the sale of slaves became more profitable than the ivory trade, which possibly had originated it, and so the one was substituted for the other, the authorities not only winking at it, but encouraging it as a source of large revenues to them. At one time a large number of so-called Christians were engaged in this unholy traffic, but the scandal became so great that European public opinion would not tolerate it, and so they had to sell their stations to Mohammedan Arabs, who if possible were even more cruel and relentless in the way they conducted the trade. Merchant princes arose among them, and they carried on their business with a thoroughness and a system worthy of a better cause. Soldiers were trained, and large armies kept for no other purpose than that of collecting slaves. Peaceful villages were surrounded, night attacks were made, whole tribes were marched off to the slave markets, the road being lined by grinning skulls to show the way in which the victims suffered *en route*.

> "Not for this
> Was common clay ta'en from the common earth,
> Moulded by God, and tempered with the tears
> Of angels, to the perfect shape of man!"

The unfortunate captives were chained together to prevent escape, and often the fastenings were secured in a way so unnecessarily cruel, that they had great difficulty in securing any sleep, either at night or during the day when the periodical halts were made. Indeed the ordinary precautions that we take in the convoy of large herds of cattle were generally neglected. This is all the more surprising when we consider what great trouble these men took to secure their victims; one would have thought that self-interest at least would often have dictated a more humane policy, but it does not appear to have been so.

In hunting for these gangs of slaves, it was a subject of deep regret to Gordon that often his action only tended to increase their sufferings. In the Central African deserts there are only a few wells, at long intervals, and the poor captives suffered terrible thirst on the march from well to well. But the surest way of intercepting the gangs was to hold the wells. When the slave-dealers knew that a certain well on which they were marching was held by Gordon, they would make a detour in order to avoid him, and their unfortunate victims would be kept from quenching their thirst for unusually long periods, with the result that many would succumb to the appalling heat. If a slave exhibited great exhaustion, and showed little chance of being able to reach the next halting-place, the drivers would not even trouble to waste a round of ammunition, but, unchaining the victim, would kill him by a blow on the back of the neck with a mallet or a piece of wood, and leave his body where it lay, to feed the vultures. Often young girls, and even infants, were marched through deserts, through which Gordon declared that he shuddered to contemplate a journey on his fleet-footed camel. It was with truth that Burns said—

"Man's inhumanity to man
Makes countless thousands mourn."

Some of the slave traders had become very rich, and one of them, Zebehr Rahama, now in captivity in Gibraltar, had become so powerful that even the Khedive dared not molest him. His field of operations lying at a considerable distance from Gordon's province, these two did not come in contact, until the latter was made Governor-General of the whole of the Soudan, and so it is not at the present time necessary to do more than merely allude to him as the king of slave hunters. Many more carried on a successful business, and some of them conducted their operations in the Equatorial Province; and it is hardly necessary to say that the first thing the new governor did was to break up the organisations of these men. He was only appointed in Cairo during the month of February, and after that time he had to spend many weary days and nights in travelling. But in June we find him seizing an Arab dealer named Nassar, at the head of a large convoy of slaves, and casting him into prison. By this brilliant stroke he not only got possession of a well-known culprit, but struck terror into the hearts of smaller dealers. But, as in the case of the Taiping rebels, whom he at once turned into soldiers to fight for him, so Nassar was enlisted into his service. "Do you know," he wrote, "I have forgiven the head slaver Nassar, and am employing him; he is not worse than others, and these slavers have been much encouraged to do what they have done. He is a first-rate man, and does a great deal of work. He was in prison for two weeks, and was then forgiven." Other quotations could be made from his letters showing that he had formed a high opinion of the abilities of the Arabs engaged in slave dealing, with a correspondingly low one of the Egyptian soldiers who were employed to put them down. The Arabs were enterprising, plucky fellows, with the spirit of a man in them, whereas the soldiers were a cowardly and contemptible lot. When in large numbers, they used to ill-treat and bully the natives, who consequently took every opportunity of retaliating. Gordon, with his quick perception, saw that the best way to remedy this was to scatter the soldiers about in small detachments, just strong enough to defend their posts, but not to take advantage of the people:—

"I have the garrisons small on purpose to make them keep awake; and it has its effect, for they are all in a fearful fright along the line. I cannot help feeling somewhat of a malicious enjoyment of their sufferings. If I personally am at any station, even if there are thirty or forty men there, the sentries all go to sleep in comfort. Not so in my absence; every one is awake, I expect. Having nothing to do—or rather not doing anything, though there is plenty to be done—they sit and talk over the terrors of their position, until they tremble again. I never in the course of my life saw such wretched creatures dignified by the name of soldiers. Fortunately, though I can do the work of the province without an interpreter, I cannot speak to the men except by my looks, or tell them my opinion in words, though my letters are pretty strong."

The results of this policy were excellent. Not only were the garrisons kept on the alert and prevented from oppressing the people, but the country was opened up and travelling rendered safer. Writing home, Gordon says:—

"It is such a comfort having my roads open. One man came down from Bedden to-day alone. Before I came it would have needed thirty or at least twenty men to go along this route. The blacks would have concealed themselves in the grass, and stuck a spear into the hindermost man; now they are quite friendly. A Bari in my employment stole a sheep yesterday, and down came the natives to complain and have justice, which they got. Is it not comfortable? All this has effected a great change among my men. They no longer fear the blacks as they did, and altogether a much better feeling exists. Going up to Kerri, where in September last the convoy of Kemp was harassed all the route, I went on alone with four or five soldiers behind me, and never felt the least apprehension; for the natives talk much amongst themselves, and the virgin tribes had heard we were not to be feared, and that their cattle was safe from pillage. A year ago an escort of five or six soldiers used to accompany each nuggar either coming up or down. Even the steamers carried an escort of the same number. Now not one soldier either goes with one or the other. This has prevented all pillaging *en route*, for our people dare not do it now, not having the escort of soldiers."

In spite of his contempt for the soldiers under him, he treated them kindly and made great efforts to improve them. Now and then he would give them a magic-lantern lecture, and in other ways try to benefit them mentally and morally. No doubt in this he succeeded to a great extent, and at all events he had the satisfaction of feeling that he was liked by them. In another letter he says:—

"The men and officers like my justice, candour, and my outbursts of temper, and see that I am not a tyrant. Over two years we have lived intimately together, and they watch me closely. I am glad that they do so. My wish and desire is that all should be as happy as it rests with me to make them, and though I feel sure that I am unjust sometimes, it is not the rule with me to be so. I care for their marches, for their wants and food, and protect their women and boys if they ill-treat them; and I do nothing of this. I am a chisel which cuts the wood; the Carpenter directs it. If I lose my edge, He must sharpen me; if He puts me aside and takes another, it is His own good will. None are indispensable to Him; He will do His work with a straw equally as well."

Gordon had not been long in his province when he saw that the only effectual way to abolish slavery was to open up the country, and encourage traders by making it safe for them to travel about. Much as he did personally to punish slave-hunting, and to break up gangs of men so engaged, he always considered that his best efforts should be devoted to the opening up of the country for trade. At the time he was there, and now also, the leading men were all more or less engaged in slave-hunting, and no one dared to say a word against them. Gordon wanted to introduce an independent class of traders, who would soon be sufficiently powerful to give evidence against the leaders of the slave-hunting system. His desire afterwards to serve the King of the Belgians in the Congo territory was with the object of developing trade, and thus ultimately of preventing slave-dealing. With regard to Egypt, he formed his ideas during the first year he was in the country, and he steadily adhered to them to the end. Writing from Tultcha, on 17th November 1873, he says:—

"I believe if the Soudan was settled, the Khedive would prevent the slave trade; but he does not see his way to do so till he can move about the country. My ideas are to open it out by getting the steamers on to the lakes, by which time I should know the promoters of the slave trade and could ask the Khedive to seize them." And again: "God has allowed slavery to go on for so many years; born in the people, it needs more than an expedition to eradicate it; open out the country, and it will fall of itself."

Though he was not permitted during his life to see much permanent result from his arduous labours, yet far from his efforts having been in vain, he it was who revived in Europe an interest in the subject, and conclusions arrived at by the recent Anti-Slavery Conference, at Brussels, clearly indicate that the more thoughtful philanthropists who are moving in the matter recognise that the lines he laid down are the right ones to follow. The number of years that he was permitted to devote to this struggle with slavery were not many, but the seeds were sown which will bring forth a rich harvest in the future. In that noble crusade, which he undertook single-handed against tyranny and oppression, he supplied the best possible answer to the cynic's question whether or not life is worth living:—

"Is Life worth living? Yes, so long
As there is wrong to right,
Wail of the weak against the strong,
Or tyranny to fight;
Long as there lingers gloom to chase
Or streaming tear to dry,
One kindred woe, one sorrowing face,
That smiles as we draw nigh."*

Not only had Gordon to contend with the slave trade, corrupt officials, an unsympathetic government at Cairo, and incompetent troops, but to add to his troubles his staff broke down with sickness and even death, while

* Mr. Alfred Austin in the *English Illustrated Magazine.*

he for the first time in his life suffered from ague and liver disorders. Here are descriptions of the climate from some of his letters:—

"This is a horrid climate. I seldom, if ever, get a good sleep. It is a very great comfort to feel that God will rectify one's defects in this life, and make right all mistakes, also that He governs everything. Is it my present temperament, or is it truly the case that things go untowardly more in this land than anywhere else? You wrap up an article in paper, the paper is sure to tear, the string you least want to be broken is broken; every, *every* thing seems to go wrong. It may be my liver which makes me think this, but it has been the same with all travellers." . . . . "The mosquitoes are horrible here; the proboscis is formed like a bayonet, with a hinge at the bend; they turn it down for perforation and press on it with their head, muscles, and chest. I am very susceptible of their bite or dig; the least touch of the 'bayonet' makes a lump."
. . . . "Variety is pleasing! Got away from mosquitoes to find sand-flies and harvest-bugs instead. However, they are quiet by day, and here there are no flies with irritating feet. There must be some wonderful mystery about this life. Why should these countries be so full of annoyances to man? Why should even the alighting of a fly, *his footprints*, cause such irritation to the skin. It must be for some good object eventually to be made known to us."

Most of Gordon's efforts were directed to the abolition of slavery, and the amelioration of the sufferings of the people he governed, but as an explorer and a surveyor he also did good work, and he might, had he cared for such distinctions, have received honours from the Royal Geographical Society. Though suffering a good deal from sickness and from mental worries, he endeavoured to explore the seventy miles of country between Foweira and the Albert Nyanza. In one of his letters he says:—

"It was contended that the Nile did not flow out of Lake Victoria and thence into Lake Albert and so northward, but that one river flowed out of Lake Victoria and another out of Lake Albert; and that these two rivers united and formed the Nile. This statement could not be positively denied, inasmuch as no one had actually gone along the river from Foweira to Hagungo. So I went along it with much suffering, and settled the question."

As he did not personally come into contact with M'tesa, the King of Uganda, it is not necessary to do more than mention the fact that this strange monarch wrote a letter to him, and even asked him to plant a stockade for his troops within Uganda territory. Gordon, however, did not trust M'tesa, and at one time, on account of some misbehaviour on the part of that monarch, even contemplated attacking him. But Mr. Stanley, the great explorer, sent a vigorous protest against any aggression on the part of a Christian representative, even of a Moslem Government, towards a newly Christianised state, if one may apply that term to Uganda. Gordon evidently recognised the wisdom of Stanley's contention, for the attack was never made, and Stanley received from Gordon a letter giving him much information.

Gordon reached Lake Albert at the end of July 1876, and from then till he left to return home he was busily engaged in surveying the country, wading through rivers, cutting his way through dense jungles, encountering natives armed with assegais, and in other ways risking his valuable life, all for the sake of his fellow-creatures, and in the hope of ultimately opening up the country. Was there ever a man more strongly actuated by the spirit of altruism?

His three years were drawing to a close, and not having received the support he thought he deserved, he decided to leave the service of the Khedive. On October 6th he commenced his journey, and by Christmas Eve of that year he had reached England.

CHAPTER XI.

GOVERNOR-GENERAL OF THE SOUDAN.

COLONEL GORDON'S visit to England was a very short one, for no sooner did the Khedive Ismail realise the fact that such an able public servant had definitely decided to quit his service, than he wrote imploring him to return on his own terms, which were nothing less than that he should be invested with the Governor-Generalship of the whole Soudan, including the Equatorial Province, over which he had for three years ruled. The Khedive was sufficiently wide awake to know what an able, conscientious servant he had in Gordon, and, cost what it might, was determined not to lose him. The truth of the matter was that Gordon had made himself indispensable to the Khedive, and when a man does that he may practically demand his own terms. His heart was thoroughly in the work, and the only reason for his having resigned was that he was disgusted with Ismail Yacoob, the Governor-General of the Soudan, who, although Gordon was not under him, was from his position in many ways able to hamper his reforms. The Khedive wisely decided to recall Ismail Yacoob from Khartoum, and to put Colonel Gordon in his place. "Setting a just value," wrote the Khedive, "on your honourable character, on your zeal, and on the great services that you have already done me, I have resolved to bring the Soudan, Darfour, and the provinces of the Equator, into one great province, and to place it under you as Governor-General. As the country which you are thus to govern is so vast, you must have beneath you three vakeels (or deputy governors): the first for the Soudan properly so called, the second for Darfour, and the third for the shores of the Red Sea and the Eastern Soudan." Thus, at the age of forty-four, Gordon had committed to his charge the absolute control, including power over life and death, over a province as large as France, Germany, and Spain together! He had already served the Khedive for three years in the unhealthy Equatorial Province, and now he was to govern for nearly three years more this larger and still more unwieldy province, his reign only ceasing with the abdication of Ismail.

When Gordon left England for Cairo, the appointment had not been conferred upon him. He merely went out to see the Khedive, and it was not till February 13, 1877, that the matter was finally decided. Writing home in reference to the Khedive's kindness, he quotes that text "Ask of me, and I will give thee to the half of my kingdom," and then he goes on to say:—

"And now for the reverse of the medal. It is the sacrifice of a *living* life. To give your life to be taken at once, is one thing; to give a life such as is before me is another and more trying ordeal. I have set my face to the work, and will give my life to it. I feel as if I had nought to do with the Government. God must undertake the work. . . . I think how many would be weighed down by this immense charge; how they would shrink from accepting it without some other help, for fear of their reputation. But for me, I never gave the question a thought. I feel sure of success; for I do not lean on my own understanding, and He directs my path."

On March 19th he writes with regard to his grand escort:—

"Here I met two hundred cavalry and infantry, who had come to meet us. I am most carefully guarded—at six yards' radius round the tree where I am sitting are six or eight sentries, and the other men are in a circle round them. Now, just imagine this, and put yourself in my position. However, I know they will all go to sleep, so I do not fret myself. I can say truly, no man has ever been so forced into a high position as I have. How many I know to whom the incense would be the breath of their nostrils. To me it is irksome beyond measure. Eight or ten men to help me off my camel! as if I were an invalid. If I walk, every one gets off and walks; so, furious, I get on again."

After being appointed Governor-General of the Soudan, the first thing Colonel Gordon did was to attempt to bring about a definite peace between the Khedive and the King of Abyssinia, whose territory adjoins the Soudan. It will be remembered that in the year 1868 an English expedition, under the late Lord (then Sir Robert) Napier, went against Theodore, King of Abyssinia, to punish him for imprisoning and ill-treating British subjects. Being defeated, that monarch committed suicide. Before his defeat, as he was much hated, some of his chieftains had broken into open revolt, and one of them had proclaimed himself king of a certain province. Sir Robert Napier presented this chieftain with four guns and a thousand rifles, and this recognition on the part of the conquerors enabled the chief in question to mount the Abyssinian throne, taking for himself the name of Johannis.

In 1874 a Swiss adventurer, who was at that time governor of Massowah, under the Khedive, seized Bogos, a piece of territory belonging to Abyssinia, and held it for his master, at the same time urging him to add another province, that of Hamaçen, to his ill-gotten gains. At this time the Khedive was rich, having just received £4,000,000 from the British Government for the Suez Canal shares, and instead of spending the money in developing the resources of the territory he already possessed, he was ill advised enough to go to war, and got defeated. Foremost among the Abyssinians in the conflict was Walad el Michael, the hereditary prince of Bogos and Hamaçen, who before the war was imprisoned for having sought the aid of Napoleon III. against the Abyssinian king. He was released at the commencement of hostilities, and proved very successful. But, having defeated the Egyptians, Walad got disgusted with the Abyssinian king for depriving him of his share of the spoils of war, and consequently, when the Egyptians in 1876 sought to avenge their defeat, Walad turned against his own king. The Egyptians were however again defeated, 9000 of them being killed, and an enormous number taken prisoners. The spoils of war were great, for all the Egyptian tents, twenty-five guns, 10,000 rifles, and a large amount of English gold, were captured by the Abyssinians. So ignorant were they of the value of this spoil, that they mistook English sovereigns for brass counters, and thirty of them were sold for four dollars! The Abyssinian king was so incensed at the conduct of Walad, who had 7000 men and 700 rifles, that, as one of the conditions of peace, he demanded that the Khedive should give him up. This of course the Khedive could not do, and a long delay followed, during which the Abyssinian monarch sent an envoy to Cairo. But the Khedive treated the envoy badly, and he, rightly or wrongly, imagined that his life was in danger. He managed to get away, and the ill-feeling between the two monarchs was intense when Colonel Gordon arrived on the scene. Just at this time the great bulk of the Egyptian troops were required for the Turkish war against the Russians, and Gordon was left helpless, as he had not sufficient force with him to compel Walad to cease his intermittent attacks on Abyssinia.

Seeing the hopelessness of his position, Gordon decided to waste no more time over the question, more especially as he had not yet been to Khartoum, the capital of his huge province, to take up his duties, and all the time there was a revolt going on in Darfour, on the extreme west of his dominion. Having once made up his mind, he lost no time in getting to Khartoum, leaving Walad to be dealt with at his leisure later on. On reaching Khartoum, which he did by travelling forty-five miles a day in the extremely hot months of April and May, he had to submit to the ordeal of installation. It was on this occasion, after the firman had been read and the royal salute had been fired, that he made the memorable speech which so delighted the people, and which may be summed up in one sentence that he made use of, "With the help of God I will hold the balance level." By this he meant to say, that as long as he was Governor-General there should be none of the cruel, grinding tyranny that had existed in the time of his predecessor. It may be well here, anticipating events, to illustrate the desperate condition of the people under the tyranny of the Egyptian rule. Mr. Frank Power, correspondent of the *Times*, in a private letter to his mother in the year 1884, describes the way in which the poor people were ground down with taxation. He says:—

"Every Arab must pay a tax for himself, children, and wife or wives. This he has to pay three times over—once for the Khedive, once for the tax collector or local Beys, and once for the Governor-General. The last two are illegal, but still scrupulously collected to the piastre. To pay this he must grow some corn, and for the privilege of growing corn he must pay £3 per annum. To grow corn the desert earth must have water: the means of irrigation is a 'Sakeh,' a wheel like a mill-wheel with buckets on it, which raise the water into a trough, and then it flows in little streams over the land. A sakeh is turned by two oxen. Every man who uses a sakeh must pay £7: if he does not use it, he must go into prison for life, and have his hut burned. Every one must pay for the right of working to earn money; every one must pay if they are idle; in any case every one must pay to make the officials rich. If you have a trading boat, you are fined £4 if you do not continually fly the Egyptian flag, and you must pay £4 for the privilege of flying it."

In another letter he says:—

"If they wish to grow corn they must pay for permission to do so, pay for liberty to take water from the broad Nile, and pay for liberty to sell the corn. If the crop is good, pay double taxes (one for private purse of the Pasha and one for the Government at Cairo). If they don't grow the corn they can't pay the taxes at all, and get kourbashed (flogged) and put into prison. No matter how they make a few piastres, the dragoman of some Bey or Pasha will steal it for his master. They frequently pull down huts and tear up yards and fields to find where the coins are hidden. If the peasant buys a few rags for his wife or child, or mends a hole in his hut to keep out the sun, he is told he must have got money somewhere, and he is doubly taxed; and after all, his sole possessions are a hut made of mud and river reeds, a rush bed, a rush mat, and an earthen pot."

In still another letter he says:—

"Some of these merchants, who sit all day in their little stalls in the bazaar, are really millionaires, and would buy up many of the London merchant-princes. They live like kings in what, outside, looks like a mud hut. If one shows any outward signs of wealth, the Pasha lets him know quietly that he will at once be charged as a rebel or something, and put in prison if he does not make him a little present, generally from £300 to £1000. One Pasha left here last year, admitting, report says, that in three years he had made £60,000. He came here three years ago as a clerk on £2 a month. Abdul-Kereem Pasha, the Governor, took a fancy to him, and made him chief of the tax-gatherers; in three years he gained the rank of Pasha and £60,000—meaning 5000 ruined homes, several million strokes of the bastinado, rapine, robbery, and men driven to exasperation, and shot down at their doors."

Need we wonder that people so ground down by tyranny were delighted to hear their Governor-General announce that he would hold the balance level, and that no longer should the rich and powerful trample on the weak and poor?

The prominent characteristic of the Egyptian rule in the Soudan was fittingly summed up in the sentence, "*Kourbash, kourbash, et toujours kourbash,*" which being interpreted means, "Flogging, flogging, always flogging." As to administration of justice, there was no such thing. He who could bribe the judges the highest got judgment delivered in his favour, while his opponent received the kourbash. The symbol of authority might well have been a kourbash, which corresponds to the English cat-o'-nine-tails. Men were often kourbashed for no other reason than that they would not, or could not, bribe any official who had the power of administering this form of punishment not to inflict it on them. Nor must it be supposed that an ordinary flogging, such as we understand by that term, would satisfy these tyrannical perpetrators of cruelty. Often the use of the kourbash meant that the victim was maimed for life, and the unfortunate one might always consider himself lucky, if he escaped without any permanent injury. In many cases it amounted to nothing more or less than a form of torture, such as used to be inflicted in England in the barbarous Middle Ages, and if the sufferer had not actually got the money he was supposed to have, he would often have to borrow as much as he could of the required amount, in order to avoid further torture. We can imagine how Gordon's blood must have boiled with indignation at such gross miscarriages of justice; and during the whole time he served the Khedive, his object was to do away with this kind of tyranny. Often his journeys from place to place were marked by signs of fallen greatness, as he would not tolerate tyranny. "In one month," he says, "I have turned out three generals of division, one general of brigade, and four lieutenant-colonels. It is no use mincing matters."

He allowed every one to approach him and to make complaints. A box always stood at his tent or palace, into which any one who had a grievance could drop his written complaint, with a certainty that it would receive immediate investigation. Such a method gave publicity to instances of cruelty and oppression, and often, directly Gordon heard of cases of this kind, he would jump on his camel, pay a personal visit to the individual concerned, and having investigated the case on the spot, would deal out justice upon the culprit. Of course, in such an extensive province as his, without railways, it was absolutely impossible to investigate all the cases, but by taking the more prominent and the grosser ones, he could strike terror into the hearts of evil-doers in high places; and in this way he considerably reduced the evil of tyrannical rule, and taught the oppressed people that they had as much right to live as their oppressors had.

Of course Gordon was a much-hated man among the oppressor class, as reformers of deep-seated abuses usually are; but he knew that the weak and helpless at all events would appreciate him. When Wilberforce, the great slavery abolitionist, was accused by an opponent of interference with the rights of man, he asked what those rights were, and received for answer, "The right that every man has to lick his own nigger!" To rights of this kind, however long established, Gordon was an inveterate enemy; his object was to show that the weak and the helpless had rights as well as their oppressors, and in this he succeeded to a marvellous extent. "My great desire," said he, "is to be a shelter to the people, to ease their burdens, and to soften their hard lot in these inhospitable lands." And again:—

> "I have an enormous province to look after; but it is a great blessing to me to know that God has undertaken the administration of it, and it is His work, and not mine. If I fail, it is His will; if I succeed, it is His work certainly. He has given me the joy of not regarding the honours of this world, and to value my union with Him above all things. May I be humbled to the dust and fail, so that He may glorify Himself. The greatness of my position only depresses me, and I cannot help wishing that the time had come when He will lay me aside and use some other worm to do His work."

Besides putting an end to cruelty and injustice, he introduced into Khartoum a system of water supply. But important as his work at Khartoum was, he was on May 19 compelled to leave, a revolt having broken out at Darfour, where his immediate presence was required. So off he went on his camel into the very heart of the slave-hunting district. Writing from Fogia, on the frontier of Darfour, he says :—

"I have a splendid camel—none like it; it flies along, and quite astonishes the Arabs. I came flying into this station in marshal's uniform, and before the men had time to unpile arms, I had arrived with only one man with me. I could not help it; the escort did not come in for an hour and a half afterwards. The Arab chief who was with me said it was the telegraph. . . .It is fearful to see the Governor-General arrayed in gold clothes flying along like a madman, with only a guide, as if he was pursued. . . . Specks had been seen in the vast plain around the station moving towards it (like Jehu's advance), but the specks were few—only two or three—and were supposed to be the advanced guard, and, before the men of Fogia knew where they were, the station was taken!"

Writing from Oomchanga near Fascher, the capital of Darfour, he says :—

"All this revolt is the fault of the Bashi-Bazouks. I said the other day, 'If the people of this country were Ryahs or Christians, I might understand your bad treatment of them, but I do not when I see they are Mussulmans, as you.' Upon which the Darfourians were delighted, and clapped their hands. Now the Darfourians were so fanatical that they would never let a Christian into their country, and now they ask me to send Christian Governors!"

Their hatred of the Bashi-Bazouks was well illustrated by an incident Gordon mentions, which was told him by one of the officers. "An officer declared to me," he said, "that a woman with an officer escaped with the child he had by her, and taking the child to the chief of the insurgents, asked him to kill it, as 'the child of a Turk,' which the chief did."

On June 29 Gordon was able to write, "We have made peace with the tribes around here half-way to Fascher;" but he records, "I speak my mind, and I cannot help saying to some" (of the Darfourians who had come in to ask for peace), "'You ought to pardon me.' Really no people could have been treated worse than these people."

No sooner was one trouble settled than he was off on another expedition, and this time his steps were directed towards Dara, the stronghold of the great prince of slave-dealers, Zebehr Rahama. *En route* he was nearly starved as well as poisoned by putrid water. Writing from Toashia on July 3, he says, "We have been two whole days without meat," and he finds a garrison who for three years have been without pay! He left Toashia on July 11 with 500 men, of whom 150 only were any good. On this march there was a threatened attack, which fortunately did not come off, but that he felt he was in great danger we may gather from the extract: "We have, thank God, passed our dangers. Whether they were imaginary or not, I do not know, but we were threatened by an attack from thousands of determined blacks, who knew I was here. Now very few Englishmen know what it is to be with troops they have not a bit of confidence in. . . . I do not fear death, but I fear, from want of faith, the results of my death—for the whole country would have risen."

At Dara he came across a gang of 210 slaves, who

had been rescued, but who had received no food for thirty-six hours. His heart was filled with pity for them, and he wrote:—

"I am a fool, I dare say, but I cannot see the sufferings of these people without tears in my eyes. . . . It is a sad sight to see the poor starved creatures looking so wistfully at one. What can I do? Poor souls! I cannot feed or look after them. I must leave it to God, who will arrange all in kindness. Some of them were so miserably thin. I have sent them some dhoora. I declare solemnly that I would give my life willingly to save the sufferings of these people; and if I would do this, how much more does He care for them than such imperfection as I am! You would have felt sick had you seen them. Poor creatures! thirty-six hours without food!"

The more experience Colonel Gordon had of his Bashi-Bazouk soldiers, the more he seems to have disliked them:—

"I am worn to a shadow by the utter uselessness of the Bashi-Bazouks. The very sight of them excites my ire. I never saw such a useless, expensive set. I hate (there is no other word for it) these Arabs; and I like the Blacks—patient, enduring, and friendly, as much as the Arab is cowardly, cruel, and effeminate. All the misery is due to these Arab and Circassian Pashas and authorities. I would not stay a day here for these wretched creatures, but I would give my life for these Blacks."

Writing from Dara, he mentions an instance which occurred on the march to that place to show the cowardly nature of his men, as well as the bravery of the Blacks. His force of 3500 men was attacked by the Leopard tribe, numbering only 700 men. In spite of these overwhelming odds in their favour, Gordon says that his men were nearly beaten. "I was sickened," he said, "to see twenty brave men of the tribes in alliance with me ride out to meet the Leopard tribe, unsupported by my men, who crowded into the stockade. It was terribly painful. The only thing which restrained me from riding out to the attack was the sheep-like state in which my people would have been had I been killed. What, also, would have become of the province?"

Notwithstanding the inferior quality of his troops, Colonel Gordon was determined to march on and pay a visit to Zebehr Rahama's camp, one of the boldest acts of his life. Zebehr, himself the head of the cursed slave traffic, was at this time practically a prisoner in Cairo. He had, foolishly enough, gone there with £100,000, in the hope that he could bribe the Khedive and his officials, and he even had the effrontery to ask Gordon to intercede for him. Unfortunately for Zebehr, he was too powerful a man for the Khedive to care to have at large. He was practically an independent chief, his power and influence being greater in the Soudan than that of the Khedive. He lived in regal style, and every one trembled at his name. Dr. Schweinfurth thus describes the surroundings of this remarkable man. He was "surrounded with a court that was little less than princely in its details. Special rooms, provided with carpeted divans, were reserved as ante-chambers, and into these all visitors were conducted by richly-dressed slaves. The regal aspect of these halls of state was increased by the introduction of some lions, secured, as may be supposed, by sufficiently strong and massive chains." Dr. Birkbeck Hill says, "He owned no less than thirty stations. These fortified posts were carried far into the heart of Africa; and all along the line from one to another, and round each one of them far and wide, the slave-dealer exercised despotic rule."

The only foolish act this prince of slave-hunters ever did was to put himself into the power of the Khedive, by going to visit him at his capital. Once at Cairo, the Khedive kept him there as a prisoner. Zebehr's son, Suleiman, was at the head of his army of some 3000 fighting men, as plucky as Gordon's men were cowardly. When the father was detained at Cairo, he telegraphed in cipher to his son to break into open revolt, and even to attack the Government. Gordon knew that his men were utterly unable to meet Suleiman's troops in the field, so he tried another method to intimidate the rebels. He rode on alone ahead of his escort, covering eighty-five miles in a day and a half, in the heat of August, and dashing into the camp of these robbers, summoned their chief to an interview. Suleiman and his followers were dumbfounded by this bold act, and offered no resistance. The Governor-General then told Suleiman that he was aware of the meditated revolt, and that if he did not submit to his authority, his band should be broken up and disarmed. Suleiman and his chiefs went off to consider their course of action. Of course many were for making Gordon a prisoner, and he had, humanly speaking, a narrow escape. However, Suleiman decided to submit, and though afterwards we hear of him again in open revolt, for the time being Gordon carried the day. Nothing but his daring courage preserved him on that occasion. He even accepted an invitation to visit Suleiman at Shaka, where he spent two days. When Suleiman asked for an appointment, it was refused, on the ground that he had not yet shown his loyalty to the Khedive. Gordon, however, made him a present of his own gun, and taught him to use it.

Gordon often used to speak of this adventure as a most remarkable answer to prayer. He had prayed for Suleiman before starting, and had also asked for guidance for himself, and God heard him. It has sometimes been represented as a mad freak on Gordon's part to put himself into the lion's den in this way, but it was nothing of the kind. Suleiman was in revolt, supported by a splendid army. Gordon was absolutely at his mercy, for he could not rely on his troops. It was only Gordon's daring courage that intimidated Suleiman, and made him think Gordon was stronger than he really was.

After obtaining the submission of Suleiman, Gordon returned to Khartoum, and again for a time resumed his ordinary official duties. But this was not for long; he had before him another visit to Walad el Michael, the turbulent Abyssinian chief, whom he had visited before taking up his duties at Khartoum. Gordon's object was to persuade Walad to submit to the authority of King Johannis of Abyssinia. But nothing would induce Walad to do this. He was surrounded by 7000 soldiers, and Gordon felt himself, in spite of the denials of the rebel chief, practically a prisoner. Walad demanded authority to go on attacking Johannis, but to this of course the Governor-General could not assent. He therefore compromised matters by offering Walad £1000 per mensem, on condition that he should leave his old king alone.

Having settled Walad, Gordon left, intending to return to Khartoum, but was intercepted by a telegram from the Khedive begging him to go to Cairo to help him in his financial difficulties, and he started for Cairo on February 3, 1878, having completed one year's service as Governor-General of the Soudan.

In spite of the hard rough life of the Soudan, he infinitely preferred it to the more artificial civilised existence which the officials were living at Cairo. He arrived there on March 7th, and left again on the 30th; and during the whole of his stay he was wretched. At first the Khedive paid great attention to him, receiving him with a splendour which suggested the "Arabian Nights." He asked him to be the president of a commission of inquiry into the finances of the country, with the condition attached that he should use his influence to arrange with the representatives of the different countries that the commissioners of the debt or the representatives of the creditors who had lent money to Egypt should not serve on that commission of inquiry. After a good deal of discussion, it was finally ascertained that this condition would not be consented to by the foreign Governments. This of course relieved Colonel Gordon of any obligations in the matter, and he, seeing that he could be of no further service, decided to return to his province. Considering how much Gordon had done to try and accomplish the desires of the Khedive, there can be little question that he was in this matter treated very badly. "I left Cairo," said he, "with no honours, by the ordinary train, paying my own passage. The sun which rose with such splendour set in the deepest obscurity. I calculate my financial episode cost me £800. His Highness was bored with me after my failure, and could not bear the sight of me."

Fortunately for Gordon, he cared very little for official favour. "I now only look," said he in a letter written a short time after this, "to benefiting the people." It was in this spirit he visited Harrar, a small province detached from the Soudan, and lying to the south of Abyssinia, on the eastern coast of Africa, almost opposite to Aden. This province had once belonged to Turkey, but had been transferred to the Khedive in exchange for £15,000 per annum extra tribute. The governor of the province was Raouf Pasha, whom Colonel Gordon, it will be remembered, had refused to employ on account of his cruel treatment of the natives in the Equatorial Province four years before. Again he had been playing the tyrant, and Gordon felt it to be his duty to turn him out. As this man afterwards succeeded Colonel Gordon as Governor-General of the Soudan, it is to him more than any one that the present Khedive is indebted for having lost the whole of the Soudan. By his tyranny, following after Gordon's kindness, the province was stirred into revolt, and the Mahdi enabled to usurp authority. We are, however, anticipating events.

Having freed Harrar of this tyrant, he went to Massowah, and thence on May 22nd to Khartoum. Back once more at his capital, he devoted himself first to a thorough reform of the prisons and the administration of the law. "The prisons," he wrote, "were dens of injustice, and I am glad to have had time to go into the question of each individual prisoner."

Although he used to tell amusing stories against himself and his own personal expenditure of money, yet Gordon had great aptitude for finance, and could make money go farther than most men. Had his views been adopted for Egypt, it is more than likely that we should have been saved the Egyptian war, to say nothing of the loss of the Soudan, and all that was associated with it. In the Soudan province there was an annual deficit amounting to something like £259,000. By dint of cutting down expenditure and increasing the receipts, Gordon reduced this during the second year to £50,600! Had he continued Governor-General for many years, there can be no question that he would have not only made the two ends meet, but would have obtained sufficient to carry out his schemes of opening up the country by railways and steamers, thus at the same time developing trade and reducing slavery. He calculated that with great economy, and utilising the machinery and the rails that were already lying idle in the country, a highway from Cairo to Khartoum might have been opened up for £70,000, a sum of money which over and over again has been frittered away in building great useless palaces for the Khedive or some other Egyptian official, which bring in no income, and are a great expense to keep up. The traffic, especially the conveyance of ivory and other merchandise, would soon have recouped the Government for their original outlay. The way in which Colonel Gordon was thwarted in every possible manner at this time troubled him a good deal. "As for myself," he writes, "I am exceedingly weary, and wish, with a degree of bitterness, that it was all over. I am cooped up here now, but am much occupied with finances, which are in a very low state. My life is burthensome and weary, but I feel that it is better to be employed here than to be idle elsewhere."

Writing on November 20, 1878, he says:—

"I will give you an instance of the miserable way the Cairo Government treats the Soudan. I asked H.H.* a long time ago to send up a man A. H.H. replied he wanted the man A., and could not send him. To-day I got a request for £7, 10s., stating that I had asked for A., who was at Port Said; that in consequence A. went to Cairo and said that he did not want to come; so they ask me to pay the £7, 10s. for his passage from Port Said to Cairo and return, which I have refused to do."

Closely associated with this question of finance was the still more important question of slavery. The Khedive's Government were at this time at their wit's end for money. They wrote to Colonel Gordon asking him to send them £12,000, and he replied that he had no funds available. Nubar Pasha, who was Minister at the time, was casting about to see how money could be raised, and not being troubled with conscientious scruples on the subject of slavery, he made overtures to the great slave-dealer Zebehr, who, it will be remembered, was practically a prisoner in Cairo. Zebehr jumped at the offer, and promised to send £25,000 per annum to Cairo from the Soudan, if he were made Governor-General in place of Gordon. This of course meant that he would be allowed a perfectly free hand to kidnap as many slaves as possible, in order to make up the annual deficit in addition to this subsidy of £25,000. Writing from Khartoum on February 18, 1879, Gordon says that he was ordered to return to Cairo for consultation. This, however, he steadily refused to do, on the ground of certain disturbances which had occurred. There was a simultaneous rebellion of slave-dealers in the Bahr-Gazelle, and also risings in Darfour and Kordofan, and Gordon

* The abbreviation he generally used for His Highness the Khedive.

felt it to be his duty to go and assist his lieutenant, Gessi, who was endeavouring to crush Zebehr's gang. Again all the horrors of the slave-trade were forced upon Gordon's mind.

"I declare if I could stop this traffic I would willingly be shot this night. This shows my ardent desire; and yet, strive as I can, I can scarcely see any hope of arresting the evil. Now comes the question, Could I sacrifice my life and remain in Kordofan and Darfour? To die quickly would be to me nothing; but the long crucifixion that a residence in these horrid countries entails appals me. Yet I feel that, if I could screw up my mind to it, I could cause the trade to cease, for its roots are in these countries. . . . I have written to the Khedive to say I will not remain as Governor-General, for I feel I cannot govern the country to satisfy myself. . . . Now as I will not stay as Governor-General of the whole of the Soudan, query, shall I stay as Governor of the West Soudan, and crush the slave-dealers? I agree, if the death was speedy; but oh! it is a long and weary one, and for the moment I cannot face it."

Again, writing from Kalaka at the beginning of May 1879, he says:—

"All the road from here to Shaka is marked by the camping-places of the slave-dealers, and there are numerous skulls by the side of the road. What thousands have passed along here! I hear some districts are completely depopulated, all the inhabitants having been captured or starved to death."

But though Gordon could not do all he desired, he was enabled to do more perhaps than any other man could have accomplished in the circumstances, and by the end of June 1879, Suleiman, the son of the great Zebehr, had been hunted down by Gessi, who discovered papers clearly proving the guilt of both father and son. The latter was tried by court-martial and shot, and Gordon sent the evidence against the father to the Khedive. No notice was taken of it, and Gordon bitterly complains that, instead of being punished, Zebehr was *pensioned!* "What pensions," he asks, "have the widows and orphans whom Zebehr has made by the thousand? What allowance have the poor worn-out bodies of men, strong enough till he dragged them from their homes, who are now draining the last bitter dregs of life in cruel slavery? What recompense has been made to those whose bleached bones mark the track of his trade over many and many a league of ground?"

Space does not permit a detailed account of the interesting and exciting campaign in which Gessi delivered this crushing blow against the great slave-dealer. No man had imbibed more of Gordon's detestation to the slave trade than Gessi, and with quite a small force he captured the redoutable Suleiman, who had a large force at his disposal. Gordon made him a Pasha and gave him a reward of £2000, which he richly deserved.

CHAPTER XII.

ABYSSINIA, INDIA, AND CHINA.

COLONEL GORDON'S work of putting a stop to slave-hunting and other evils in the Soudan was about to terminate. At Fogia on the 1st July 1879 he received a telegram announcing that Ismail had abdicated, and that his son Tewfik reigned at Cairo in his place. Gordon at once decided to go to Cairo. He writes:—

"I am a wreck, like the portion of the *Victory* towed into Gibraltar after Trafalgar; but God has enabled me, or rather has used me, to do what I wished to do—that is, break down the slave-trade. . . . To-day I had a telegram from Darfour, saying, 'Haroun [another great slave-dealer, second only in importance to Zebehr] had been killed and his forces dispersed.' God has truly been good to me. 'Those that honour Me I will honour.' May I be ground to dust, if He will glorify Himself in me; but give me a *humble heart*, for then He dwells there in comfort."

"The new Khedive is most civil," he writes from Cairo, "but I no longer distress myself with such things. God is the sole ruler, and I try to walk sincerely before Him." In spite of his treatment by the deposed Khedive, he always had a real affection for him, and he says: "It pains me what sufferings my poor Khedive Ismail has had to go through;" but later on he writes: "Do not fret about Ismail Pasha; he is a philosopher, and has plenty of money. He played high stakes and lost. He is the cleverest man in Europe. I am one of those he fooled, but I bear him no grudge. It is a blessing for Egypt that he has gone."

Colonel Gordon had quite determined not to remain under the new Khedive, so he terminated, as he then thought for ever, his connection with the Soudan, little thinking how inseparably his name was yet to be associated with that country. It may give us some idea of the energy of the man when it is mentioned that during the last three years he had ridden 8500 miles on camels or mules. Such violent exertion in a hot country was greatly to the detriment of his health. In one of his letters he says:—

"From not having worn a bandage across the chest, I have shaken my heart or my lungs out of their places; and I have the same feeling in my chest as you have when you have a crick in the neck. In camel-riding you ought to wear a sash round the waist, and another close up under the armpits; otherwise, all the internal machinery gets disturbed."

Before finally quitting the service of the Khedive, Gordon felt that he would like to put affairs between Egypt and Abyssinia on a more satisfactory footing, though it was through no fault of his that they were in such a bad condition. In spite, therefore, of his state of health, he left Cairo on August 30, 1879, on a mission to the Abyssinian king, Johannis. Writing home he playfully alludes to a ridiculous report that was being circulated, that he intended to throw off allegiance to Egypt, and set up as an independent Sultan, similar to what the American adventurer, Burgevine, proposed to do in China. "The Khedive said, after some circumlocution, 'Was I not too friendly with Johannis?' In fact, the general report in Cairo was that I was going in for being Sultan ; but it would not suit our family. I hope to finish off Johannis soon, and then to come home." There seem to have been some other evil reports circulated at this time about Colonel Gordon, for he says again in his humorous manner:—"I wrote to the secretary of the Foreign Office man, who is a friend of mine, asking him to tell his chief, who is of the council, 'That if, on my return, I hear any of the Council of Ministers have said anything against me, I will beg the Khedive to make the evil speaker Governor-General of the Soudan,' which is equivalent to a sentence of death to these Cairo Pashas."

Though he was sick in body his brave spirit showed no signs of yielding as long as there was duty to be done, and off he went to Abyssinia. On September 2nd, 1879, he writes:—

"The heat is terrible, but I am quiet and that is a great thing. I fear, through this Abyssinian affair, I shall have to wend my weary way to Senheit; however, God knows what is best for me. I would sooner have come home straight, but I had it not in my heart to forsake Tewfik till this affair is finished. I have begun to be very tired of the continual wear and tear of my last six years. However, I cannot think of leaving Egypt exposed to her enemies."

On September 12th he writes, when *en route* to meet Aloula, the Abyssinian commander-in-chief:—

"We have met a caravan coming from Aloula's. They confirm the news that Walad el Michael and all his officers are prisoners, by orders sent to Aloula by King Johannis, and Metfin [Walad el Michael's son, whom Gordon disliked very much] is dead—killed by some one. I heard just as I left Massowah that Abdulgassin—the last of the leaders of Zebehr's slave-dealers—had been taken, and I ordered him to be shot.* Thus gaps, one by one, are made in my prayers for my enemies."

This last remark is made in reference to his custom of always praying for his enemies by name.

He went on this Abyssinian embassy with a heavy heart, for the Khedive had telegraphed to him, "Give up nothing, but do not fight." It really mattered little what happened, considering that soon Egypt was to give up even the lands over which she had a legal right, but in November 1879 this could not be foreseen. Khedive Ismail had undoubtedly behaved very badly to Abyssinia, and had treated the Abyssinian envoy with a great want of courtesy. Tewfik, however, was not to blame for this, and he wanted to express his regret at the past and his desire to renew the old friendship between Egypt and Abyssinia. Johannis was a tyrannical king, hated by his own people, who thought him partly mad, and he took to heart Ismail's conduct to his representative and refused to distinguish between one Khedive and another. Gordon's description of the Abyssinian king is as follows:—

"Johannis, oddly enough, is like myself—a religious fanatic. He has a mission, and will fulfil it, and that mission is *to Christianise ! ! all Mussulmans.* He has forbidden the smoking of tobacco in his country, and cuts off the right hand and left foot of any man he catches doing so! When Christ comes again, how truly He may say to us all, 'I know ye not.'"

---

* This man had started his career by a cold-blooded murder. When he first set up his standard of revolt, the wind blew it down, so in order to turn away the anger of heaven four oxen were slaughtered, and then a negro boy. In the poor wretch's blood a flag was dipped, and the standard was raised a second time, a second time to fall.

Gordon had foreseen that the Abyssinians would probably revenge themselves upon him for the treatment which their envoy had received at Cairo, and this probability was rendered a certainty by the fact that he had nothing to offer by way of compensation. From the day he entered Abyssinia to the day he left it, he was constantly insulted, and he gained very little by the journey, in which he risked his life. He saw King Johannis, and got him to make certain definite demands, but the king would not put them into writing. When Gordon referred him to the Khedive's letter it was not forthcoming, and could not even be found for some time. When it was found the chief clerk received forty blows for not having before translated it! Amid a pile of letters which were disregarded Gordon saw one from the British Government and one from the French Government.

At first the king tried to distinguish between Gordon and the Khedive, but the former was too loyal to allow this, and informed the king that he must look on him as a Mahommedan and an Egyptian, and not as a Christian and an Englishman. On this point Gordon held very conscientious views. In the event of a foreigner entering the service of an Oriental Power, he contended, "He shall for the time entirely abandon his relations with his native land; he shall resist his own government, and those of other powers, and keep intact the sovereignty of the Oriental State whose bread he eats."

When Johannis saw that Gordon had nothing to offer, and nothing was to be got out of him, he dismissed him. It is unnecessary to retail all the unpleasant incidents of his journey to Massowah. The only thing of importance is, that Gordon, anticipating that there might be disturbances at Massowah, telegraphed to the Khedive to send a battalion of infantry there, a request to which no attention was paid. This neglect on the part of the Khedive ultimately led to an open rupture between him and Gordon. Fortunately the British Government had sent a gunboat across from Aden at Gordon's request. "The whole town was in a ferment," Gordon writes, "and had it not been for H.M.S. *Seagull*, Massowah would no doubt have been attacked and sacked." The Khedive asked Gordon to come at once to Cairo, but this he refused to do till the battalion arrived, as he felt that his presence was necessary there, "in order to give confidence to the people, until the troops came."

Ultimately, however, Gordon went to Cairo, and gave the Khedive a piece of his mind, with regard to the publication of confidential telegrams, as well as other things. It was on this occasion that he received the reply from the ruler of Egypt, "I am a young man; it is not my fault," which caused some little amusement in England, when it was made known. The rupture was made, Gordon had decided to serve the Khedive no longer, and at the beginning of the year 1880 he returned home for the rest that he required, mentally and physically, after six years' incessant hard work in the thankless task of governing the Soudan.

When Gordon was leaving Alexandria he was medically examined by Dr. Mackie, the surgeon to the British Consulate, who stated that he was "suffering from symptoms of nervous exhaustion, and alteration of the blood, giving rise to hæmorrhagic spots on the skin, &c." "I have," said the same authority, "recommended him to retire for several months for complete rest and quiet, and that he may be able to enjoy fresh and wholesome food, as I consider that much of what he is suffering from is the effect of continued bodily fatigue, anxiety, and indigestible food. I have insisted on his abstaining from all exciting work—especially such as implies business or political excitement." Gordon possessed an exceptionally strong constitution, but there is a limit to the burden which the most powerful can bear, and that limit had been exceeded. There was nothing for it, therefore, but to put into dock for constitutional repairs.

After spending three months in England, he went to Switzerland on the 9th April 1880. During this period of inactivity he was offered by the Government of the Cape of Good Hope the command of their colonial forces on £1500 per annum, but his reply was, "Thanks for telegram just received; I do not feel inclined to accept an appointment." In the beginning of May, however, he accepted the post of private secretary to Lord Ripon, who was going out to India as Viceroy. Considering that Colonel Gordon had been ruling a territory as large as France, Germany, and Spain put together, it was thought strange at the time that he should accept such a very subordinate post as that of secretary to the Viceroy, himself only a subordinate to the Secretary of State for India, who practically governs that vast empire from Downing Street by means of the telegraph. The appointment was indeed a peculiarly unfortunate one. The P. & O. steamer that conveyed the Viceregal party had on board two kings, the greater man being, so to speak, the uncrowned one. The Viceroy, who has since shown himself to be a man of ability, had not at that time gained the confidence of the public. Consequently, his principal qualification for the post was that he possessed the aristocracy of birth. It is impossible to secure everything in any given man, and as social distinctions weigh heavily in such a post as that of Viceroy of India, only average abilities are as a rule looked for. Consequently India has been termed the "land of mediocrity," from the fact that the average statesmen who direct her affairs, are neither very brilliant nor very dull.

The Viceroy must have been more than human not to have felt somewhat keenly the awkward position in which he was placed on that voyage. To make matters worse, the ship was compelled to pass through the very territory where Gordon's name was best known, and he was most beloved, and thus the Suez Canal voyage was a kind of royal progress. Unfortunately the homage paid was to the subordinate, the uncrowned king, and not to him who held the higher position. It was Gordon's opinion that was sought for, it was to him that every one looked, and it is said by the well-informed, that at least once on the voyage this led to difficulties. Be that as it may, the experience of that voyage showed Colonel Gordon that he was utterly out of place, and that it was neither fair to himself, nor to his chief, that he should continue in it, so he decided to resign at Bombay, which place he reached on June 1st. All sorts of reasons for this resignation were suggested at the time, but none of them went very near the mark. Of course some said that the difference of opinion on religious matters was the cause, while others alleged a political reason, saying that Colonel Gordon was opposed to the treatment of Yakoob Khan, the late Ameer of Afghanistan. Colonel Gordon's brother, the late Sir H. Gordon, has given publicity to this latter as the reason, but as a matter of fact it is not the correct one, and there is no use handing down false reports to posterity. More than this I am not at liberty to say.

The only published statement on the subject from Gordon himself was as follows:—

"In a moment of weakness, I took the appointment of private secretary to Lord Ripon, and repented that I had done so at once, but I did not like to say so. I went out, and saw at Bombay that in my irresponsible position I could not possibly hope to do anything really to the purpose, in the face of vested interests out there; so seeing this was the case, and also observing that my views were diametrically opposed to those of the official classes, I gave it up. It certainly was a great consideration with me—Lord Ripon's position—for it was assumed by some, that my views of the state of affairs were those of the Viceroy, and then I felt I would do him harm by staying with him. Lord Ripon and I left perfect friends. The brusqueness of my leaving was unavoidable, inasmuch as my stay would have put me in the possession of State things that I ought not to know. Certainly, I might have stayed a month or two, and had a pain in the head and gone quickly; but the whole duties were so distasteful that I felt—being perfectly callous as to what the world says—it was better to go at once, and did so."

Subordinate posts of that kind may do very well for men of ability, who have a name to make; but it is not in accordance with human nature, that a man of brilliant genius, who had already made a great reputation as a soldier and an administrator, could serve with satisfaction to himself, or justice to his chief, in such a position, and Gordon was not the man to serve unless he could be thoroughly loyal.

Having resigned his post on the 3rd June, he received a telegram from London inviting him to go again to China. Mr. Robert Hart, then in China as Inspector-General of Customs, telegraphed to Mr. Campbell, his agent in London, to invite Gordon to go out on six months' leave. Mr. Campbell, seeing Gordon's resignation announced, at once passed on the invitation to Bombay. Gordon's reply was, "Inform Hart Gordon will leave for Shanghai first opportunity; as for conditions, Gordon indifferent." He then telegraphed to the War Office for leave till the end of the year. It was thought that China would shortly be involved in war with Russia, and as our own relationships with the Czar were not too friendly at that time, the War Office authorities felt bound to act cautiously, lest it should appear as if we shrank from fighting Russia ourselves, but were encouraging another nation to do so, by allowing one of our most brilliant officers to lead their forces. Consequently Gordon received the following telegram, "Must state more specifically purpose and position for and in which you go to China." Gordon's reply was, "Am ignorant; will write from China before the expiration of my leave." On the 11th he received a further message, "Reasons insufficient: your going to China is not approved." To this Gordon replied, "Arrange retirement, commutation or resignation of service; ask Campbell reasons. My counsel, if asked, would be for peace, not war. I return by America." The War Office were not, however, going to lose an officer of such ability so easily, so when Gordon arrived at Pont de Galle on the 16th June, he found the following telegram awaiting him, "Leave granted on your engaging to take no military service in China;" to which he replied, "I will take no military service in China; I would never embarrass the British Government."

He arrived at Hong-Kong on July 2nd and went immediately to Shanghai, but hearing that his old friend, Li Hung Chang, was at Tientsin, he proceeded there at once, and found things in a very unsatisfactory condition. Prince Chun and the Empress Regent were anxious for war with Russia, being supported in this folly by all the Court, while Prince Kung and Li Hung Chang practically stood alone in their desire for peace. Li was so delighted to see Gordon that he fell on his neck and kissed him. Gordon at once threw his influence into the scale of peace. He had previously, before leaving India, expressed his views on the subject in the press:—

"My fixed desire is to persuade the Chinese not to go to war with Russia, both in their own interests, and for the sake of those of the world, especially those of England. To me it appears that the question in dispute cannot be of such vital importance that an arrangement could not be come to, by concessions upon both sides. Whether I succeed in being heard or not is not in my hands. I protest, however, at being regarded as one who wishes for war in any country, still less in China. Inclined as I am, with only a small degree of admiration for military exploits, I esteem it a far greater honour to promote peace than to gain any paltry honours in a wretched war."

As a matter of fact Gordon did succeed in convincing the Government at Pekin of the advisability of coming to terms with its opponent, and thus once more he rendered China an invaluable service. In his earnest advocacy he appears to have used such emphatic language that the interpreter dared not repeat it, so Gordon seized a dictionary, looked up the word "idiotcy," and pointed it out to them. Far better was it, in Gordon's opinion, to ruffle the self-esteem of a few bigwigs, than to allow two great nations to drift into a war which, after an enormous sacrifice of life and much suffering, must have ended fatally for the Chinese, who were quite unable to meet the trained hordes of Russia.

CHAPTER XIII.

MAURITIUS, CAPE, AND PALESTINE.

GORDON left China immediately he had saved that country from war, arriving in England on October 21, 1880. From then till about the end of the following April he spent on leave. During this month the post of officer commanding Royal Engineers at the Mauritius fell vacant, and two officers to whom the command was offered retired rather than go to Mauritius. Sir Howard Elphinstone was then offered the command, and would also probably have retired, but Colonel Gordon offered to go for him, and refused any money on account of the exchange, though usually £700 or £800 was paid for an exchange of this kind. Yet Gordon was so poor that he had actually to borrow the money to pay for his passage when he went from India to China a few months before this! He left England for the Mauritius on the 2nd May, travelling *viâ* the Suez Canal and Aden.

The voyage opened up to his ever-active fertile brain the whole question of the advantage to England of the Suez Canal, and of our proper route to India. This, he maintained most strongly, should, in the event of war, be *viâ* the Cape, and not through the Canal, his opinion concurring with that of Lord Palmerston, Mr. W. E. Forster, and many men of ability. The Suez route may save a few days, but the risk is terrible. In some parts of the Canal only one ship can pass at a time, and a sunken barge, a little dynamite, or even a severe sandstorm may block the Canal for days. An enemy could easily bribe the owners of a few petty craft to sink their vessels, and thus completely to block up troopships in the Canal. Even without such designs our troopships are frequently delayed in passing through owing to accidents of all sorts.

The heads of many Englishmen have been completely turned by the opening of the Suez Canal, and Gordon was one of the few who stood out against the idea of considering it as *the* proper route to India. It has been said that our trade has increased very largely since the Canal was opened, and that is true; but then the period in question has been one of special activity, and probably our trade would have increased no less had the Canal never been constructed. Moreover, the trade of other countries has increased even more rapidly. Italy, France, Russia, Germany, and Austria, have gained more in proportion than we have. In the olden days, when all the trade with the East came to Europe *viâ* the Cape, England was the great centre of the world. Everything was shipped to England, and then despatched to different parts of Europe. We were the great carriers of the ocean. But the Suez Canal has disturbed this arrangement, and the European nations can more easily obtain their supplies direct through the Canal, to the detriment of our labour market. Gordon recognised that it was too late for the mistake to be remedied, but he was most anxious that we should attach more importance to our hold on the Cape, as the natural route to India in the event of war, and not be deceived by the fictitious advantages of the Suez Canal, which only offers the saving of a few days at enormous risk.

He took the opportunity of stopping at Suez to pay a visit to the grave of his friend and lieutenant, Gessi, who had lost his life and died at Suez from the hardships through which he passed on the Nile, partly owing to the blocking of that river by the "sudd," which had re-formed after Gordon left the Soudan, all precautionary measures having been neglected, and partly owing to the cruel neglect of the authorities, who might have taken more prompt measures for his relief. As his master was to do a few years later, Gessi practically sacrificed his life in the crusade against slavery. He had been an interpreter in the Crimean war, and in the Soudan he exhibited such great military skill that he was given a high independent command, with the result that he was, it will be remembered, the means of capturing and breaking up Suleiman's band of slave-dealers.

Colonel Gordon arrived at the Mauritius at the end of May 1881, and he left in March 1882, so he was only for about ten months on the island. He went out to command the Royal Engineers, but as the officer commanding the island was promoted and sent home, he succeeded by seniority to the chief command. During this period there is not much to mention beyond the fact that here, as elsewhere, he used every opportunity to do acts of kindness to others. Two men of the Royal Artillery had, when the worse for liquor, gone out in a boat, without oars. For eight days they were drifting about in the currents that surround the Mauritius. At last they reached the Island of

Bourbon, and in attempting to land, one of them got drowned. The other was sent back to his battery, and the owner of the lost boat at once demanded compensation. Thinking that the poor fellow had already suffered enough for his misdeeds, Colonel Gordon paid for the boat, and took the receipt to the man's commanding officer, stipulating that he should not tell the man who had got him out of trouble. He always took the greatest interest in the men, and also in the agent of the Army Scripture Readers' Society, who worked among them. He told the officer who collected funds for that Society to put him down for a subscription of Rs.40 per annum, and said that if more was wanted he would be delighted to give it.

In March 1882 he received a telegram from the Premier of the Cape Government, asking for his aid in bringing about a termination of the Basuto war. He had previously in April 1881 offered his services on £700 per annum for this purpose, but the Government then in office at the Cape had not even replied to his telegram, either by mail or by wire, and so Gordon had thought no more about the matter. Troubles had thickened, and a new Government had come into office. Hence the offer, accompanied by the statement that they did not expect him to be bound to the salary formerly proposed. Gordon at once accepted the offer, but he could not get a ship going to the Cape direct. Fortunately there was a small coasting vessel called the *Scotia* bound for the Cape, so Gordon at once took his passage, and stated that he would arrive on board at a certain hour. The hour came, but no passenger arrived. The afternoon wore away, evening came and passed, night arrived, and still the Colonel did not put in an appearance. At last, about midnight, a gentleman quietly came on deck, saying that he was Colonel Gordon, and hastened to explain his reasons for being so late. Some of the officers and people on the island, hearing that he was going to sail, had intended to give him an ovation. In order to escape this, he had walked twelve miles into the interior, returning after dark so that no one should know where he was. Next day, however, crowds came on board to wish him "good-bye," among them many children in whom he had as usual taken an interest. One of these, whom he introduced as his "pet lamb" to the wife of the captain of the ship, brought him a couple of bottles of sherry, and other friends gave him a case of champagne. As he was almost a total abstainer and frequently did not touch stimulants for days together, he had no use for the wine, but he accepted the gifts in order to please the givers.

He made himself perfectly at home on board the little ship, and soon became very friendly with the captain and his wife. He spoke a great deal about the Seychelles Islands, situated to the north-east of Madagascar, which he believed to be the site of the Garden of Eden, and he showed them wood from the coco-de-mer, or nut of the sea, which he believed to be the veritable tree that produced the forbidden fruit which our ancestors tasted. The voyage, though not more than three thousand miles in length, lasted a whole month, and there was some rough weather, which he felt terribly, for he was not a particularly good sailor, and the ship was very small. Writing to his sister he said:—

"You will not care overmuch for my secular history, but will say, 'What did you learn on the passage?' Well, the passage was truly a fearful trial; dirt prevailed in everything; the bilge-water literally, when pumped out from decayed sugar, tore up the very inmost parts of the stomach, and showed me that, if that was wrong, life was unendurable. I am not generally sick at sea, but I was nearly dead with it; perhaps it was Mauritius fever coming out. Salt water had got into the tank and we had to drink it. I was very, very ill, but through it all I would not have changed one iota of the voyage. . . .

I am a *rag;* that voyage in the *Scotia* has killed me. I went to Dr. Abercromby, and he told me I was on the verge of an attack of jaundice. I am certainly better, but feel far from well. Listless, worried in *body*, not a bit in spirits, and as if I had eaten copper. I want to get into the position of delighting to accept and do His will, yet I feel so very much inclined to wish His will might be my release. . . .

Earth's joys grow very dim, its glories have faded. My Mauritius sojourn has quenched to a great degree my desire for anything but to be with Jesus. Everybody is very kind here and complimentary, but all compliments are to me but sounds of the wind. If it was Jesus' will, how delighted I should be to be called away, to be a nail in His footstool, and how willingly I would have every one to be higher than me in heaven!"

There was, however, some mitigation to the horrors of this voyage, for, during it, he heard of his promotion to the rank of major-general, which gave him very great satisfaction, as he was beginning to fear that, as the War Office authorities had failed to offer him an appointment worthy of his merits, they might also see fit to pass him over in the matter of promotion. Before he had heard the news he had written:—

"Why am I not in the *Gazette?* I will not move, but it seems odd. Anyway, if they do not promote me, I shall hope for strength to bear it. *He* is ruler, and I love Jesus irrespective of His mighty rank and power. At Communion this morning I asked Christ to let me rest, and then He should take the post of COMMANDANT-GENERAL, and that I should be passive in the matter. Good-bye, my dear Augusta, *fifteen years more.*"

He arrived at the Cape on May 3rd, 1882, and at once made the acquaintance of the Governor, Sir Hercules Robinson, and the Premier, Mr. Merriman. He found things in a very unsatisfactory condition, and nearly decided to have nothing to do with them. The Cape Government were in an awkward position, the affairs of the Basuto war being in the hands of Mr. Orpen, in whom the Government had no confidence, but whom, for party reasons, they did not like to remove. Consequently they could not entrust matters entirely to General Gordon. He good-naturedly yielded to pressure, accepted the post of Commandant-General, on £1200 per annum, and undertook to report to the Cape Government his suggestions for the improvement of the army generally, as well as the best means for bringing the Basuto trouble to a speedy termination. The arrangement was a very unsatisfactory one, but, with that public spiritedness which so characterised him, Gordon threw himself thoroughly into the business, and, before the end of the month, he drew up a most able, statesman-like paper on the whole subject. With most it would have been a piece of presumption for a man during a single month, much of which was spent in travelling, to attempt such a task, more especially as some of the questions were extremely difficult. But such was Gordon's capacity for work, and for grasping complex questions, that not only was the paper he drew up most exhaustive, but, read in the light of subsequent events, it shows how well-informed he was, and what an impartial mind he brought to bear on the subjects before him. He read very quickly, he could at a glance grasp the salient points of any question, and, having a wonderfully retentive memory, no important detail was lost sight of. He wrote both quickly and clearly, and had the faculty of presenting his points in a lucid manner. Like many military men, who are, when young, taken from their studies, he did not always write in the best of English, but he made up for this in the remarkable manner in which he could marshal facts and arguments, and the ease with which he carried his reader along. In his letters and journals he does not do himself justice as a writer, but in his official despatches and memoranda he shows that, not least among his accomplishments, was the gift of being able to write well, and to the point. His memorandum on the reform of the Cape army was very able, though too long to reproduce here. Briefly stated it showed how an army of 8000 men could be maintained instead of the 1600 men then under arms, and at a reduced cost of £7000 per annum! He also pointed out how unjustly the Basutos had been treated, and suggested as a remedy that they should be invited to assemble a general council in which to ventilate their grievances, and that steps should be taken to remove these grievances. He advocated giving them a semi-independent position, with power to manage their own affairs, and to administer justice without the intervention of foreign magistrates, some of whom, in Gordon's opinion, were very corrupt.

Those who have studied the affairs of South Africa, and the history of Christian missions there, will not need to be told what an interesting people the Basutos are. But for others, it may be as well to say that this branch of the Kaffir race are not only among the most civilised of all the African races, but a large proportion of them are Christian in something more than name.

The old chieftain Moshesh, who reigned some fifty years ago, was a man of marked ability, and, though a great soldier, he hated war. Having heard of the work of the celebrated Dr. Moffat among the Korannas, he sent to invite this "man of prayer, and teacher of the Christian religion," to visit him. To cut a long story short, some French Protestant missionaries responded to the invitation, and were wonderfully blessed in their work. Hundreds of converts were received into the Christian Church, and instead of war and bloodshed prevailing, men were instructed how to cultivate fields and build houses.

In the Kaffir war of 1852 Sir George Cathcart was informed that Moshesh was the centre of intrigue, and, ill-advised, he attacked that chieftain and was defeated. When the attack was about to be renewed, he received from Moshesh the following message: "O my master, I am still your servant; I am still the child of the Queen. Sometimes a man beats his dog, and the dog puts his teeth into his hands, and gives him a bite: nevertheless the dog loves the master, and the master loves the dog, and will not kill it. I am vexed at what happened yesterday; let it be forgotten." Fortunately Sir George Cathcart had sufficient nobility of character to appreciate this message. Peace was made, and Sir George afterwards said of Moshesh, "I found him not only to be the most enlightened, but the most upright chief in South Africa, and one in whose good faith I put the most perfect confidence, and for whom, therefore, I have a sincere respect and regard." Moshesh died in 1870, and the policy he had initiated was carried on by his successor Masupha.

Unfortunately the Cape Government wanted to

deprive the Basutos of their right to carry arms, and this they resented. Gordon's sympathies were entirely with them. There were other abuses, such as bad magistrates, which were even admitted by the Secretary for Native Affairs, and Gordon came to the conclusion that the Basutos had been very badly treated. They were loyal to the Queen, but objected to being put under the Cape Government, disliking the Dutch element which has such influence at the Cape.

On the 18th July 1882 the Cape Government proposed that General Gordon should visit Basutoland, but he was of opinion that unless the Government saw their way to grant what he suggested, there was little use in his going. In August, Mr. Sauer, the Secretary for Native Affairs, came to King William's Town, and asked Gordon to accompany him into the Basuto country. Much against his own opinion Gordon yielded, and went as far as Leribe; but finding that the idea in the mind of Mr. Sauer was that he might employ one portion of the Basutos to fight against the other, he remonstrated very strongly. Mr. Sauer then asked him privately to visit Masupha, but gave him no instructions officially. Gordon consented to do this much, but he let Mr. Sauer clearly understand that nothing would induce him to fight the Basutos, with the object of forcing bad magistrates on them, or treating them unjustly. Hoping to avert the horrors of war, Gordon, unarmed and without a flag of truce or any commission, went into the middle of a hostile people, who had never even heard his name. The charm of manner which he ever manifested in his dealings with native races gained the day, and he secured the confidence of these people. In his speech to them he said:—

"I have come here as a friend of the Basutos. I showed myself a friend, for when asked to come and fight, I would not. Now, when I come, I want first to do good for Basutos. The Basutos are of a good disposition. I say to the chief and people, How can Basutoland belong to Basutos? I tell all that the Government want to do good to the people. The Queen does not want the Colony to take land of Basutos, and what the Colony and the Queen are afraid of is that if abandoned the Basutos would be eaten up. I like the Boers; they are brave, and like their own government; and when they fought, they fought for their own government. England could have beaten the Boers if they liked, but thought it unjust. Which do Basutos think Dutch like best—Basutos or land? I think they like land best. Supposing Colony abandoned this country, by-and-by they have trouble with Free State; after that begins fighting; then I look forward ten years, and I see Dutch farms close here. I do not want that, the Colony does not, and the Queen does not, and no Basuto either. Then I say, Basutos, make friends with the Government. . . .

"Suppose Boers drive you away, for me it would be all the same, and not much difference when you are put in the ground. I wish the Basutos would do what I say. What I want is for all to speak with one tongue. I cannot make myself black. I cannot make Masupha and his people do what I want, so I leave it to Jesus, who works everything. This is all I have to say—Do what you like; think well; pray to Jesus for advice."

No sooner had General Gordon gone on his peaceful mission than he discovered that Mr. Sauer had actually induced Lerethodi, a rival chief, to attack Masupha. This action not only endangered Gordon's life, but outraged his sense of honour to such an extent, that he decided forthwith to sever all connection with the Cape Government. It was, to say the least, extraordinary conduct, to send a messenger of peace to a rebel chief, and then, without waiting for any reply, to induce some of his own countrymen to attack and coerce him. It would perhaps not be fair to hold the whole of the Cape Government responsible for the action of a single man, but this curious proceeding confirmed General Gordon in an opinion he held, that white men often fail to practice towards the despised coloured men that honourable, upright dealing that might be expected from the leaders of civilised nations.

Mr. Arthur Pattison, writing to the *Times* on the 20th August 1885, after Gordon's death, said of Masupha, "If you trust him straightforwardly, he is as nice a man as possible, and even kind and thoughtful; but if you treat him the other way, he is a fiend incarnate. The late General Gordon divined his character marvellously, and was the only man Masupha had the slightest regard for." If our Government had more men of the type of General Gordon, we may rest assured that we should have fewer of these petty little "nigger wars," which, more often than not, are brought on by incapacity and want of sympathy on the part of our representatives abroad. One great charm about Gordon's character was his sympathy for the weak and helpless. It mattered not whether the helpless one were a king or a slave, so long as he was weak he was sure of having Gordon's sympathies and assistance in his troubles. Before leaving the Cape, Gordon made a most noble offer, which was that he should go on £300 per annum and live as a magistrate among the Basutos, so as to protect them from their enemies, but the offer was not accepted.

The way in which Gordon regarded his position is shown in the following passages from two of his letters:—

"KING WILLIAM'S TOWN, *October* 6, 1882.—The telegrams will show you that the Cape Colony chapter of my life is over. I am so glad to be free of all this turmoil. There will be a fearful row, but these things have not moved me at all. I have thought more of a scuttler who shed tears when I spoke to him of God's living in him, than I have of all this affair."

"SS. KINFAUN'S CASTLE, *October* 20, 1882.—I shall, D.V., be in England when you get this. I shall go by sea to Gravesend, and on to Southampton at once. Whether men praise you, it does not make you better, or whether they blame you, it does not make you worse. God judges by motives, men by actions (Thomas à Kempis). When I went to the Cape I prayed for glory to God and the welfare of the people, so I am glad *I* got no glory out of it."

It may be well to introduce here a few words he wrote of the celebrated Zulu king whom we deposed and imprisoned at the Cape.

"*May* 20, 1882.—I went to see Cetewayo, and felt for him, and tried to cheer him. I gave him a stick with an ivory head —a beauty—which had been given me by the Sultan of Perak, who was a prisoner at the Seychelles. When I told Cetewayo that I had always been interested in him and that he must have hope, with a deep '*Ah!*' he pointed upwards. He is a fine savage."

General Gordon arrived in England on the 8th November 1882, after the close of the Egyptian war, little thinking how closely that war would affect him. After a short stay at Southampton he left on December 28th for Palestine, and nearly the whole of the year 1883 was spent in Palestine. Writing from Jerusalem he says:—

"Everything looks small and insignificant, but quite meets the idea I had of the *worldly* position of the Jews and of our Lord.

In fact, the Scriptures tell the story without any pretence that either the country, people, or our Lord were of any great importance *in the world.* They are expositors of how very low the position to which He, the Lord of lords, descended. You can realise the fact as well in England as here, by substituting a Scripture-reader of dubious birth and humble parents, exposing the fallacy of a ceremonial church-going religion, and pointing out how impossible it is to please God by such religious formalities. . . .

"The Temple of Solomon was fine for those days, but, setting aside its Divine significance, it was only about six times as long as the room you are in, and not much wider—60 cubits = 90 feet = 30 yards long, by 20 cubits = 30 feet = 10 yards wide. You could walk round the city in less than an hour; it is not quite three miles round. . . .

"The ravines round Jerusalem are full of the dust of men, for over a million bodies must have been slain there. What a terrific sight the resurrection there will be! I suppose there is no place in the world where so many bodies are concentrated. . . .

"It is nice sauntering about, conjuring up scenes of days gone by—real scenes, actions on the stage of life; all gone! It quiets ambition!

"I came back from Gaza yesterday, after a ten days' sojourn there, returning through Askelon, where there are very fine ruins, enormous columns, marbles, &c., lying in all directions: it is a wonderful place. Like all the coast, it is most dreary, yet one sees that all the country was once thickly populated. Sand from the shore is creeping in steadily, and makes it mournful. Napoleon I., Alexander the Great, Sennacherib, Nebuchadnezzar, and a host of great men passed by this route. Titus came up by Gaza to Jerusalem. Richard Cœur de Lion was years at Askelon. All gone, 'those old familiar faces'!"

The supposed sites of the holy places seem to have had peculiar fascination for his active brain, and he came to the conclusion that most, if not all, of them were wrong. It would, however, occupy too much space to give the reasons which led him to this conclusion. Though we cannot gather it from his own letters, a good deal of his time was more profitably spent than in hunting up old sites. Dr. Cunningham Geikie, who was in Jerusalem when Gordon was killed at Khartoum, tells us :—

"A poor dragoman told me that General Gordon used to come often to his house in Jerusalem when he and his wife lay ill, and that he would take a mat, and put it on the floor as a seat, there being no chairs or furniture, and sit down with his Testament to read and speak to them about Christ. Ascertaining that a doctor's account had been incurred, he went off secretly and paid it. He gave away all he had to the poor in Jerusalem and the villages round, and the people mourn for him as for their father."

He made friends with some of the missionaries of the Church Missionary Society, with whom he found himself much in sympathy. Speaking of the Rev. J. R. L. Hall, he says, "I have found a nice man now here (Jaffa), but his mission is at Gaza. He is a Jew * by birth, but a man after my own heart. I may drop down there ere long and help him. He belongs to the C. M. S."

This Mr. Hall, in a speech afterwards made at Exeter Hall, told some interesting things about General Gordon at this period of his life, which for want of space cannot be reproduced at length here. He thoroughly identified himself with mission work, showing how much he valued Christianity over all other religious systems. When he met Mr. Hall he said, "I am very restless ; I came here for rest and quiet, to study the Word of

* General Gordon was under a misconception as to the parentage of Mr. Hall. As a matter of fact this missionary is descended from a very old family in the county of Hampshire, and was no more related to that ancient race than the General himself.

God, and at the same time to discover different sacred sites. I am not satisfied; I am restless; I want Christian work. Do you think that if I were to come to Jaffa, you could give me any work to do?" He went to live at Jaffa for eight months. While he was there instructions came from the central society for a mission-house to be built at Nablous. There was no architect nearer than at Jerusalem, and his fee and expenses would have been very high. The missionaries agreed to consult General Gordon about drawing up the plans for the house, but were afraid of presuming too much on his kindness. When the deputation from them arrived, he cut them short in their apology. "I know what you want; you want a contribution," said he. When told that they wanted something much more valuable, he was delighted, and seizing a pencil and paper wrote down exactly all they needed in the way of accommodation. He set to work, and before the day was over he had drawn up admirable plans and calculations. The mission-house was built on those plans, and his estimate proved to be almost exactly the cost of the building. He said to Mr. Hall:—

"You thought that I should be annoyed at being asked to draw out plans for a mission-house. If there is anything that I can do for the cause of missions I am delighted to do it. What did I come to Jaffa for? Did I not tell you at Haifa that if you could give me some work to do for the Lord, that would set my mind at rest? I was restless because I had been shutting myself up in Palestine, and had not been putting out my powers for service in the Lord's work."

There are among Christian people some who take a deep interest in the spread of the Gospel at home, but do not exhibit the same interest in the spread of

Christianity abroad, and *vice versâ.* During Gordon's stay at Gravesend he showed what a real interest he took in home mission work, and in his letters he frequently used to say that he should like to end his days working in the east end of London. The time he spent among the missionaries in Palestine shows that he took an equally deep interest in foreign missions, and before leaving that country he wrote, in reference to a conference of missionaries that was about to be held at Gaza, "I should like to go down there and meet the brethren who assemble; it may be the last time that I can have any intercourse with a number of missionaries."

On the 15th October 1883 General Gordon received a telegram from the King of the Belgians, asking him to go to Central Africa to govern the territory that had been acquired by the International Association. The King had once before pressed him to join this movement, which had for its object the opening up of Africa to trade and civilisation, and the consequent abolition of slavery and cruelty. Mr. H. M. Stanley was at the head of the movement, and Gordon offered to serve under him, and had promised the Belgian king that when his services were required they would be given. Stanley had resigned his post, and the time had come for Gordon to redeem his promise. He at once telegraphed home for leave, and the reply came back, "The Secretary of State has decided to sanction your going to the Congo." A telegraph clerk had made a mistake, and the correct message was, "The Secretary of State has *declined* to sanction your going to the Congo." As Gordon had, however, already promised the King of the Belgians to go, there was no alternative but for him to sever his connection with the British army. With the full intention of placing his resignation in the hands of the Secretary of State for War, as well as to interview King Leopold, he left Palestine at the end of the year 1883. He was travelling on the last night of the old year, and he tells us that he spent that night in prayer in the railway carriage, of which he was the solitary occupant. As the new year was ushered in, the lonely traveller between Genoa and Brussels little thought that it was to be almost his last,* and that soon he would be permitted to throw off the earthly tabernacle, and put on the crown of glory. His active brain was busily employed at this time in considering how best he could wage war with human cruelty. He was to have started on January 26, 1885, for the Congo, but a telegram reached him at his sister's house at Southampton, from Lord Wolseley, requesting his presence in London, as an outcry was being made by certain well-informed persons that the only man who was capable of solving the Soudan difficulties was being permitted to leave the British army, and to go into the service of a foreign power, to busy himself in the wilds of Africa.

* General Gordon is supposed to have been killed on 26th January 1885.

CHAPTER XIV.

KHARTOUM.

In order to understand aright the events that suddenly intervened and prevented General Gordon from fulfilling his engagement to the King of the Belgians, it will be necessary to go back to the year 1882, and briefly survey what occurred after that time. It will be remembered that Gordon left the Soudan at the end of 1879, when the young Khedive Tewfik was reigning in place of his father Ismail, who had been compelled to resign. Tewfik unfortunately was not fit to rule, and Egypt above all things wanted a man who was not a mere puppet. His father, with all his faults, had great force of character, and made himself respected in the kingdom. The son was as weak as the father was strong, with the result that his rule soon became nominal. When weak men get into such positions, there is great temptation for stronger ones to rise up and seize the reigns of government. It is unnecessary to sketch the history of Arabi Pasha, or to recount in detail the circumstances that brought him to the front. Enough for our purpose to mention that his name, little known before, was suddenly associated with a great military revolt, and that the powers of Europe took alarm lest the Suez Canal should be blocked. But for that Canal, events in Egypt might have taken a very different turn, and that country might now have had, what it sorely needs, a strong man at the head of affairs. England, having far more ships passing through the Canal than all the rest of the world together, intervened. Our fleet attacked Alexandria, and our troops under Lord Wolseley broke up the Egyptian army at Tel-el-Kebir. From that time we have virtually been the rulers of the ancient kingdom of Egypt, the Khedive being little more than a puppet in our hands. He has all the social position and dignity of a Khedive, without the trouble or responsibility of having to govern.

Unfortunately, soon after General Gordon relinquished the Governor-Generalship of the Soudan, the Khedive, in spite of Gordon's protest, appointed to the post about as bad a man as he could possibly have selected. This was no other than Raouf Pasha, whom Gordon had twice turned out of different appointments for playing the tyrant. No sooner was he appointed than there was a revival of all the horrors of cruel government, which Gordon had done so much to abolish. The following are his own words in explanation of the origin of the rebellion :—

"The movement is not religious, but an outbreak of despair. Three times over I warned the late Khedive that it would be impossible to govern the Soudan on the old system, after my appointment to the Governor-Generalship. During the three years that I wielded full powers in the Soudan, I taught the natives that they had a right to exist. I waged war against the Turks and Circassians, who had harried the population. I had taught them something of the meaning of liberty and justice, and accustomed them to a higher ideal of government than that with which they had previously been acquainted. As soon as I had gone, the Turks and Circassians returned in full force; the old Bashi-Bazouk system was re-established; my old *employés* were persecuted; and a population which had begun to appreciate something like decent government was flung back to suffer the vast excesses of Turkish rule. The inevitable result followed; and thus it may be said that the egg of the present rebellion was laid in the three years during which I was allowed to govern the Soudan on other than Turkish principles."

There was a belief among the Mohammedans that the year 1882 would be an eventful one for them. It closed the twelfth century of Mohammedanism, and the popular expectation was that a Mahdi, or another prophet, would arise to reform Islam, and to abolish the tyranny of the rich and powerful. Predictions of this kind frequently bring about their own accomplishment. Before the time stated, a man named Mohammed Achmet had arisen, declaring that he was the long-looked-for Mahdi, and crowds were flocking to his standard.* With a powerful governor, such as Gordon, the movement would have been quickly stamped out; indeed, so few abuses existed under his rule, that there was then no demand for such a reformer. But with Raouf Pasha the case was reversed; not only were there many abuses to be reformed, but there was a corresponding want of ability to subdue such a

* One writer thus describes the Mahdi:—"Mohammed Achmet was a native of Dongola, the son of a shipwright, formerly well known there. From his early youth he was fond of meditation and studying the Koran, rather than of working like his brothers; and his tastes were encouraged. He became the disciple of a fakir, or dervish, near Khartoum. In 1870 he took up his residence on an island, where he gained reputation as a learned and devout man. For a time he used this reputation only for selfish and sensual ends. He took wives from among the Arabs, and thus made many alliances, which he afterwards turned to account. After some years he began to assume more ambitious claims, and declared himself to be the true Mahdi."

movement. The Mahdi's forces grew apace, for there existed plenty of material in the way of recruits. Passing over smaller engagements in which the Egyptian troops met the forces of the Mahdi, we come to one crowning disaster on the 5th November 1883, when an Egyptian army, numbering something like 12,000 men, under the command of Colonel Hicks, a retired Indian officer, was massacred on the road between Khartoum and El Obeid. No blame can be attached to the commander on this occasion. Mr. Frank Power, the *Times*' correspondent at Khartoum, writes of him as follows: "I pity Hicks; he is an able, good, and energetic man, but he has to do with wretched Egyptians, who take a pleasure in being incompetent, thwarting one, delaying and lying." The unfortunate men who composed his army had been dragged from their homes in chains, and many of them had never learnt to fire a shot, or to ride a horse. Mr. Power predicted, before the army left Khartoum, that fifty good men would rout the whole lot. The Mahdi not only had upwards of 69,000 men on his side, but a large proportion of them were fine plucky fellows, worthy of a better foe.

Mr. Power says: "The last that was seen of poor old Hicks was his taking his revolver in one hand, and his sword in the other; calling on his soldiers to fix bayonets, and his staff to follow him, he spurred at the head of his troops into the dense mass of naked Arabs, and perished with all his men." They had fought for three days and nights without a drop of water, the whole day under a scorching sun on a sandy plain. Gordon writing to a friend says: "What a defeat Hicks's was! It is terrible to think of over 12,000 men killed;

the Arabs just prodded them to death, where they lay dying of thirst, four days without water! It is appalling. What a hecatomb to death!"

That victory changed everything. Nothing succeeds like success; the Mahdi became the hero of the hour in the Soudan, and his forces, it was supposed, at one time numbered something like 300,000 men. Here then were all the elements ready for a new Mohammedan crusade, and considering how much trouble the first Mohammedan crusade had given in Europe, it was not to be wondered at that there was fear and trembling in Egypt, the first country on the line of march of this huge fanatical army, flushed with victory, believing their leader to be none other than the long-expected reformer of Islam and conqueror of the world. A hurriedly-scraped-together force, consisting mainly of gendarmerie, was at once despatched under Baker Pasha, *via* Suakim, to relieve Khartoum, and attack the Mahdi. This force was so completely smashed up by Osman Digna within a few miles of Suakim that it had little effect upon the campaign, except to show that Egyptian troops were absolutely unfit to meet the forces of the Mahdi. If the tide of conquest was to be rolled back it must be done by British troops. But England might well ask what claim was there resting on her that she should give valuable lives to be sacrificed, to say nothing of incurring the cost of a fresh campaign, simply because the corrupt Egyptian Government was too weak to rule its own territory?

When once it became clear that Egyptian troops could not hold the Soudan, our Government rightly decided that the province must be given up. Unfortunately, there were scattered about in different parts of that immense territory various Egyptian officials and bodies of troops. It was calculated that including the women and children their number must have been about 30,000. We had practically broken up the Egyptian army, and virtually become the rulers of the country, so we as a nation had a certain amount of responsibility in the matter. The problem was how to withdraw that enormous number of human beings from the Soudan into Egypt. What appeared to be needed far more than troops was a man with a head on his shoulders, acquainted with the country, familiar with the people and their habits of thought, and possessing force of character to stand against the turbulent elements that had to be dealt with. No sooner were the difficulties of the position recognised in England than an outcry arose that Gordon ought to be sent to undertake the herculean task. Mr. Gladstone, in the House of Commons, has given credit to Sir Charles Wilson as the first to suggest sending Gordon, as the only man competent to deal with all the difficulties of the situation. Both Mr. Gladstone and Sir Charles Dilke asserted in public that the English Cabinet advised the Egyptian Government that Gordon was the best man to send, but that the Khedive's ministers did not approve of this step. Sir Henry Gordon, in his biography states that Sir Evelyn Baring, our representative in Egypt, does not even seem to have consulted the Egyptian Government, but of his own accord declined to accept Gordon. It is quite clear that Sir Evelyn Baring and General Gordon were not the best of friends, for Gordon later on complains: "I hear very little from Cairo. Baring only telegraphs officially." It does not, however, much matter now who is to blame for the want of wisdom in not recognising in time that Gordon was the man for the occasion. That blunder, whosever fault it was, not only lost the Soudan to Egypt, but caused the death of many of our brave soldiers, to say nothing of Gordon himself. The Egyptian government blundered on a little longer, till it was too late, and then the request that Gordon might be sent was telegraphed home.

Nubar Pasha, who was the first to invite Gordon to Egypt many years before, was now the first to see that he ought to be sent for. This astute minister had only just come into office, and within eight days he got Sir Evelyn Baring to telegraph to England for Gordon. There can be little question now that the fatal delay of a single month sealed the fate of the Soudan. Hicks Pasha's force was annihilated in November 1883, but it was not till January 11, 1884, that General Gordon received a telegram from his old friend and comrade, Lord Wolseley, urging him to come to town at once for consultation, and though he did not lose a single day he did not reach Cairo till January 24th. By that time he ought to have been at Khartoum.

Before proceeding further, it may be well to say that so little was General Gordon known at this time by his countrymen, that a country gentleman, who was a magistrate and a deputy-lieutenant in Pembrokeshire, a county in which Gordon had formerly been stationed, remarked, on seeing the fact mentioned in the paper that "Chinese Gordon" was going out, "I see the Government have just sent a Chinaman to the Soudan. What can they mean by sending a native of that country to such a place?" This story, which is mentioned by Sir William Butler, is quite characteristic of the ignorance that prevailed about the Khartoum hero, previous to his being selected as the one man who could save Egypt from its troubles, and our Government from an awkward position.

In a letter to his brother, dated 17th January, Gordon says, "I saw King Leopold to-day; he is furious." It must have been a great trial to that kind-hearted monarch to have all his philanthropic plans thus upset, and he made Gordon promise that he would, if spared, go to the Congo when the Soudan was settled. So hard up for money was Gordon at this time that he had to borrow from the king enough to pay for his journey to London. Fortunately it occurred to Lord Wolseley to ask Gordon, a few hours before he was to start by the evening mail, if he had sufficient money. Gordon had none, and as the banks had closed his lordship had some amusing adventures going about to raise £200, which he did by borrowing small sums. As far as Gordon was concerned, his lordship might have saved himself the trouble, as £100 of the amount was generously bestowed by him on Mahomet, his old blind secretary at Cairo.

The *Pall Mall Gazette*, which was the first journal to advocate sending Gordon to the Soudan, and which first published his views on that country, was represented at Charing Cross when the gallant General was starting, and described the scene as a very unusual and interesting one. Lord Wolseley carried the General's portmanteau; Lord Granville, the Foreign Secretary, took his ticket; and the Duke of Cambridge held open the door. Considering how little Gordon cared about grandees, it is amusing to note that he was waited on in a way that many tuft-hunters would envy.

Writing before he had actually started, he said: "I am averse to the loss of a single life, and will endeavour to prevent any happening *if I go.* I have a Bank, and on that I can draw; He is richer than the Khedive, and knows more of the country than any one; I will trust Him to help me out of money or any other difficulties." Again he writes, when at sea, 21st January: "If people ask after me, tell them they can greatly help me with their prayers, not for my earthly success, but that my mission may be for God's glory, the welfare of the poor and wretched, and, for me, what He wills, above all for a humble heart." And to his friend Prebendary Barnes, he says: "You and I are equally exposed to the attacks of the enemy—me not a bit more than you are."

On January 24th he reached Cairo, where a good deal of excitement prevailed. Gordon apparently took it all very calmly. He had to remain a couple of days, and during that time had a stormy interview with Zebehr, who accused him of the murder of his son. Gordon's reply was practically that had full justice been done, Zebehr too would have paid the death penalty. Though he had such a short time at Cairo, he found opportunity to interest himself in the affairs of a poor lad, the son of a native pastor of the Church Missionary Society at Jaffa. The boy had been in a telegraph office at Jaffa, but had been unjustly dismissed. He went to Cairo for employment, and got into the telegraph office. General Gordon had not forgotten him, and went to call on the young fellow, who was of course in quite a subordinate position, and must have been not a little astonished at the visit of a man upon whom, at that time, the eyes of the whole civilised world were turned. "How is your mother?" was the first question Gordon put, the woman having been unwell when he was in Palestine. He then spoke to the head of the department, with the result that the boy's position was improved considerably. Writing from Khartoum, Gordon said: "I saw two pleasant things at Cairo—Baring's and Wood's chicks; * and I heard one pleasant thing—Mrs. Amos wanted me to see her lambs."

General Gordon had brought with him from England a very able staff officer, Colonel Stewart, of the 11th Hussars, who knew Egypt well. Having done all that was necessary in the way of interviewing officials at Cairo, the two proceeded together on January 26th, reaching Korosko on February 1st, at which point they took to their camels, and dashed into the Nubian Desert. All sorts of alarming rumours reached England as to Gordon's fate during this hazardous ride, but on February 13th he reached Berber in safety, and we heard that he had reached Khartoum on the 18th. Mr. Power, the *Times'* correspondent, writing from Khartoum on January 24th, said: "I hear that Chinese Gordon is coming up. They could not have a better man. He, though severe, was greatly loved during the five years he spent up here." Again Mr. Power writes: "Just got a telegram from Mr. Bell, the *Times'* agent for Egypt, to say, 'Gordon leaves Cairo to-night, and will be in Khartoum in eighteen days.' The shortest time on record is twenty-four days; but Gordon (sword and Bible) travels like a whirlwind. No Arab of

* Sir Evelyn Baring, the British representative, and Sir Evelyn Wood, the commander-in-chief.

the desert could, when he was up here, vie with him in endurance on camel back;" and yet again, on February 9th, "I don't believe the fellows in Lucknow looked more anxiously for Colin Campbell than we look for Gordon." The same pen described the scene he created on arrival, and the speech he made. Thousands of the people crowded to kiss his hands and feet, calling him the "Sultan of the Soudan."

"His speech to the people was received with enthusiasm. He said, 'I come without soldiers, but with God on my side, to redress the evils of the Soudan. I will not fight with any weapons but justice. There shall be no more Bashi-Bazouks.' It is now believed that he will relieve the Bahr-Gazelle garrisons without firing a shot. Since they heard that he was coming the aspect of the people has so changed that there are no longer any fears of disturbance in the town. They say that he is giving them more than even the Mahdi could give. He is sending out proclamations in all directions. Such is the influence of one man, that there are no longer any fears for the garrison or people of Khartoum."

General Gordon immediately reduced the taxation of the people by one half, and directed Colonel Stewart to examine into the case of each person in prison. It was found that some prisoners had been awaiting trial for months and some even for years, one poor woman having been detained for fifteen years for a paltry offence committed when a child. As many as possible were released, only the worst cases being detained. One poor old Sheikh had to be carried into Gordon's presence, the ex-governor of Khartoum having bastinadoed him so severely on the feet that the flesh had all gone, and only the sinews and bones were showing. Gordon was so indignant at this that he telegraphed to Cairo to have £50 stopped out of the pay of Hussein Pasha Cheri, and handed to his victim by way of compensation for such brutal treatment. He had a collection made of kourbashes and other instruments of torture, and had them all destroyed in a bonfire.

Writing on February 22nd, Gordon says:—

"I have all my old servants back, and it is like old times again. I have not minced matters with the Pashas; it was useless to do so. We have thousands of petitions daily. I have ordered an Arabic text, 'God rules the hearts of all men,' to be put up over my throne, to which I can refer when people come to me in fear. . . . There is, of course, a very mixed sort of feeling here about the evacuation of the Soudan; the civil employés do not desire it, for the half taxes will cause their pay to be diminished by half, and the *personnel* reduced."

From Mr. Power's interesting correspondence we get pleasant little peeps at the private life of the great hero:—

"Gordon is a most lovable character—quiet, mild, gentle and strong; he is so humble too. The way he pats you on the shoulder when he says, 'Look here, dear fellow, now what would you advise?' would make you love him. When he goes out of doors there are always crowds of Arab men and women at the gate to kiss his feet, and twice to-day the furious women, wishing to lift his feet to kiss them, threw him over. He likes my going so much amongst the natives, for not to do so is a mortal sin in his eyes. . . . It is wonderful that one man could have such an influence on 200,000 people. Numbers of women flock here every day to ask him to touch their children to cure them; they call him the 'Father and the Saviour of the Soudan.' He has found me badly up in Thomas à Kempis, which he reads every day, and has given me an 'Imitation of Christ.' He is indeed, I believe, the greatest and best man of this century. . . .

"I like Gordon more and more every day; he has a most lovable manner and disposition, and is so kind to me. He is glad if you show the smallest desire to help him in his great trouble. How one man could have dared to attempt his task, I wonder. One day of his work and bother would kill another man, yet he is so cheerful at breakfast, lunch, and dinner; but I know he suffers fearfully from low spirits. I hear him walking up and down his room all night (it is next to mine). It is only his great piety carries him through. He and I agree in a great many religious views."

Mr. Power being an Irishman and a Roman Catholic, while General Gordon was a Scotchman and a member of the Church of England, such testimony speaks volumes for the General as well as for the writer. There can be little doubt that General Gordon had not known the brave young Irishman long, before he had cast over him that fascinating spell which invariably attracted and charmed young men. Cowper tells us that—

"Truth embodied in a tale,
Shall entrance find at lowliest doors."

Might not the poet have added that truth embodied in a life shall be even more efficacious in obtaining an entrance? Power's life was cut short before he had an opportunity of doing much in the world, but the little that he was permitted to do shows us that he too was made of that stuff which produces heroes; and as long as our country has such men in reserve to fall back upon in times of emergency, there need be no fear of her not being able to maintain her supremacy among nations.

How unwavering was Gordon's faith in the providence of God, even in the midst of difficulties that would have appalled most men, is shown by the following letter:—

"*February* 27, 1884.—I have sent Stewart off to scour the river White Nile, and another expedition to push back the rebels on the Blue Nile. With Stewart has also gone Power, the British Consul and *Times'* correspondent, so I am left alone in the vast palace of which you have a photograph, but not alone, for I feel great confidence in my Saviour's presence.

"The peculiar pain, which comes from the excessive anxiety one cannot help being in for these people, comes back to me at times. I think that our Lord, sitting over Jerusalem, is ruling all things to the glory of His kingdom, and cannot wish things were different than they are, for, if I did so, then I wish *my will* not *His* to be done. The Soudan is a ruin, and, humanly speaking, there is no hope. Either I must believe He does all things in mercy and love, or else I disbelieve His existence; there is no half-way in the matter. What holes do I not put myself into! And for what? So mixed are my ideas. I believe ambition put me here in this ruin; however, I trust and stay myself on the fact that not one sparrow falls to the ground without our Lord's permission; also that enough for the day is the evil. 'God provideth by the way, strength sufficient for the day.'

"*March* 1, 1884.—We are all right at present, and I have hope, but certainly things are not in a good way; humanly speaking, Baker's defeat at Suakim has been a great disaster, and now it has its effects up here. 'It is nothing to our God to help with many or with few,' and I now take my worries more quietly than before, for all things are ruled by Him for His glory, and it is rebellion to murmur against His will. Excuse a long letter." *

It may be well at this point to consider the position of General Gordon in his official relationship to the Egyptian and English Governments, for it is impossible to understand subsequent events accurately, without a proper apprehension of the exact state of affairs. When Gordon was first sent out, his instructions were merely

* This letter of 27th February and 1st March has been presented to the Trustees of the British Museum, and is now exhibited in the Manuscript Department.

"to report to Her Majesty's Government on the military situation in the Soudan, and on the measures which it might be deemed advisable to take for the security of the Egyptian garrisons still holding positions in that country, and for the safety of the European population in Khartoum, &c. &c." Added, however, to these instructions was an insignificant clause to which no one at the time attached much importance, and which ran as follows, "You will consider yourself authorised and instructed to perform such other duties as the Egyptian Government may desire to intrust to you, and as may be communicated to you by Sir E. Baring." The Egyptian Government decided to make Gordon Governor-General of the Soudan, and the Khedive gave into his hands all the absolute power that he himself possessed; this appointment was sanctioned by the British Government, and officially communicated to Gordon by Sir E. Baring. In view of this appointment, most readers will concur in the opinion of Mr. Egmont Hake, the editor of Gordon's Journals, that "it is as unfair as it is illogical to talk about General Gordon having exceeded the instructions conveyed to him by Her Majesty's Government." The real truth is that it was impossible for Gordon to exceed his instructions. He himself again and again contended that while it was open to the Khedive to cancel the appointment, until that was done he was absolutely master of the situation, to do as he thought best for the good of the country.

It must not, however, be supposed that General Gordon availed himself of a flaw in his instructions to carry out a policy of his own. On the contrary, he clearly understood from the British Government that evacuation was what was required, and all that the Egyptian employés must be given a chance of leaving the Soudan if possible. From beginning to end this was the one thing he held out as the object at which he aimed. All the suggestions he put forward were made with this end in view, and he never swerved from it. He was in reality more true to the instructions he received than were those who issued them. No sooner had he got into the country, and grasped the actual state of affairs, than he saw that things were looking very serious. The interval between Hicks's defeat and his own arrival had been too prolonged. People who might have been loyal had lost heart and gone over to the Mahdi. Added to this, Gordon had himself made public the fact that the country was to be evacuated, so all who intended to remain behind saw that their best policy was to throw in their lot with the Mahdi. Gordon blamed himself sometimes for having made known the intentions of the Government, but it is questionable if such an important fact could have been long kept secret. At all events, when he openly promulgated it as Governor-General, he thought, and many thought with him, that he was taking the line most likely to lead to a peaceful solution.

General Gordon did not take long to make up his mind, and soon after his arrival in Khartoum he astonished the English people by two steps he took. The first was the issue of a proclamation announcing that the institution of slavery was not to be interfered with in any way; the second was an application that his old enemy, Zebehr Rahama, the great slave-dealer, should be sent up to govern the Soudan. At first sight

Gordon's action was amazing; but when it is more carefully examined in the light of facts, it cannot be blamed. To take the proclamation first, it must be apparent to any one that when it was decided that the Soudan was to be given up, and that thenceforth neither Egypt nor England should interfere in its internal affairs, it would have been ridiculous to go on talking about the abolition of slavery. Gordon had to face a fanatical body of Mohammedans who, rightly or wrongly, looked upon slavery as a religious institution. The feeling of the country was strongly in favour of slavery, and if the country was to be left to itself slavery would continue to exist. Gordon did but make a virtue of a necessity, and announce that henceforth outsiders would not interfere in the matter. Thus he took the wind out of the sails of the Mahdi and his party, who could not say that they were fighting on behalf of one of their religious institutions.

The proposal to the English Government that Zebehr should be made ruler of the Soudan, was, as Mr. Hake truly says, "one of those daring strokes of policy which made his tactics unlike those of other men." The telegram reached England on February 18, and must at first have caused some of the Cabinet Ministers to think that Gordon had lost his head. The last that they had heard on the subject of Gordon's relationship with Zebehr, was the suggestion of the former that the latter should be sent as a prisoner to Cyprus, to get him out of Egypt, where he thought he might give trouble. No wonder, then, if the ministers were astonished to hear that their representative had changed his mind so completely as to propose that instead of being imprisoned in Cyprus, his enemy should be sent to govern the Soudan!

Those who have followed Gordon's tactics closely will not wonder so much at the proposal. Indeed it seems to have been a part of his creed to utilise his enemies, and thus if possible to turn them into friends. In China he frequently enlisted hundreds of prisoners of war, converted them into staunchest allies, and led them to victory against their old comrades. He now wanted to apply in the case of Zebehr the principles he had found so effective elsewhere. So long as he did not see his way to utilising this king of slave-hunters, he desired to have him kept out of the way, but when his brilliant genius saw a way of turning his old foe into a friend, he asked for his services. Unfortunately, Gordon was not in the position of a Napoleon: he was hampered in the carrying out of his brilliant designs by those at home, who had neither his knowledge nor his capacity.

With regard to the proposed appointment of the great slave-hunter to be King of the Soudan, opinions even now differ greatly. Lord Wolseley, Sir Evelyn Baring, and most well-informed people are agreed that the recommendation ought to have been acted upon, and that its adoption would have been the means of saving many valuable lives, including Gordon's, and of placing the Soudan under an authoritative government, which it has not yet obtained. But the English Cabinet felt that public opinion would be strongly opposed to such a step, and therefore they would not sanction it.

When Gordon left Cairo for Khartoum he thought that the best plan for the Soudan, when the Egyptian

Government withdrew, would be to replace it by the heirs of the petty Sultans, who had been deprived of their power when the Soudan was annexed by Mehemet Ali. But when he saw the real state of affairs, he felt that these disunited kinglets would not be strong enough to resist the power of the Mahdi. As for the Mahdi, he was too much of a religious fanatic to have the government of the Soudan put into his hands. He was ambitious as well as fanatical; his object was to overrun the whole world. Directly he ceased to be a conqueror, his people would cease to believe in his Divine mission, and he would lose his power. At that time he possessed great power, and Gordon felt that there must be a still more powerful man set up. There was only one such man alive, and he was a prisoner at Cairo. The argument against Zebehr was that he had been an inveterate slave-hunter, and that to put him into supreme power would be to give him unlimited means of gratifying his vices. Against this it must be urged that under the Mahdi's rule the kidnapping of slaves would be just as cruelly carried on as under that of Zebehr. Also that with Zebehr, being a prisoner, it would be possible to make certain stipulations on the subject of slave-hunting. Moreover, it was Gordon's intention eventually to annex, for the Congo State, the great slave-hunting district, and to rule that himself, so that Zebehr could not interfere. Apart from these arguments, Gordon did not believe that Zebehr loved slave-hunting for its own sake, but rather for the wealth and position it gave him. He believed that if Zebehr were made Sultan of the Soudan, his ambitious nature would be satisfied, and he would cease to hunt slaves, the *raison d'être* for such an occupation being gone.

There can be no question that Zebehr was a most able man, a born ruler and leader of men. He was an inveterate enemy of Gordon's, and at the meeting which took place between Gordon and Zebehr at Cairo, when the former was *en route* to Khartoum, lookers on considered that on no account ought these two men ever to be in the Soudan together.

It was, however, one of Gordon's characteristics, and a great charm in his nature, that he was not only forgiving, but that he never allowed personal feeling to affect his judgment. He thought only of what was good for the Soudan, and he was convinced that the only way to restore law and order there was to place Zebehr in power. One of the faults of our system of party government is that the Cabinet does not consider so much what is right in the abstract, as what will most affect the public mind. The national hatred of slavery is, in England, rightly very strong; but circumstances alter cases. The Cabinet could not face public opinion, although the public were at that time ill-informed, and ignorant of many important elements in the case, and they consequently refused to let Zebehr go.

Public opinion in England is generally in the right when the public have been properly informed, and have had time to form an opinion. But it is not to be expected that the first impressions, formed by a large mass of people who have not been supplied with full information, are very reliable. We ought therefore always to have a government in office strong enough to resist, if need be, the first impression of public opinion, but willing to yield when the public have thoroughly made up their minds. The government in office at that time were not united among themselves, and consequently were weak, and afraid to face the public. As a result, Gordon's policy was not carried out, and he fell a victim. The Soudan is still without a settled government, and the problem how it should be governed is as far as ever from being solved. As for slavery, that institution alone has gained by the weak policy of those who were afraid to send up the old slave-hunter to govern the unfortunate Soudan.

CHAPTER XV.

THE SIEGE.

ONE of the most remarkable characteristics of General Gordon was the marvellous fertility of his resources. Knowing that there would be a great deal of prejudice against employing Zebehr, he almost simultaneously suggested an alternative scheme, which was that, as the Egyptians could not govern the Soudan, and the English would not, rather than let it fall into a state of anarchy it should be offered to the Turks. There was much to be said for this suggestion. Turkey had once ruled Egypt, and still exercised a suzerainty over it and all its belongings, and if Egypt was not strong enough to rule itself and its annexations, it only seemed fair that the suzerain power should intervene to prevent its being grasped by an upstart like the Mahdi. Besides, the Sultan of Turkey is the head of the Mohammedan religion, and had therefore a special interest in suppressing the claims of a False Prophet.

That the scheme was no hastily-formed one, which he would see fit to change later on for something else, may be gathered from the fact that Gordon adhered to it to the very last. Nor was it a scheme suggested by the immediate difficulties of his position, for in the month of October, when Lord Wolseley was on the way to relieve him, he writes:—

"Give the country to the Turks, when once you have come to Khartoum, with one or two millions sterling (which you will have to spend in three months' occupation up here if you delay), make arrangements at once with the Porte for its Soudan cession, let 6000 Turks land at Suakim and march up to Berber, thence to Khartoum; you can then retire at once before the hot weather comes on. . . .

"I do not advocate the keeping of the Soudan by us, it is a useless possession, and we could not govern it, neither can Egypt (after the late events). I am only discussing how to get out of it in honour and in the cheapest way (we must remember we caused its troubles), and that way is, either by some sort of provincial government under Zubair, or by giving it to the Turks; it is simply a question of getting out of it with decency. The Turks are the best solution, though most expensive. *They would keep the Soudan:* give them £2,000,000. The next best is Zubair, with £500,000 and £100,000 a year for two years: he will keep the Soudan for a time (in both cases slave trade will flourish), thus you will be quiet in Egypt, and will be able to retreat in January 1885. If you do not do this, then be prepared for a deal of worry and danger, and your campaign will be entirely unprofitable and devoid of prestige, for the day after you leave Khartoum the Mahdi will walk in and say that he drove you out."

But the Government that had refused the assistance of Zebehr for fear of public opinion at home, were equally decided not to allow the assistance that might be obtained from the Turks, and this time, it must be admitted, they had more reason on their side. There were already too many complications connected with the government of Egypt to make it prudent to admit another possible element of discord. Earl Granville, the Foreign Secretary, therefore telegraphed as follows:—

"Gordon should be at once informed by several messengers . . . that we do not propose to supply him with Turkish or other force for the purpose of undertaking military expeditions, such being beyond the scope of the commission he holds, and at variance with the pacific policy which was the purpose of his mission to the Soudan; that, if with this knowledge, he continues at Khartoum, he should at once state to us the cause and intention with which he so continues."

This despatch shows how little the powers in England actually understood the questions at issue, or the practical working of their own instructions. Gordon had been asked to undertake the withdrawal of the Egyptian garrisons and civil employés. Having accepted this duty, he goes out, and finding the Mahdi's forces stronger than was supposed in this country, he sends home word that the task is a far more complicated one than the authorities in England knew of, and he suggests other methods. His suggestions are not accepted, and he is asked why he continues at Khartoum, as if he could have left his duty unperformed with honour to himself, or credit to his country.

Gordon was anxious to evacuate the country as quickly as possible; in this he was quite at one with his employers; but, on the spot, and knowing all the difficulties of the situation, he saw what they in the distance could not see, that the evacuation was a practical impossibility. The most distant garrison held by Egyptians was at Senaar, and if Gordon could have got to that place, a feat which it is more than doubtful if even he could have performed, it is perfectly certain that with the wretched troops he would have had to command he could not have safely escorted the host of the Egyptian employés thence to Khartoum, while the whole intermediate country was in the hands of the fanatical hordes owning allegiance to the Mahdi.

The commencement of his march from Senaar to Khartoum would have been the signal for a repetition of the horrors of the march of our retreating army from Cabul to Jellalabad in 1842, the sole survivor of which has been immortalised in Miss Elizabeth Thompson's (Lady Butler) celebrated picture, the only difference being that the heat and sand of the Soudan would have been substituted for the cold and snow of Afghanistan. The Mahdi's forces would have at once occupied Senaar, and spread reports to the effect that they had driven out the Egyptians, while Gordon's party with very limited provisions would have been exposed to incessant attacks during the whole of their journey. A retreating army has always plenty of enemies; and it is doubtful if a single survivor would have reached Khartoum.

On the other hand, if either of Gordon's suggestions had been accepted and the country handed over to the Turks or to Zebehr, the towns at both ends would have been held in force, and a suitable escort could have been provided for the Egyptian employés. Gordon states his position very fairly in the following brief telegram to Sir Evelyn Baring:—

"You ask me to state cause and intentions in staying at Khartoum, knowing Government means to abandon Soudan, and in answer I say, I stay at Khartoum because Arabs have shut us up, and will not let us out. I also add that if the road was opened the people would not let me go, unless I gave them some government or took them with me, which I could not do. No one would leave more willingly than I would if it was possible."

There were some in authority who advocated leaving such a distant garrison as Senaar to its fate, and wanted

Gordon to retreat with the Khartoum force only, picking up the Berber force on the way home. Against this Gordon's generous heart revolted, and he was determined that so long as he was Governor-General it should never be said that he left his subordinates to perish. He thus telegraphs to Sir Evelyn Baring:—

"Put yourself in my position, if you say 'rapid retreat, and leave Senaar to its fate.' I will say, 'No, I would sooner die first,' and will resign my commission, for I could not do it. If you say, 'Then you are no longer Governor-General,' then I am all right, and all the responsibility is on you (for I could not be supposed, if you turn me out of being Governor-General, to be obliged to aid such a movement, which I think is disgraceful)."

Writing as late as October 24th, and assuming that Lord Wolseley had conquered the country, he says:—

"I declare I do not see how we will get out of it (the Soudan) even now; allow that you come to Khartoum, that you drive off the Arabs, open the road to Senaar. What are you going to do? You will say, 'Take out those who wish to leave.' Well, you begin with Senaar, and of course will have to fight all the way down. It will take three months. During these three months, how are you to feed Khartoum? for the moment you leave Senaar you leave your granary. You get to Khartoum, you are face to face with 30,000 people who will not leave, and who are hedging with the Mahdi; and with 3000 Shaggyeh all armed. You fight your way to Berber; another three months, you have no food at Berber; then it will need another two months to get to Dongola, which (seeing your policy) will be hostile.

"It is indeed a terrible problem, and I wish I could see my way out of it. Then you come into the hot months, and low Nile. This time next year will not see you out of the Soudan with decency. Of course you can go back now, but what was the use of your coming? I will not allow that you came for me. You came for the garrisons of the Soudan. Now, by the Turkish arrangement, if you act promptly, you can get away quietly in January 1885."

Not only, however, did the British Government refuse to adopt either of Gordon's alternative proposals, but they neglected until August 12th to take any other measures for relieving the garrisons. Yet all the time the gallant General felt that he had not a free hand, and could not take independent action, for he writes in his Journal:—

> "Truly the indecision of our Government has been, from a military point of view, a very great bore, for we never could act as if independent; there was always the chance of their taking action, which hampered us. . . . It is truly deplorable, the waste of men and money on account of our indecision."

The mistake our Government made was the old one of endeavouring to control details in distant countries from Downing Street, instead of sending out the best man to the spot, and giving him more or less of a free hand.

At last, on April 16th, Gordon telegraphed to Sir Evelyn Baring at Cairo:—

> "As far as I can understand, the situation is this: You state your intention of not sending any relief up here or to Berber, and you refuse me Zebehr. I consider myself free to act according to circumstances. I shall hold on here as long as I can, and if I can suppress the rebellion I shall do so. If I cannot, I shall retire to the Equator, and leave you the indelible disgrace of abandoning the garrisons of Senaar, Kassala, and Dongola, with the certainty that you will eventually be forced to smash up the Mahdi under great difficulties, if you would retain peace in Egypt!"

But though Gordon saw that it was impossible to attempt an immediate evacuation with something like 50,000 men, women, and children, he did everything that lay within his power to get rid of as many refugees as possible during the few weeks that he was in Khartoum before the means of communication were cut off. The measures he took were described by Colonel Duncan, M.P., at that time in command of a station on the Nile, through which the refugees had to pass *en route* to Egypt, in a speech made some time afterwards, as follows :—

"Last year, after the arrival of General Gordon at Khartoum, I was sent to the northern end of the Korosko desert to facilitate the passage of the refugees from Khartoum to Egypt. It was then that I realised the true nature of Gordon, who was not a mere sentimental philanthropist, but a man of business as well as a man of courage. At that time the telegraph wire between Khartoum and where I was stationed was still uncut; and with marvellous monotony, I might say, batch after batch of the sick and the injured, of women and children, used to be sent by Gordon to me. They used to arrive in an almost perfect state of comfort, with all the necessary papers enabling me to disperse them among their different villages in Egypt. One of the first messages the General sent to me was this, 'Do try and find a motherly European woman to receive these poor women and children, for they have never been in Egypt yet before.' With the regularity of clockwork over 2000 refugees arrived, all the arrangements for their transport from Khartoum to Berber having been made by Gordon. . . . Two thousand five hundred men, women, and children were saved by the direct action and the direct humanity of Gordon himself, long before the expedition set out for Khartoum."

It is evident that the impression among the three Englishmen at Khartoum was, that the English Government had deserted Gordon, and intended to leave him there to die. Both Colonel Stewart and Mr. Power nobly decided that they would not forsake him in his hour of need, and that, happen what might, they would remain with him.

Though plenty of skirmishes took place, there was no real fight that might be dignified by the name of a battle till the middle of March. Some 4000 of the Mahdi's force had cut off about 800 of Gordon's men at a village called Halfaya, on the north of Khartoum, and, as the detachment could not retreat, Gordon decided to attempt to relieve them. By means of steamers he succeeded in extricating them from danger, but he could not drive away the rebels who held Halfaya in strong force.

On the 16th, therefore, he sent Colonel Stewart to attempt to dislodge the enemy, and the following is his own description of what actually occurred :—

"At 8 A.M. on the 16th, two steamers started for Halifaya. Bashi-Bazouks and some regulars advanced across plain towards rebels. At 10 A.M. the regulars were in square opposite centre of rebels' position, and Bashi-Bazouks were extended in their line to their right. The gun with regulars then opened fire. Very soon after this a body of about sixty rebel horsemen charged down a little to the right of centre of Bashi-Bazouks line. The latter fired a volley, then turned and fled. The horsemen galloped towards the square, which they immediately broke. The whole force then retreated slowly towards the fort with their rifles shouldered. The horsemen continued to ride along flanks, cutting off stragglers. The men made no effort to stand, and the gun was abandoned with sixty-three rounds and fifteen cases of reserve ammunition. The rebels advanced, and retreat of our men was so rapid that the Arabs on foot had no chance of attacking. Pursuit ceased about a mile from stockade and the men rallied. We brought in the wounded. Nothing could be more dismal than seeing these horsemen, and some men even on camels, pursuing close to troops who, with arms shouldered, plodded their way back."

The result of this, the first real battle, showed Gordon the hopelessness of his position. Colonel Stewart was wounded, though not very seriously, and Gordon saw that not only were his men cowards, but they were treacherous as well. At one time the rebels were actually retreating when two of Gordon's generals, Hassan and Seyid by name, actually rode after them and summoned them back. Need it be added that an army, seeing itself thus betrayed by its own leaders, lost all heart and bolted, leaving two valuable guns in the hands of their opponents. It is satisfactory, however, to be able to record that both these traitors were tried by court-martial and shot.

General Gordon made every effort to avoid further bloodshed by opening negotiations with the Mahdi, and even going so far as to offer to make him Sultan of Kordofan. The False Prophet briefly replied, "I am the Mahdi," which was a polite way of saying that it would be beneath his dignity to accept such a subordinate post. He, however, sent Gordon a courteous letter, urging him to become a Mohammedan. As Gordon declined this offer all negotiations between the two were closed.

Towards the end of April Gordon wrote that the Nile was beginning to rise. It continues to rise during May, June, and July, and is so high during the last mentioned month that boats can pass the numerous cataracts with comparative safety. This is the season of which an expedition should have taken advantage for the Nile campaign. Unfortunately the greatest empire of the world was at this time ruled by a disunited Cabinet, and party conflicts were going on at home. There may be much to be said in favour of party government, but there can be no question that to it is due the disgrace of England in the eyes of the whole civilised world, for having sent one of her bravest heroes into the heart of a hostile country in Africa, and then left him to perish. The blame in the matter is often cast solely upon the Liberals. Those who are not political partisans must see that this is not a fair way of stating the truth. The government in office was a Liberal one, but it cannot be said that it is a part of their programme to leave English heroes to perish. Lord Palmerston, the old Whig leader, would have been the first to denounce such a policy. The fact is, the fault was not due to either party as such, but to the party form of government that unfortunately prevails in this country. The opposite party might have fallen into the same mistake, had they been in the same position. The Government was afraid to split up its supporters by engaging in another war so soon after the Egyptian and Suakim campaigns. But, be the cause what it may, the fact remains that much valuable time was lost, in spite of Lord Wolseley's remonstrances, who said with truth—

"Remember, we can command many things, but all the gold of England will not affect the rise and fall of the Nile, or the duration of the hot and cold seasons in Egypt. Time is a most important element in this question, and it will be indeed an indelible disgrace if we allow the most generous, patriotic, and gallant of our public servants to die of want, or fall into the hands of a cruel enemy, because we would not hold out our hands to save him."

Public opinion at last grew too strong for the Government, and orders were given on August 12th to commence making the boats that were to convey the troops up the river Nile. The official report of the campaign states that there were only 104 vessels on the Nile that were able to pass the cataracts on the upper part of the river, so that boats of some sort had to be taken out. From August 12th till the final disaster took place no reasonable time was lost, but it takes time to transport a large army over such obstacles as had to be surmounted. It has been truly said that the campaign of the Nile was far more a conflict with Nature than with man. We might, however, have overcome Nature's had we only taken the field earlier in the day.

When Gordon realised how thoroughly the enemy had invested Khartoum, and that all supplies from outside were cut off, he wisely decided to reduce the number of persons inside the beleaguered city. There were, it was estimated, something like 10,000 who were in sympathy with the enemy, and who not only ate food, which was most valuable, but were a source of weakness to the defenders. Consequently the General gave them permission to go over to the enemy, which they did with alacrity. He was after all only acting on the sensible advice he gave the leader of the Taipings in China, who was retaining a large force of white men against their wills in the city of Soo-chow, of whom Gordon's rival, Burgevine, was one (see page 60). The Khartoum general gained considerably more than the enemy by this bold yet humane stroke of policy, as he got rid of 10,000 traitors, who would have very soon demoralised his whole force.

The greater the difficulties became the nobler Gordon's character appears. No sooner was he absolutely cut off from the outer world than he fell back on his boundless fertility of resources, and showed himself to be at the same time a skilful general, a brave soldier, a far-seeing statesman, and a clever financier. The defences of the town were attended to, and the whole place so well covered with obstacles and mines, that it might have been defended for years, had the food supply only held out. Cartridges were manufactured on an enormous scale; the General calculated that over half a million were fired away during four months of the siege. Eight steamers, which were nothing more than ordinary vessels, similar to the "Penny Steamers" on the Thames, were armour-plated, and made to act as miniature men-of-war, new ones were built, old ones were fitted up and adapted, and landsmen were trained to take them into action. "Our steamers," Gordon said, "are blinded and bullet proof, and do splendid work, for you see they cannot run away, and must go into action." The food supply, such as it was, was regulated so that nothing should be wasted, and paper money was issued, redeemable in six months. So great was the faith of the inhabitants in Gordon's ultimate success that £2500 worth of this paper money was in circulation by the end of April, and £26,000 worth was issued before the end of July. In addition, the merchants advanced to him upwards of £50,000.

For six long weary months General Gordon held out at Khartoum. Till the 9th of September he had at all events the companionship of his two brave countrymen, Colonel Stewart and Mr. Power. But for the remaining months of the siege he was deprived of even this comfort, and had to stand at the post of duty single-handed, as far as his own countrymen were concerned. On the 26th August the authorities at Cairo received a telegram from Gordon to the effect that now that the Nile had risen, and the way from Khartoum to Dongola was opened for a steamer, he intended to attack Berber and capture it, and thence to despatch Colonel Stewart and Mr. Power to Dongola. His object was to publish to the outside world the real facts of the terrible position at Khartoum, and to enable Colonel Stewart to urge on the authorities the necessity of at once despatching troops to the rescue; for he had not received any notification that a few days before this time—namely, on August 12th—the Government had decided to send an expedition for his relief. Colonel Stewart brought Gordon's Diary of Events up to the date of his starting, and was accompanied by Mr. Power, M. Herbin, the French Consul, and about fifty soldiers. They went in the *Abbas*, a small paddle-boat drawing only two feet of water. The following remark is made in Gordon's Journals in reference to the departure of Colonel Stewart in this vessel:—

"Stewart said he would go if I would exonerate him from deserting me. I said, 'You do not desert me. I—I cannot go, but if you go you do me a great service.' I then wrote him an *official*. He wanted me to write him an order. I said, 'No, for though I fear not responsibility, I will not put you in any danger which I am not in myself.' I wrote then a letter couched thus: '*Abbas* is going down. You say you are willing to go in her if I think you can do so with honour. You can go in honour, for you can do nothing here, and if you go you do me service in telegraphing my views.'"

The *Abbas* started together with two other steamers on the night of September 9th, and having shelled Berber proceeded on her way to Dongola, the two other vessels returning. On the 18th the *Abbas* struck on a rock. When Colonel Stewart saw that further progress was hopeless, he spiked the guns and threw them, with the ammunition, into the river. He then went on shore to arrange for the purchase of some camels to take his party on to Dongola. He was accompanied to the house of a blind man, named Fakri Etman, by Power and the French Consul. The Sheikh Suleiman Wad Gamr was present and invited them on shore, only insisting that the soldiers must not come armed for fear of frightening the people. To this Colonel Stewart agreed, and was the only one who was armed, he carrying a small revolver. Suleiman accepted from Colonel Stewart a sword and a dress as gifts. When Stewart and his party were in the house, Suleiman came outside and made some signs to his people, who were hanging about in large numbers. Immediately they divided into two parties, one proceeding to the house, the other to the steamer's crew landed on the bank, and the whole were massacred. News has recently reached Cairo to the effect that the perpetrator of this cold-blooded and treacherous murder, has at last paid the penalty of his crime, being slain in a conflict with Saleh Bey. All the official documents that Gordon had sent for the British authorities fell into the hands of the Mahdi, giving him the most exact information as to the supply of ammunition and food within the walls of Khartoum. These documents were at once sent to the Mahdi, and it is generally supposed that at this present moment they are lying in the Fort at Omdurman, outside Khartoum.

The loss of the *Abbas* was a cause of great grief to General Gordon, and again and again he refers to it. Writing on November 5th he says:—

"I cannot get out of my head the *Abbas* catastrophe ; that the *Abbas* (with her 970 bullet marks on her, her gun, and her parapets, which were bullet proof) could be captured by force seems impossible ; that she ran upon a rock seems unlikely, for she had her sides defended by buffers, sunk one foot in water. I also warned them against ever anchoring by the bank, also to take wood from isolated spots ; in fact as far as human foresight goes, I did all my possible. . . . You will notice the number of Greeks (on board). They were a bodyguard I ordered and paid highly, to prevent any treachery on the part of the crew. Thus the question of treachery was duly weighed by me, and guarded against, as far as I could—both on the part of the crew, and on the part of the inhabitants—and I told them to anchor mid-stream, and not to take wood except in isolated spots."

One can only echo the words of Mr. Egmont Hake: "It is impossible to read this without a feeling of admiration for the thorough way in which General Gordon examined into the minutest details of everything himself. Every precaution human foresight could conceive he took to ensure the safety of the *Abbas* and her crew; having done this, her fate was in higher hands than his."

CHAPTER XVI.

THE FALL OF KHARTOUM.

FORTUNATELY for the public, as soon as Colonel Stewart left, Gordon commenced, in addition to all his other duties, writing journals of events at Khartoum, in which doubtless he recapitulated much of what had been given in the Diary of Events he had sent with Stewart. On September 21st, the General received authentic news that an expedition was actually on its way to Khartoum. On September 30th he sent five steamers to Metemmah to meet the advancing army, so that there should be no delay on his part in rendering help. By the steamers he sent his Journals made up to date, and it is from these that authentic information is obtained. The despatch of these steamers to Metemmah was a most unselfish act on his part; indeed, it is by no means certain that their presence at Khartoum might not have prevented the crowning disaster later on. He calculated that each steamer was worth to him at least 2000 men, so that he practically reduced his force by something like 10,000 men in order to assist the Relief Expedition. Since the Nile had risen these vessels had considerably increased in utility, and they had been most valuable in the defence of Khartoum. Each was well provisioned, so that they would not have required to draw on the slender resources of the garrison.

On November 5th Gordon says:—

"A curious thing has happened; my friend Kitchener sent up the post; he wrapped the letters in some old newspapers (he gave me no news in his letter), the old newspapers were thrown out into the garden: there a clerk who knew some English found them blowing about, and gave them to the apothecary of the hospital, who knows English. The doctor found him reading them, saw date 15th September, and secured them for me; they are like gold, as you may imagine, since we have had no news since 24th February 1884! These papers gave us far more information than any of your letters. Did K. send them by accident or on purpose?"

In the newspaper appeared the following statement in the form of a heading: "Lord Wolseley seen off at Victoria Station for the Gordon Relief Expedition." To this Gordon appended, "*No! for the relief of the Soudan garrisons;*" and he extracted another statement to the following effect, "An official telegram received here from Wady Halfa states that, owing to the unprecedented lowness of the Nile, no confidence is felt in the practicability of hauling boats over the cataracts till the end of September." General Gordon pasted this into the Journal, and wrote opposite to it, "It was not a low Nile, it was an average Nile, only you were *too late*"—a verdict which events only too completely justified. It will be of interest to give here a few brief extracts selected from Gordon's remarks regarding the Relief Expedition:—

"If it is right to send up an expedition now, why was it not right to send it up before?"

"We are a wonderful people; it was never our Government

which made us a great nation; our Government has been ever the drag on our wheels."

"I am afraid to say what numbers have been killed through this present policy, certainly some 80,000; and it is not over yet."

"I altogether decline the imputation that the projected expedition has come to relieve me. It has come to save our national honour in extricating the garrisons, &c., from a position in which our action in Egypt had placed these garrisons. I was relief expedition No. I. They are relief expedition No. II. As for myself I could make good my retreat at any moment if I wished. Now realise what would happen if this first relief expedition was to bolt and the steamers fall into the hands of the Mahdi; this *second* relief expedition (for the honour of England engaged in extricating garrisons) would be somewhat hampered. We, the *first* and *second*, are equally engaged for the honour of England. This is fair logic. Earle * comes up to extricate garrisons and (I hope) succeeds. Earle does not come to extricate me. . . . I am not the *rescued lamb*, and I will not be."

In spite of his great anxiety, and the worries through which he was called to pass, Gordon never seemed to lose his sense of humour. There are many amusing entries in his Journals, of which the following may be taken as fair specimens:—

"A horse escaped from the Arabs, formerly belonging to Government. It gave *no* information; but from its action, may be supposed *not to believe in the Mahdi.*"

"It is really amusing to find (when one can scarcely call one's life one's own) one's servant, *already* with one wife (which most men find is enough), coming and asking for three days' leave, in

---

* Gordon thought that General Earle was to be in command of the whole force. As a matter of fact he was in command of the brigade that was going by water the whole way to Khartoum. He was killed on the way.

order to take another wife. Yet such was the case, a few days ago, with one of my servants."

His comments on the Mahdi are also amusing:—

"The Greek (refugee) who came in told the Greek Consul that the Mahdi puts pepper under his nails, and when he receives visitors then he touches his eyes and weeps copiously; that he eats a few grains of dhoora openly, but in the interior of the house he has fine feeding and drinks alcoholic drinks. . . . After this pepper business! I think I shall drop any more trouble in writing him letters, trying to convince or persuade him to reasonable measures. I must confess that the pepper business has sickened me; I had hitherto hoped I had to do with a regular fanatic, who believed in his mission, but when one comes to pepper in the finger nails, it is rather humiliating to have to succumb to him, and somehow I have the belief that I shall not have to do so. . . .

"One cannot help being amused at this pepper business. Those who come in for pardon, come in on their knees, with a halter round their neck. The Mahdi rises, having scratched his eyes and obtained a copious flow of tears, and takes off the halter. As the production of tears is generally considered the proof of sincerity, I would recommend the Mahdi's receipt to Cabinet Ministers, justifying some job."

It is not necessary to enumerate the number of encounters that took place betwen Gordon's men and the Mahdists; he took little personal part in these engagements. The fiery spirit of the young soldier, who led his own troops in China, had not expended itself, but was kept in subjection by a higher spirit. He knew that much was staked on his life, and that the risk was too great. There was no one to succeed him; his death meant defeat to his cause, and ruin to the country for which he had done so much. Speaking generally, therefore, he did not expose himself more than he could help. But though he avoided rashness in any form, he was a good deal exposed to danger, and the palace in which he lived was an object on which the enemy expended much of their ammunition.

The Mahdi had kept himself as far from Gordon's reach as possible, by remaining at Obeid, while his troops conducted the investment of Khartoum. But when the new year of the Mohammedan Calendar commenced, on October 21st, and the Mahdi had heard, through the capture of Colonel Stewart's papers, of the difficulties that Gordon was in, he appears to have mustered his courage and to have brought up 30,000 men to intimidate Gordon. When called upon to surrender the following was the reply that Gordon returned: "If you are the real Mahdi, dry up the Nile and come over, and I will surrender." It is said that the Mahdi took him literally, and lost 3000 men in an attempt to walk across the Nile! Be that as it may, the Mahdi ordered an attack, which was conducted with some vigour. It was resisted successfully by Gordon, aided by his twelve steamers and 800 men, but the fighting must have been severe, for it lasted for eight hours. The bursting of mines and torpedoes carried more havoc into the ranks of the enemy than Gordon's men did. Material things of this kind at least responded to the will of him who organised them, and did not prove cowardly or treacherous.

The Mahdi then retreated to a more respectful distance, and, it is said, hid himself in a cave, prophesying that there should be sixty days of rest, and that then blood would flow like water. The real truth of the matter is that the Mahdi's military advisers saw that there was little use in attempting to capture Khartoum by direct assault. Having full information from Stewart's papers that the food supply could not last long, they prudently decided to starve out the garrison.

English officers have before now gone through trying sieges, as, for instance, Lawrence and Havelock at Lucknow, and Sale at Jellalabad, but it would be difficult in the whole of the military history of England to find a case in which an officer was left single-handed to contend with such frightful odds for so long a time. The siege lasted 317 days, very nearly as long as the siege of Sebastopol. English officers have usually had a few of their own countrymen, on whom they could rely and with whom they could take counsel, to share their hardships. But Gordon stood alone, and the troops he had were not only foreigners, but, with a few exceptions, they were cowards, and he knew that very few of them were really loyal to him. Nothing but his extraordinary personality kept the force together. His opinion of these miserable troops is frequently expressed in his Journals. The following passages are examples:—

"*October* 31*st.*—I have ever felt the greatest insecurity respecting the lines, for I believe 100 determined men would carry them with ease, if they made their attack on the Shaggyeh or Bashi-Bazouk part. . . . The Cairo Turkish Bashi-Bazouks, the Shaggyeh, and the Fellaheen soldiers, I will back against any troops in the world for cowardice."

"*November* 17*th.*—I certainly lay claim to having commanded, more often than any other man, cowardly troops, but this experience of 1884 beats all past experiences; the worst of the matter is that you cannot believe one word the officers say."

On November 2nd he writes: "Six weeks' consumption! and then the sponge must be thrown up." Fortunately, he discovered on November 11th that a robbery by some corrupt Egyptian officials had been going on, and that 2½ million lbs. of biscuit —worth £9000 at any time, but at least £26,000 during the siege—had been stolen. The recovery of this helped him to hold out a little longer. On December 13th he writes:—

"We have in hand 1,796,000 rounds Remington ammunition; 540 rounds Krupp; 6000 rounds mountain gun ammunition; £140 in specie; £18,000 in paper in treasury! £60,000 in town in paper; 110,000 okes of biscuits; 700 ard ebs of dhoora. . . .

"We are going to send down the *Bordeen* the day after to-morrow, and with her I shall send this Journal. *If some effort is not made before ten days' time the town will fall.*"

The following day, December 14th, was the last as far as his ability to communicate with the outer world was concerned. Though he held on for nearly six weeks longer, nothing is known accurately after the *Bordeen* left Khartoum. Writing to the commander of the approaching Expeditionary Force, he says:—

"I send down the steamer *Bordeen* to-morrow, with vol. vi. of my private journal, containing account of the events in Khartoum from November 5 to December 14. The state of affairs is such that one cannot foresee further than five to seven days, after which the town may at any time fall. I have done all in my power to hold out, but I own I consider the position is extremely critical, almost desperate; and I say this without any feeling of bitterness with respect to Her Majesty's Government, but merely as a matter of fact. Should the town fall, it will be questionable whether it will be worth the while of Her Majesty's Government to continue its expedition; for it is certain that the fall of Khartoum will ensure that of Kassala and Senaar."

Another letter of the same date was received by Sir Gerald Graham in Cairo, saying: "Farewell. You will never hear from me again. I fear there will be treachery in the garrison, and all will be over by Christmas." The following message, addressed to a friend in Cairo, and also dated December 14, was received only on February 24: "All is up. I expect a catastrophe in ten days' time. It would not have been so if our people had kept me better informed as to their intentions. My adieux to all." He also wrote to his sister:—

"This may be the last letter you will receive from me, for we are on our last legs, owing to the delay of the expedition. However, God rules all, and, as He will rule to His glory and our welfare, His will be done. I fear, owing to circumstances, that my affairs pecuniarily are not over-bright. . . . .—Your affectionate brother, C. G. GORDON.

"*P.S.*—I am quite happy, thank God, and like Lawrence, I have '*tried* to do my duty.'"

It has already been mentioned that August 12th was the day when the English Government yielded to the pressure of public opinion and gave orders to commence the building of the boats which were to convey the troops to relieve Khartoum. It is unnecessary to follow in detail the history of that force. Suffice it to say that the commander, Lord Wolesley, received at Korti a message from General Gordon, dated 14th December 1884, "Come quickly, come together; do not leave Berber behind you." But the verbal message which the messenger delivered was far worse, "Famine was in Khartoum; the Arabs knew it: there was not a moment to be lost."

At once Sir Herbert Stewart, with a small force, was sent to dash through the desert from Korti to Metemmah. He, Colonel Burnaby, and several other brave men, fell on that famous march, for the enemy at two points warmly disputed their passage. The loss in these conflicts, at Abu Klea on the 17th, and at Metemmah on the 19th, was appalling for the Arabs, but such victories often repeated would soon have done for the conquerors. The entire force reached Gubat on the Nile on January 20th, and there they found the four steamers which Gordon had sent down. Originally there were five steamers, but one had been sunk. The six journals were handed over to Sir Charles Wilson, who, by right of seniority, had taken command on the death of Sir Herbert Stewart. A note was also given to Sir Charles, which had been brought by a messenger from Khartoum, to the following effect: "Khartoum all right, could hold out for years.—C. G. Gordon, 29th December 1884."

It was at first generally believed that this document was but one of many sent out in order to deceive the enemy, but it is now thought that his real object was not to deceive the enemy, who knew only too well the actual state of affairs, so much as to get them to let his messengers pass, if caught by them, and that then the messengers could deliver a *viva voce* message, and tell the appalling truth.

Sir Charles Wilson, with two officers and a small detachment of Englishmen belonging to the Sussex regiment (late 35th), started on the morning of the 24th for Khartoum in two of Gordon's steamers. The delay that occurred between the arrival of the English force at Gubat, and the start up the river for Khartoum, has been freely criticised by the press. The journey from Gubat to Khartoum being entirely by water, Lord Charles Beresford, a well-known naval officer, had been attached to Stewart's force, with orders "at once to take over and man any steamer or steamers that were either there or in the vicinity," and to "use every means in his power to get one or more of the steamers into an efficient state." Unfortunately, the British force that reached the Nile was in a very different condition from that which left Korti in such high spirits. Rapid marching and hard fighting had demanded a heavy penalty, and the death-roll and sick-list were very high; among others, Lord Charles Beresford himself was on the latter.

The whole force under Sir Charles Wilson did not equal a battalion of infantry on its war strength, and it included a large percentage of sick and wounded to be looked after. In addition to this, reports came into camp that large bodies of Arabs were advancing from the north as well as from the south, with the object of annihilating the force. The commander, therefore, had an anxious time of it, and was compelled to undertake a reconnaissance to ascertain the truth of the rumours, and to make all sorts of preparations for defending his little camp with its sick and wounded against any sudden onslaught. He was unconscious of the fact that time was so pressing, and that instead of his camp being attacked, it would be Khartoum, where Gordon had for so long held out against overwhelming odds. Thus the valuable hours of the 21st, 22nd, and 23rd glided away, all too rapidly.

Even when Wilson's force was ready to start, Lord Charles Beresford was not able to accompany it, and

Sir Charles had to go without him. The distance to Khartoum was about 100 miles, but it was not until January 28th that the steamers got clear of the Sixth Cataract, which was about half way between Gubat and Khartoum. For about a dozen miles large boulders and rocks caused delay and danger. No sooner had the steamers got clear of these obstacles than all eyes were strained to catch sight of the Egyptian flag floating over Khartoum. The steamers made rapid progress in the open water, and as the distance was reduced, the square roof of the palace where Gordon had resided came into view. But there was no Egyptian flag flying from it, and the reception accorded to the relieving force, although a warm one, was not such as Gordon would have given. His eyes had often been strained looking to the quarter whence he thought his grateful countrymen would surely send aid, but he had looked in vain. Now, when the tardy help was at hand, it received no welcome from him, for just two days before, on January 26th, he had yielded up his heroic spirit. From every side the Mahdists poured shot and shell upon Sir Charles Wilson and his little band; and it was matter for grateful surprise that they escaped the fate of him whom, too late, they had come to rescue. They approached within eight hundred yards of the city, and then, convinced that it had fallen, retreated to a safer position, from which they could institute inquiries as to the fate of the gallant hero, hoping, yet hardly daring to hope, that his life might have been spared.

It is not necessary to follow further in detail the history of Sir Charles Wilson's party, the narrow escape they had from being treacherously run on to a rock.

and the way in which they were gallantly rescued by Lord Charles Beresford, who by February 1st was sufficiently recovered to enable him to take command of another of Gordon's steamers, and relieve the would-be relievers. There followed at least six days of suspense, as the accounts brought in by natives were very conflicting, but by the 11th of February it was known in England that a consensus of evidence pointed to the fact that the noble hero of Khartoum had been killed at his post.

Probably it will never be accurately known either how Khartoum fell into the hands of the Mahdi, or how the gallant defender actually met his fate. There have been many wild rumours regarding both events, but it is probable that the most authentic account is that obtained by Colonel Kitchener, who of all men was most likely to be well informed, for not only was his experience of the Arabs great, but he had personal opportunities of examining witnesses. He thinks that the ordinary food supply at Khartoum was quite exhausted by the 1st January 1885, and that on the 6th the General issued a proclamation, offering to any of the inhabitants who liked free permission to leave the town and go to the Mahdi. Great numbers availed themselves of this permission, and Gordon wrote letters to the Mahdi, requesting him to protect and feed these poor Moslem people, as he had for the last nine months. In this way the population of the city was reduced to about 14,000 out of the 34,000 inhabitants who were there in September. About the 18th of January, a sortie was made which resulted in desperate fighting, and a large number of the Mahdi's troops and about 200 of Gordon's men were killed. Colonel Kitchener says:—

"The state of the garrison was then desperate for want of food; all the donkeys, dogs, cats, rats, &c., had been eaten; a small ration of grain was issued daily to the troops, and a sort of bread was made from pounded palm-tree fibre.

"On the 23rd General Gordon had a stormy interview with Farag Pasha [the commander of his black troops]. An eye-witness states that it was owing to Gordon having passed a fort on the White Nile which was under Farag Pasha's charge, and found to be inadequately protected. Gordon is said to have struck Farag Pasha on this occasion. It seems probable to me that at this interview Farag Pasha proposed to Gordon to surrender the town, and stated the terms the Mahdi had offered, declaring in his opinion that they should be accepted. Farag Pasha left the palace in a great rage, refusing the repeated attempts of other officers to effect a reconciliation between him and Gordon. On the following day (24th) General Gordon held a council of the notables at the palace. The question of the surrender of the town was then discussed, and General Gordon declared, whatever the council decided, he would never surrender the town. I think it very probable that on this occasion General Gordon brought Farag Pasha's action and proposals before the council, and it appears that some in the council were of Farag Pasha's opinion, that the town could resist no longer, and should be surrendered on the terms offered by the Mahdi. General Gordon would not, however, listen to this proposal.

"On the 25th Gordon was slightly ill, and as it was Sunday, he did not appear in public. He had, however, several interviews with leading men of the town, and evidently knew that the end was near. . . . On the night of the 25th many of the famished troops left their posts on the fortifications in search of food in the town. Some of the troops were also too weak, from want of nourishment, to go to their posts."

Meanwhile news had reached the Mahdists of their terrible defeat at Abu Klea, and also rumours that the English had taken Metemmah. Reports which have quite recently arrived from Egypt say that the Mahdi, alarmed at the approach of English troops, had already packed up his goods and chattels and was about to beat a retreat. There was a meeting of all the Emirs in the camp of the Mahdi, and, with one exception, all were in favour of abandoning the siege. A single Emir, however, said, "Let us make one more attempt. Let us fire 101 guns and proclaim a great victory over the advancing English army, and then make one more attempt on Khartoum. If we fail we shall be no worse off than we are now, for we can only retreat, but if we succeed we shall be able to defy the approaching British." Unfortunately for us the advice of the Emir was taken, and the British expedition, which was so near succeeding, failed by forty-eight hours to gain its object. The Mahdist attack took place at 3.30 A.M. on Monday, January 26th, and was only too successful. With regard to the report that the fall of Khartoum was due to foul play on the part of Farag Pasha, Colonel Kitchener says: "The accusations of treachery have all been vague, and are, to my mind, the outcome of mere supposition. In my opinion Khartoum fell from sudden assault, when the garrison was too exhausted by privation to make proper resistance!" Whether Farag Pasha was guilty or not is not definitely known, but it is certain that he was taken prisoner, and three days after the fall of the town was brought up to show where the wealth was hidden. As there was none he could not reveal it, so he was killed in the market-place at Omdurman. The Mahdi's troops massacred 4000 persons, and after they had been engaged for six hours in thus wreaking their vengeance, the Mahdi sent over to stop them, and a systematic method was adopted of searching for loot. As the Mahdi had bribed his men by promises of untold wealth, and they were disappointed, a large number deserted his cause, and afterwards actually fought against him.

The most contradictory reports have been circulated as to the manner in which General Gordon met his fate, and although it would be impossible to allude to all, it may not be out of place to refer to one which has been very widely accepted. It is to the effect that the General, hearing that the city had been betrayed, put on his uniform and rushed out, sword in hand, to die as a soldier. Narratives which have a dramatic element are always easily accepted. Dramatic effect was, however, the last thing our gallant hero thought of at any time, and still less on such an occasion as this. As a matter of fact he had not a stitch of uniform in Khartoum, and, considering his Chinese experience, it is very unlikely that he would have drawn his sword, even if he had possessed one, which he certainly did not. One person who recognised Gordon after his death says that he was dressed in light clothes. Colonel Kitchener quotes the only person who claimed to be an eye-witness of his death, who says:—

"On hearing the noise, I got my master's donkey, and went with him to the palace. Muhamed Bey Mustapha, with my master, Ibrahim Bey Rushdi, and about twenty cavasses, then went with Gordon towards the house of the Austrian Consul Hansall, near the church, when we met some rebels in an open place near the outer gate of the palace. Gordon Pasha was walking in front leading the party. The rebels fired a volley, and Gordon was killed at once; nine of the cavasses, Ibrahim Bey Rushdi, and Muhamed Bey Mustapha were killed; the rest ran away."

Whether Gordon's death was intended by the Mahdi or was entirely an accident is not known. Colonel Kitchener says that the Mahdi professed to be very angry when he heard that Gordon was killed, but the Colonel thinks that had he expressed himself strongly on the subject beforehand, this calamity would never have taken place. This, however, is very doubtful; a rushing host of victorious soldiers, firing wildly in every direction, are never very discriminating; of course many of them did not know Gordon personally, and the brave General was not the man to make himself conspicuous by any distinguishing garb. Though Colonel Kitchener is perhaps rather hard on the Mahdi in this respect, he is probably correct in thinking that "the want of discipline in the Mahdi's camp made it dangerous for him to keep as a prisoner a man whom all the black troops liked better than himself, and in favour of whom, on a revulsion of feeling, a successful revolt might take place in his own camp. Moreover, if Gordon was dead, he calculated (and rightly) the English would retire and leave him in peace." How Gordon was actually killed, and whether it was the intention of the Mahdi that he should be "accidentally" disposed of, is open to dispute. There can, however, be no question that he was slain, for his dead body was recognised. Well might Colonel Kitchener say, "Never was a garrison so nearly rescued, never was a commander so sincerely lamented." As far back as October 13th General Gordon had written :—

"It is, of course, on the cards that Khartoum is taken under the nose of the Expeditionary Force, which will be *just too late.*

"The Expeditionary Force will perhaps think it necessary to

retake it; but that will be of no use, and will cause loss of life uselessly on both sides. It had far better return, with its tail between its legs. . . . England was made by adventurers, not by its Government, and I believe it will only hold its place by adventurers."

The Government decided to take Gordon's advice, and, to save further bloodshed, withdrew the Relief Expedition. Wady Halfa, Korosko, and Assouan, were held with some force, in case the Mahdi's adherents should seek to follow up their victory. The death of the Mahdi, however, and the defeat of his followers at the end of 1885, have together helped to crush the Mahdist movement, and Egypt has been left unmolested.

CHAPTER XVII.

CONCLUSION.

The news of Gordon's death startled not England only, but the whole of the civilised world. Every eye had been watching the relief column slowly wending its way up the Nile, and over the desert route. One war correspondent had actually used the words in his telegram, "To-morrow the lonely and weary hero will joyfully grasp the hand of an Englishman." People would not at first believe the sad reality, and for a time every one hoped against hope. The news reached the War Office on February 4th, and was communicated to the public during the following day. No better proof exists of the tenacity with which many clung to the hope that Gordon might possibly have survived, than the fact that the Queen, whose womanly heart always prompts her to be one of the first to send expressions of sympathy to the relatives of those who fall at the post of duty, did not date her letter to Miss Gordon till February 17th, and even then used the sentence, "I fear there cannot be much doubt of it," in alluding to the hero's death. The Queen's letter, which did but give expression to the feelings of the country on the subject, was as follows:—

"Osborne, *17th February* 1885.

"Dear Miss Gordon,—*How* shall I write to you, or how shall I attempt to express *what I feel!* To *think* of your dear, noble, heroic Brother, who served his Country and his Queen so truly, so heroically, with a self-sacrifice so edifying to the World, not having been rescued. That the promises of support were not fulfilled—which I so frequently and constantly pressed on those who asked him to go—is to me *grief inexpressible!* indeed, it has made me ill! My heart bleeds for you, his Sister, who have gone through so many anxieties on his account, and who loved the dear Brother as he deserved to be. You are all so good and trustful, and have such strong faith, that you will be sustained even now, when *real* absolute evidence of your dear Brother's death does not exist—but I fear there cannot be much doubt of it. Some day I hope to see you again, to tell you all I cannot express. My daughter Beatrice, who has felt quite as I do, wishes me to express her deepest sympathy with you. I hear so many expressions of sorrow and sympathy from *abroad:* from my eldest daughter, the Crown Princess, and from my Cousin, the King of the Belgians,—the very warmest. Would you express to your other Sisters and your elder Brother my true sympathy, and what I do so keenly feel, the *stain* left upon England for your dear Brother's cruel, though heroic fate?—Ever, dear Miss Gordon, yours sincerely and sympathisingly, V. R. I."

Parliament at once voted £20,000, the sum usually given to a successful general on the completion of a campaign, to be set apart for the sisters, nephew, and nieces of General Gordon, and an *In Memoriam* service was conducted in every cathedral, and in nearly all the large churches of England. A statue was in course of time erected in Trafalgar Square,* and another has recently been unveiled at Chatham. A monument was erected in St. Paul's Cathedral, and it was decided to place another in Westminster Abbey, the national mausoleum of England. But better still, we know that

* It is from this monument that the picture on the cover is taken. It represents Gordon in the undress uniform of the Royal Engineers, with a Bible under one arm, and the "magic wand of victory" under the other.

his memory is enshrined in the hearts of many left behind, and that the record of his noble saintly life is still teaching many of our countrymen valuable lessons.

Few men have done more than General Gordon to elevate the tone of the soldier. The old-fashioned notion still survives that soldiers love war for its own sake, and for the honours it brings to those who take part in it; but Gordon showed us a higher ideal, that the true soldier should study his profession with the idea of mastering it, so as the better to enable him to maintain peace. If good men were all to abstain from studying the science of war, evildoers would very soon have a monopoly of it, and would become aggressors. There are plenty of bullies, who, like Napoleon, would soon upset the peace of Europe were it not that they fear to do so. Such men can only be kept in order by brute force, and brute force is absolutely of no avail, unless it is organised and directed by a brain that has studied the art and science of directing and controlling physical force. It need hardly be said that a knowledge of this kind is not acquired in a day, and although there have been some splendid soldiers of the type of Cromwell, Warren Hastings, and Washington, who have never had a military training, it is unquestionable that a knowledge of the science of war gives a general a very great advantage over one who has not had such training. Exceptions there are to every rule, and the names mentioned must be placed amongst them. It is doubtful if some of the generals named would have ever attained celebrity had their opponents been well trained. Gordon loved his profession, but he took a high view of it. Soldiering with him was not a mere profession for slaughtering his fellow-creatures, but for the prevention of that bullying and bloodshed which would be ever going on in this world, were it not for those who train themselves in order to be able to stop it. The Tai-ping rebellion, which caused the death of millions of innocent creatures, is but a specimen of what might go on throughout the world did not skilful, well-trained soldiers throw in their lot with the side of law and order. Had the Chinese Government only possessed an able general, and a proper army, that rebellion would never have made such headway as it did. And had they not received the services of such an able soldier as Gordon proved to be, the rebellion might have been indefinitely prolonged, and might have broken up the Empire of China.

In less civilised days the percentage of persons who loved fighting for its own sake was undoubtedly larger than it is now. The more civilised we become, the more we learn to value peace and to dislike war. But even in a civilised nation like the English, there is a certain percentage who really love fighting for its own sake; and besides these, there are many who do not actually love it, but think they ought to do so, as they are in the army, and so they cultivate a style of talking as if they really liked it, and thus they mislead others. In the case of Gordon there was an entire absence of either the one or the other spirit. He did not love fighting for its own sake, and he would probably have looked upon a person who did as a survival of a former age. As for the latter class he had an utter abhorrence of all shams, and he took every opportunity of speaking out of the honesty of his heart. "People have little idea how far from 'glorious' war is. It is organised murder, pillage, and cruelty, and it is seldom that the weight falls on the fighting men—it is on the women, children, and old people. Consider it how we may, war is a brutal, cruel affair." Speaking of some of his men killed and wounded in a skirmish, he says, "I wish people could see what the suffering of human creatures is—I mean those who wish for war. I am a fool, I daresay, but I cannot see the sufferings of any of these people without tears in my eyes."

It is worthy of note that some of the ablest generals who have lived and died in the latter half of this century have held similar views. The great Duke of Wellington remarked, as he crossed the field of Waterloo, the evening after the battle, that "nothing exceeds the horror of victory except a defeat;" and such men as Sir Henry Havelock, Sir Hope Grant, Sir Henry Lawrence, and the heroic General Lee of America, used expressions of similar purport. Gordon was a living illustration of the saying that "the gentlest men are ever the bravest when enlightened consciousness tells them that they have a just cause to support."

Gordon's courage was unquestioned, but, though he possessed more natural courage than most men, he never made a wanton display of it merely with a view of impressing others. In China he exposed himself almost recklessly, in order to encourage his officers and men; but in the Soudan, where he felt so much depended on his life, he carefully refrained from exposing himself, though it must at times have been a great trial to him to see his men so badly handled by their leaders.

It is not unnatural that, in the case of the death of a man like General Gordon, people should like to know his views on that event which must in due course happen to all of us, unless our Lord Himself shall come to terminate this dispensation. Apparently he sometimes wished for this, though he did not appear to think the Second Advent near at hand. In one of his letters he says:—

"I wish, I wish the King would come again and put things right on earth; but His coming is far off, for the whole world must long for Him ere He comes, and I really believe that there are but very, very few who would wish Him to appear, for to do so is to desire death, and how few do this! Not that we really ever die: we only change our sheaths."

But though he longed for the return of the Heavenly Bridegroom during his life, he also looked upon death as a welcome release from the trials and troubles of life. He frequently alluded to this subject, and dozens of extracts might be made from his letters, all more or less similar to the two following, which were written at different dates:—

"I would that all could look on death as a cheerful friend, who takes us from a world of trial to our true home. All our sorrows come from a forgetfulness of this great truth. I desire to look on the departure of my friends as a promotion to another and a higher sphere, as I do believe that to be the case with *all.*

"Any one, to whom God gives to be much with Him, cannot even suffer a pang at death. For what is death to a believer? It is a closer approach to Him, whom, even through the veil, he is ever with."

There is one point on which we ought specially to dwell in considering the lessons to be learnt from the life of General Gordon, and that is the *moral* courage he always exhibited. His physical courage has already been touched on, but great as it was, his moral courage was far greater. There are plenty of men possessing physical courage who fail to exhibit moral courage when put to the test. Man being a gregarious animal, and accustomed to go in flocks, is led by his fellows to evil as well as to good. No man can be a true leader of men who is not prepared to stand alone, if need be, against overwhelming majorities. Gordon had the courage of his convictions, and no amount of pressure, no weight of public opinion, could deter him when once the path of duty was clear. The time-server does not ask, What is right? What is my duty? but, What will pay? What will public opinion think? For such an one Gordon had a supreme contempt. It has been well said by Dr. Ryle, the Bishop of Liverpool, "It is not overwhelming majorities that shake and influence the world. Small minorities have ever had more influence than large majorities. All great men have had their seasons of loneliness. See Napoleon, Mahomet, Luther, John Wesley, and Christ Himself." To this list we may add the name of General Gordon; few men so often found themselves so much in opposition in fashionable circles and in the official world.

Among the false reports that have been circulated about General Gordon is one that he was very unsociable and morose, shunning society in general, and ladies' society in particular. It is true that he shunned a certain class of society; there was also a certain set of women that he fought shy of; but it is quite untrue to say that he was unsociable. He greatly enjoyed the society of ordinary cultivated women, who were in sympathy with his efforts to do good, and with them he was neither shy nor reserved. He could talk pleasantly for hours together, and as his own mind was a very cultivated one, he was a great element of attraction to society of a certain kind. What he did dislike intensely was the society of that class of ladies who think of little beyond the fashions of the day, the latest style of dress, and the newest forms of amusement. Such persons he used to find had no minds to think, and no hearts to feel for suffering humanity. Many of them attempted to lionise him, while others paid him the most fulsome compliments, both being things that he particularly disliked. The ordinary conventional dinner-party, where a man is condemned to take in a lady with whom he has nothing in common, and next to whom he must sit for a couple of hours or so eating and drinking things which do not agree with him, was to Gordon a special object of antipathy. Writing from Cairo on March 15, 1878, he says:—

"I am much bothered, but I get to bed at 8 P.M., which is a comfort, for I do not dine out, and consequently do not drink wine. Every one laughs at me; but I do not care."

Again, when in South Africa, he writes:—

"How I hate society; how society hates me! I never tell you the sort of life I lead, it is not worth it; for it is simply the life I led at home, being asked out, and refusing when it is possible; —when I go, getting humiliated, or being foolish. This latter is better than not being exposed—keeping one's self in cotton wool, for that brings out no knowledge of self, such as is brought out by being with others. At the same time, I think it is not right to be much in society, indeed I fight against it truly, and have only dined out about seven times since I have been here."

On October 24th, 1884, when he had made up his mind not to return to England, even if he should get away from Khartoum, he says:—

"I dwell on the joy of never seeing Great Britain again, with its horrid, wearisome dinner-parties and miseries. How we can put up with those things passes my imagination! It is a perfect bondage. At those dinner-parties we are all in masks, saying what we do not believe, eating and drinking things we do not want, and then abusing one another. I would sooner live like a Dervish with the Mahdi, than go out to dinner every night in London. I hope, if any English general comes to Khartoum, he will not ask me to dinner. Why men cannot be friends without bringing the wretched stomachs in, is astounding."

But though Gordon did not like the artificial conventional society one meets at ordinary dinner-parties, it must not be supposed that he was in any way gloomy. His friend, Prebendary Barnes, says about him: "The seriousness of Gordon's temper did not prevent him from being a bright and agreeable companion, especially when those with whom he talked could join him in smoking a cigarette. He had a keen sense of humour, and on every matter about which he cared to form an opinion he spoke clearly and decisively." And his old brother officer, Sir Gerald Graham, thus speaks of him:—

"Pictures have been drawn of Gordon as a gloomy ascetic, wrapped up in mystic thoughts, retiring from all communion with the world, and inspiring fear rather than affection. I can only describe him as he appeared to me. Far from being a gloomy ascetic, he always seemed to me to retain a boyish frankness, and to long to share his ideas with others. Our intimacy began when we were thrown together in mining the docks of Sebastopol during the winter of 1855–56—a period

Gordon always delighted in referring to whenever we met, by calling up old scenes, and even our old jokes of that time. Like all men of action, more especially soldiers, Gordon disliked argument with subordinates when once he had resolved on his course of action; otherwise he invited discussion, and I always found him most tolerant in listening to arguments against his own views, even on subjects in which he, of course, possessed a knowledge far exceeding any I could pretend to. To show the impression he made upon me at the time of my last seeing him, in 1884, I will quote from a letter which I wrote shortly after: 'Charlie Gordon's character is a very fascinating one; he has so much of the natural man about him. To his friends—and he treats all as friends whom he knows and trusts—his charm of manner is irresistible. It is utterly unlike the charm of a polished man of the world; it is the charm of a perfectly open mind, giving and demanding confidence, sometimes playfully, sometimes earnestly, and sometimes with touching humility."

There were various reasons which made him avoid worldly society; one was the incessant grumbling in which many indulge, who have little cause to complain. Writing from the Soudan, he says:—

"I have not patience with the groans of half the world, and declare there is more happiness among these miserable blacks, who have not a meal from day to day, than among our own middle classes. The blacks are glad of a little handful of maize, and live in the greatest discomfort. They have not a strip to cover them; but you do not see them grunting and groaning all day long, as you see scores and scores in England, with their wretched dinner-parties, and attempts at gaiety, where all is hollow and miserable."

Then there was a higher reason. He found that such society interfered with his spiritual life. He says, in three distinct letters:—

"Getting quiet does one good; it is impossible to hear God's voice in a whirl of visits. You must be more or less in the desert, to use the scales of the Sanctuary, to see and weigh the true value of things and sayings."

"We have no conception or idea of what God will show us, if we persevere in seeking Him; and it is He who puts this wish into our hearts. All I can say to you is: Persevere; avoid the world and its poor wretched little talk about others; never mind being thought stupid; look on everything with regard to the great day, and trust Him implicitly."

"Christ must *actually die*, not come *very near* death; and so must we, if we would rise. I once thought it possible to bargain with Christ; to say, I will give up half of my desire of the world, and gain, in the gap, a corresponding measure of Christ. It was no good: I lost the half, but did not get the measure filled. Then I tried to give up a little more, but with the same result; now I think God has shown me that it is not the least use trying these subtle bargains; that the giving up little by little is more wearisome and trying than *one* surrender, and *that* I trust He will give me power to make."

Another reason, doubtless, why he shunned fashionable society was his extreme sensitiveness to praise. His honest, straightforward nature could not tolerate the praise that so often is showered upon great men. He used to say:—

"If a man speaks well of me, divide it by millions and then it will be millions of times too favourable. If a man speaks evil of me, multiply it by millions and it will be millions of times too favourable. Man is disguised, as far as his neighbour is concerned; this disguise is his outward goodness. Some have it in a slight measure torn off in this life, and are judged accordingly by those whose disguise of goodness is more intact; the revelation of the evil by this partial tearing off is but the manifestation of what exists. Whether the disguise is torn or intact, the interior and true state (known to God quite clearly) is the same corrupt thing; the eye of the Spirit discerns through the disguise.

"Who could bear to have this disguise quite rent off, and the evil exposed to the eyes of the world? How would the world receive me, if they knew what I really was, and what God knows that I am at this minute? Yet, how hardly I judge another whose disguise, slightly rent, shows a little of the corruption I know exists in me. Nothing evil was ever said of any man which was not true, his worst enemies could not say a thousandth part of the evil that is in him.

"Praise now humbles me, it does not elate me; did the world praise Jesus? and what right have we to take this praise of men, when it is due to Him?

"When one knows the little one does of oneself, and any one praises you, I, at any rate, have a rising, which is a suppressed 'You lie.' There are several nice bits in our Lord's life, when He replied with some unpalatable truth to those men who would follow Him, and would make much of Him, but afterwards they entirely changed their demeanour."

At one time he used, for the same reason, to avoid reading all newspapers, as they contained so much praise of him. Writing in 1882, when he was Governor-General of the Soudan, he says:—

"I have come to a conclusion; may God give me strength to keep it! *Stop all the newspapers.* It is no use mincing the matter; as the disease is dire, so also must be the remedy. . . . Newspapers feed a passion *I* have for giving my opinion; therefore, as we have no right to judge and have nothing to do with this world (of which we are not), this feeding must be cut short.

"The giving up the papers may cause the starvation of my passion for politics, and that scab may drop off. God has shown me what the scabs are:—Evil-speaking, lying, slandering, backbiting, scoffing, self-conceit, boasting, silly talking, and some few more.

"I wish friends would not send me papers, &c., I pass them on to ——, who is my waste-paper basket!"

Not only did he combat that part of his nature which loved the praise of men, he also sternly resisted the temptation of ambition. For instance, he writes:—

"I wonder if I look ambitious in your eyes. Do you think I sought this place? You should know better than most people, for you have all my thoughts in my letters. Judging myself, I fear it was so when I took the work in hand; not that I cared for the money or the honours to come from it. I think, however, my main idea was the Quixotic one—to help the Khedive, mixed with the feeling that I could, with God's direction, accomplish this work.

". . . There is death in the seeking of high posts on this earth for the purpose of what the world calls doing great things; the mightiest of men are flies on a wheel; a kind word to a crossing-sweeper delights Christ *in him*, as much as it would delight Christ *in* a queen."

He was conscious, too, of a natural tendency to judge his neighbours. Like many reformers, he had a critical nature, and often found himself led into temptation through it. He never screened this failing, and did his utmost to fight against it. There are several extracts from his letters on this besetting sin. Witness these two:—

"What troubles me immensely is the way in which circumstances force me into society, for in it is the great evil of judging others, picking them to pieces behind their backs, so entirely mean and contrary to our Lord's will. All this tends to make a cloud between Him and us; and yet I declare I cannot see how I can avoid it."

"This is one great reason why I never desire to enter social life, for there is very great difficulty in knowing people and not discussing others."

Considering how thorough Gordon himself was, and how intensely he hated shams of every kind, it is not surprising to find that, with his naturally critical temperament, he used most relentlessly to expose the unreality of many who, acknowledging the truth of Christianity, practically denied its power.

"As a rule, Christians are really more inconsistent than 'worldlings.' They talk truths, and do not act on them. They allow that 'God is the God of the widows and orphans,' yet they look in trouble to the gods of silver and gold: either He can help altogether, or not at all. He will not be served in conjunction with idols of any sort. . . .

"How unlike in acts are most of so-called Christians to their Founder! You see in them no resemblance to Him. Hard, proud, 'holier than thou,' is their uniform. *They have the truth*, no one else, it is *their* monopoly."

But though he avoided Christians of this type, he had a great yearning for the society of those who were real, and had more sympathy with the weaknesses of those who were true, in spite of their failings, than most men. He was fully conscious of the natural depravity of his own heart, and so was ever tender to those who fell. Nobody was more willing than he to act to a fellow Christian on the principle laid down in the lines—

"Help a poor and weary brother
Pulling hard against the stream."

He loved Christian society of the right sort, and, under its influence, his whole nature would expand, and he would converse for hours together. Writing from Galatz, where he went after the pleasant time spent at Gravesend, he says, "I feel much also the want of some religious talk," thereby adding another illustration to the truth of that text, "They that love the Lord spake often one to another."

General Gordon's temperament was not that of the monk who shuns his fellow-creatures, and it must therefore have been all the greater trial for him to cut himself off from his friends for so many years at a time as he used to do. Indeed he used to speak of it as "a living death." But the great lesson of his life was that of self-sacrifice for the good of others. Speaking to the editor of a journal, to which reference has already been made, he once said, "When I was in the Soudan, I used to pray every day, 'O Lord, let me be crushed. Lay the punishment of their sins upon me.'" Then, as if he was afraid of being misunderstood, he said, "It was a strange prayer, was it not? As if I had not enough of my own sins to bear!" Few men have learned better than he the great lesson taught from the Cross of Calvary, and few have practised that lesson more completely.

As we so often see greatness associated with success in life, it is well that now and then we witness greatness, which has not been associated with what the world calls success, for the two are far from being inseparably connected. General Gordon frequently emphasised the distinctions between honours and honour. The former he cared very little about, but the latter he ever valued highly, and he used to say that often men attain the former at the expense of the latter. No titles precede his name, nor do any decorations of importance follow it, but his simple and yet heroic self-sacrificing life have fascinated his countrymen, and helped to make the world better by setting before it a higher ideal. On the monument in St. Paul's Cathedral his life is briefly summed up in the few following words: "To Major-General Charles George Gordon, C.B., who at all times and everywhere gave his strength to the weak, his substance to the poor, his sympathy to the suffering, his heart to God. He saved an empire by his warlike genius, he ruled vast provinces with justice, wisdom, and power, and lastly, obedient to his Sovereign's command, he died in the heroic attempt to save men, women, and children, from imminent and deadly peril." The nation felt that their Poet Laureate, Lord Tennyson, did but speak the simple truth when he penned the following lines:—

"Warrior of God, man's friend, not laid below,
But somewhere dead far in the waste Soudan,
Thou livest in all hearts, for all men know
This earth has borne no simpler, nobler man."

THE END

Printed by BALLANTYNE, HANSON & Co.
Edinburgh & London

THE "LAUREL" SERIES.

Crown 8vo. Numerous Illustrations. 2s. each.

1. WINNING HIS LAURELS; or, The Boys of St. Raglan's. By F. M. Holmes. **2s. each.**
2. THAT AGGRAVATING SCHOOLGIRL. By Grace Stebbing.
3. WHAT A MAN SOWETH. By Grace Stebbing.
4. DULCIBEL'S DAY DREAMS; or, The Grand, Sweet Song. By Mrs. Marshall.
5. THE LADS OF LUNDA. By Jessie M. E. Saxby.
6. THE YARL'S YACHT. By Jessie M. E. Saxby.
7. A NEW EXODUS; or, The Exiles of the Zillerthal. A Story of the Protestants of the Tyrol. By Catherine Ray.
8. GRACE MURRAY. A Story. By Ella Stone.
9. MR. ORDE'S GRANDCHILDREN. By Cecilia Selby Lowndes.
10. WHERE THE DEW FALLS IN LONDON. By Sarah Doudney.
11. TOM AND HIS CROWS. By Mrs. Saxby, Author of "Viking Boys," &c.
12. WATCH AND WATCH. By W. C. Metcalfe, Author of "Frank Weatherall."
13. THE VIKING BOYS. By Jessie M. E. Saxby.
14. WILL IT LIFT? By Rev. J. Jackson Wray.
15. A YOUNG STOWAWAY. By Mrs. Corbett.
16. THE SAGA BOOK OF LUNDA. By Jessie M. E. Saxby.
17. A MAN EVERY INCH OF HIM. By Rev. J. Jackson Wray.
18. GOOD LUCK. By L. T. Meade.
19. DECIMA'S PROMISE. By Agnes Giberne.
20. GARTON ROWLEY. By Rev. J. Jackson Wray.

THE "PILGRIM" SERIES.

POPULAR EDITIONS OF STANDARD BOOKS.

Crown 8vo, numerous Illustrations, 2s. each; with gilt edges, 2s. 6d. each.

2s. and 2s. 6d. each.

1. BUNYAN'S PILGRIM'S PROGRESS.
2. BUNYAN'S HOLY WAR.
3. FOXE'S BOOK OF MARTYRS.
4. THE THRONE OF DAVID.
5. THE PRINCE OF THE HOUSE OF DAVID.
6. THE PILLAR OF FIRE.
7. BEN-HUR; or, The Days of the Messiah. By LEW WALLACE.
8. THE LAMPLIGHTER. By M. CUMMINS.
9. UNCLE TOM'S CABIN. By Mrs. H. STOWE.
10. ROBINSON CRUSOE.
11. MY DESIRE. By SUSAN WARNER.
12. NOBODY. By SUSAN WARNER.
13. THE FAIRCHILD FAMILY. By Mrs. SHERWOOD.
14. THE SWISS FAMILY ROBINSON.
15. DERRY. By CHARLOTTE ELIZABETH.
16. ROMANCE OF NATURAL HISTORY. By P. H. GOSSE.
17. GREAT MEN: A Series of Lectures. By Rev. F. MYERS, M.A.
18. TOO LATE FOR THE TIDE-MILL. By Rev. E. A. RAND.
19. LITTLE WOMEN. By L. M. ALCOTT.
20. DRAYTON HALL. By JULIA MATHEWS.
21. THE END OF A COIL. By SUSAN WARNER.
22. GLEN LUNA. By ANNA WARNER.
23. DIANA. By SUSAN WARNER.
24. STEPHEN, M.D. By SUSAN WARNER.
25. MELBOURNE HOUSE. By SUSAN WARNER.
26. BIBLE WARNINGS. By Rev. Dr. NEWTON.
27. THE PHYSICIAN'S DAUGHTER.
28. THE WIDE, WIDE WORLD. By SUSAN WARNER.
29. DAISY. By SUSAN WARNER.
30. DAISY IN THE FIELD. By SUSAN WARNER.
31. NOR'ARD OF THE DOGGER. By E. J. MATHER.
32. A DREAM OF THE NORTH SEA. By J. RUNCIMAN.
33. SOLDIERS AND SERVANTS OF CHRIST; or, Chapters in Church History. By ANNA LEHRER.
34. QUEECHY. By SUSAN WARNER.
35. DARE TO DO RIGHT. By JULIA MATHEWS.
36. NETTIE'S MISSION. By JULIA MATHEWS.
37. WANDERING HOMES AND THEIR INFLUENCES.

THE "PILGRIM" SERIES—continued.

2s. and 2s. 6d. each.

38. FRANK WEATHERALL. By W. C. METCALFE.
39. SHORT LIVES OF MEN WITH A MISSION: Charles Kingsley, Lord Lawrence, Henry M. Stanley. With Portraits.
40. EXPELLED. By the Author of "Dorrincourt."
41. YOKED TOGETHER. By ELLEN DAVIS.
42. BESSIE HARRINGTON'S VENTURE. By JULIA MATHEWS.
43. OPENING OF A CHESTNUT BURR. By E. P. ROE.
44. ST. ELMO. By A. J. E. WILSON.
45. THE CHILDREN'S PILGRIMAGE. By L. T. MEADE.
46. ROMANCE OF NATURAL HISTORY. Second Series. By P. H. GOSSE.
47. NAOMI. By Mrs. J. B. WEBB.
48. BARRIERS BURNED AWAY. By E. P. ROE.
49. WYCH HAZEL. By S. and A. WARNER.
50. THE GOLD OF CHICKAREE. By S. and A. WARNER.
51. THE OLD HELMET. By SUSAN WARNER.
52. THE YOUNG MAROONERS. By F. R. GOULDING.
53. A LETTER OF CREDIT. By SUSAN WARNER.
54. LIFE OF GENERAL GORDON. By Major SETON CHURCHILL.
55. CULTURE OF PLEASURE. By W. HAIG MILLER.
56. A KNIGHT OF THE NINETEENTH CENTURY. By E. P. ROE.
57. IN THE DAYS OF BRUCE. By GRACE AGUILAR.
58. HOME INFLUENCE. By GRACE AGUILAR.
59. A MOTHER'S RECOMPENSE. By GRACE AGUILAR.
60. THE VICAR OF WAKEFIELD. By OLIVER GOLDSMITH.
61. A CANDLE IN THE SEA. By Rev. E. A. RAND.
62. JOHN KNOX AND HIS TIMES. By Miss WARREN.
63. THE VALE OF CEDARS. By GRACE AGUILAR.
64. THE GOLDEN LADDER. By S. and A. WARNER.
65. C. H. SPURGEON. The Story of his Life.
66. INFELICE. By A. J. E. WILSON.
67. AT THE MERCY OF TIBERIUS. By A. J. E. WILSON.
68. DORRINCOURT. By the Author of "Expelled."
69. A SALT-WATER HERO. By Rev. E. A. RAND.
70. SEVEN SONS. By DARLEY DALE.
71. WESTWARD HO! By CHAS. KINGSLEY.
72. HOLDEN WITH THE CORDS. By W. M. L. JAY.
73. A RED WALLFLOWER. By SUSAN WARNER.
74. JOHN HALIFAX, GENTLEMAN.
75. VINEGAR HILL. By ANNA WARNER.
76. CROSS CORNERS. By ANNA WARNER.
77. ONE LITTLE VEIN OF DROSS.
78. MISTRESS MARCHETT'S MISTAKE.
79. ARABIAN NIGHT'S ENTERTAINMENTS.

THE "PEOPLE'S" SERIES.

Crown 8vo. 1s. 6d. Illustrated.

1s. 6d. each.

THE PILGRIM'S PROGRESS.

STEPHEN, M.D. By SUSAN WARNER.

LITTLE WOMEN AND GOOD WIVES. By L. M. ALCOTT.

THE LETTER OF CREDIT. By SUSAN WARNER.

DAINTREE. By the Author of "Expelled."

BOXALL SCHOOL. By the Author of "Expelled."

ST. MARTIN'S SUMMER. By ROSE PORTER.

MRS. LESTER'S GIRLS AND THEIR SERVICE. By the Author of "Mrs. Marston's Girls and their Confirmation."

FIVE THOUSAND POUNDS. By AGNES GIBERNE.

READY, AYE READY! By AGNES GIBERNE.

JOHN HALIFAX, GENTLEMAN.

THE OLDER BROTHER. By PANSY.

GERALD AND DOLLY. By D'ESTERRE.

THROUGH SHADOW TO SUNSHINE. By Mrs. HORNIBROOK.

A SUMMER IN THE LIFE OF TWO LITTLE CHILDREN. By Mrs. HOWARD.

OLIVER'S OLD PICTURES; or, The Magic Circle. By Mrs. MARSHALL.

RUBY AND PEARL; or, The Children at Castle Aylmer. By Mrs. MARSHALL.

LADY TEMPLE'S GRANDCHILDREN. By Miss EVERETT GREEN.

A LONDON BABY: The Story of King Roy. By L. T. MEADE.

HIDDEN HOMES; or, The Children's Discoveries. By M. A. PAULL RIPLEY.

AN UNWILLING WITNESS. By Miss LYSTER.

SIR VALENTINE'S VICTORY. By EMMA MARSHALL.

THE "GOLDEN SILENCE" SERIES.

With Illustrations.

Small Crown 8vo. Attractively bound in cloth. 1s. each.

THE STORY OF OUR ENGLISH BIBLE AND WHAT IT COST. **1s. each.**
By Mrs. BAYLY.

STEPPING HEAVENWARD. By Mrs. PRENTISS.

WHAT KATY DID. By SUSAN COOLIDGE.

MORAG: A Tale of Highland Life. By Mrs. MILNE RAE, Author of "Rinaultrie," "Geordy's Tryst," &c.

AUNT JANE'S HERO; or, Sorrow and Sunshine. By Mrs. PRENTISS.

MAGGIE AND BESSIE, AND THEIR WAY TO DO GOOD. By JOANNA H. MATHEWS.

BESSIE AT SCHOOL. By JOANNA H. MATHEWS.

BESSIE AND HER FRIENDS. By JOANNA H. MATHEWS.

BESSIE IN THE MOUNTAINS. By JOANNA H. MATHEWS.

BESSIE AT THE SEASIDE. By JOANNA H. MATHEWS.

BESSIE ON HER TRAVELS. By JOANNA H. MATHEWS.

THE THREE LITTLE SPADES. By ANNA B. WARNER.

WHEN I WAS YOUNG. By Mrs. MARSHALL.

THE HOME AT GREYLOCK. By Mrs. PRENTISS.

MICHAEL'S TREASURES; or, Choice Silver. By Mrs. MARSHALL.

CISSY'S TROUBLES. By DARLEY DALE.

LITTLE BRICKS. By DARLEY DALE.

EFFIE'S FRIENDS; or, Chronicles of the Woods and Shore.

MATTHEW FROST, CARRIER; or, Little Snowdrop's Mission. By Mrs. MARSHALL.

MY LADY BOUNTIFUL. By Mrs. MARSHALL.

THREE PATHS IN LIFE. A Tale for Girls.

STELLAFONT ABBEY; or, "Nothing New." By EMMA MARSHALL.

A SUNBEAM'S INFLUENCE; or, Eight Years After. By Lady DUNBOYNE.

SUSY'S SACRIFICE.

KENNETH FORBES.

THE CHILDREN OF BLACKBERRY HOLLOW.

THE "GOLDEN SILENCE" SERIES—continued.

1s. each. THE SAFE COMPASS, AND HOW IT POINTS. By Rev. R. Newton, D.D.

MR. RUTHERFORD'S CHILDREN.

PAT'S INHERITANCE. By Mrs. Marshall.

IN THE MIST. A Tale. By Rose Porter.

THE OTHER HOUSE. A Tale. By Mary R. Higham.

NATURE'S GENTLEMAN. By Mrs. Marshall.

THE BRIDE'S HOME. By Mrs. Marshall.

MILES MURCHISON. By Miss Giberne.

HOUSE IN TOWN. By the Author of "The Wide, Wide World."

TRADING. By the Author of "The Wide, Wide World." Sequel to above.

LETTICE LAWSON'S LEGACY. By Mrs. Marshall.

THREE LITTLE BROTHERS. By Mrs. Marshall.

THREE LITTLE SISTERS. By Mrs. Marshall.

KARL KRINKEN; or, The Christmas Stocking.

THE KING'S HIGHWAY. By Rev. R. Newton, D.D.

A VANISHED HAND. By Miss Doudney.

SOME COMMON INSECTS. By Emily Dibdin.

THE FOOTSTEPS OF FORTUNE. By Esmé Stuart.

MY SON'S WIFE. By Rose Porter.

MASTER MARTIN. By Mrs. Marshall.

THE STORY OF JOHN MARBECK; A Windsor Organist of 300 Years Ago. By Mrs. Marshall.

MY GRANDMOTHER'S PICTURES. By Mrs. Marshall.

PETER PENGELLY. By Rev. Jackson Wray.

NELLIE GRAHAM; or, The Story of a Commonplace Woman. By Ella Stone.

JACK HORNER THE SECOND. By Rev. Jackson Wray.

KITTEN PILGRIMS. By R. M. Ballantyne.

Printed in Germany
by Amazon Distribution
GmbH, Leipzig

28358348R00167